THE GOOD COOK
TECHNIQUES & RECIPES

Poultry

BY
THE EDITORS OF TIME-LIFE BOOKS

TIME-LIFE BOOKS/ALEXANDRIA, VIRGINIA

Cover: A roast turkey, among the most traditional of poultry dishes, is carved easily with a two-pronged fork and a sharp, flexible blade (pages 42-43). For best results, the turkey should be allowed to rest for about 20 minutes at room temperature before the first cut is made.

Time-Life Books Inc.
is a wholly owned subsidiary of
TIME INCORPORATED

Founder: Henry R. Luce 1898-1967
Editor-in-Chief: Henry Anatole Grunwald
President: J. Richard Munro
Chairman of the Board: Ralph P. Davidson
Corporate Editor: Jason McManus
Group Vice President, Books: Reginald K. Brack Jr.

TIME-LIFE BOOKS INC.

Editor: George Constable. Executive Editor: George Daniels. Director of Design: Louis Klein. Editorial Board: Roberta Conlan, Gerry Schremp, Gerald Simons, Rosalind Stubenberg, Henry Woodhead. Editorial General Manager: Neal Goff. Director of Research: Phyllis K. Wise. Director of Photography: John Conrad Weiser. Design: Ellen Robling (assistant director). Copy Room: Diane Ullius. Production: Anne B. Landry (director), Celia Beattie. Quality Control: James J. Cox (director), Sally Collins. Library: Louise D. Forstall

President: Reginald K. Brack Jr. Senior Vice President: William Henry. Vice Presidents: George Artandi, Stephen L. Bair, Robert A. Ellis, Juanita T. James, Christopher T. Linen, James L. Mercer, Joanne A. Pello, Paul R. Stewart

THE GOOD COOK
The original version of this book was created in London for Time-Life International (Nederland) B.V.
European Editor: Kit van Tulleken. Chief Designer: Graham Davis. Director of Photography: Pamela Marke. Planning Director: Alan Lothian. Chief of Research: Vanessa Kramer. Chief Sub-Editor: Ilse Gray. Production Editor: Ellen Brush

Staff for Poultry: Series Editor: Windsor Chorlton. Deputy Editor: Deborah Thompson. Picture Editor: Anne Angus. Anthology Editor: Liz Clasen. Designer: Douglas Whitworth. Staff Writers: Norman Kolpas, Anthony Masters. Researchers: Irsula Beary, Sally Crawford, Suad McCoy, Karin Pearce. Sub-Editors: Gillian Boucher, Nicoletta Flessati. Permissions Researcher: Mary-Claire Hailey. Design Assistant: Martin Gregory. Editorial Assistants: Kathy Eason, Joanne Holland, Rosemarie Hudson, Eleanor Lines, Molly Sutherland, Julia West

U.S. Staff for Poultry: Series Editor: Gerry Schremp. Designers: Peg Schreiber, Abbe Stein. Text Editor: Ellen Phillips. Staff Writer: Susan Bryan. Chief Researcher: Lois Gilman. Researchers: Eleanor Kask, Barbara Peters, Christine Schuyler. Copy Coordinators: Tonna Gibert, Barbara Quarmby, Ricki Tarlow. Art Assistant: Cynthia Richardson. Picture Coordinator: Alvin Ferrell. Editorial Assistants: Pamela Gould, George McDaniel

CHIEF SERIES CONSULTANT

Richard Olney, an American, has lived and worked for some three decades in France, where he is highly regarded as an authority on food and wine. Author of The French Menu Cookbook and of the award-winning Simple French Food, he has also contributed to numerous gastronomic magazines in France and the United States, including the influential journals Cuisine et Vins de France and La Revue du Vin de France. He is a member of several distinguished gastronomic societies, including L'Académie Internationale du Vin, La Confrérie des Chevaliers du Tastevin and La Commanderie du Bontemps de Médoc et des Graves. Working in London with the series editorial staff, he has been basically responsible for the planning of this volume, and has supervised the final selection of recipes submitted by other consultants. The United States edition of The Good Cook has been revised by the Editors of Time-Life Books to bring it into complete accord with American customs and usage.

CHIEF AMERICAN CONSULTANT
Carol Cutler is the author of a number of cookbooks, including the award-winning The Six-Minute Soufflé and Other Culinary Delights. During the 12 years she lived in France, she studied at the Cordon Bleu and the École des Trois Gourmandes, and with private chefs. She is a member of the Cercle des Gourmettes, a long-established French food society limited to just 50 members, and she is also a charter member of Les Dames d'Escoffier, Washington Chapter.

PHOTOGRAPHERS
Alan Duns was born in 1943 in the north of England and was a student at the Ealing School of Photography. He specializes in food photography, and his photographs have appeared in major British publications.
Aldo Tutino, a native of Italy, has worked in Milan, New York City and Washington, D.C. He has won a number of awards for his photographs from the New York Advertising Club.

INTERNATIONAL CONSULTANTS
GREAT BRITAIN: Jane Grigson has written many books about food and has been a cookery correspondent for the London Observer since 1968. FRANCE: Michel Lemonnier, the cofounder and vice president of Les Amitiés Gastronomiques Internationales, is a frequent lecturer on wine and vineyards. GERMANY: Jochen Kuchenbecker trained as a chef, but has worked for 10 years as a food photographer in

several European countries. Anne Brakemeier the co-author of three cookbooks. THE NETHERLAND Hugh Jans has published cookbooks and his rec ipes have appeared in a number of Dutch mag zines. THE UNITED STATES: François Dionot, a gradua of L'École des Hôteliers de Lausanne in Switze land, has worked as chef, hotel general manage and restaurant manager in France and the U.S. H now conducts his own cooking school. Shirley Sa vis, a freelance food writer and consultant, is th author and co-author of a dozen cookbooks. Th late José Wilson wrote many books on food and i terior decoration.

Correspondents: Elisabeth Kraemer-Singh (Bonn); Margo Hapgood, Dorothy Bacon (London); Miriam Hsia, Susan Jonas, Lucy T. Voulgaris (New York); Maria Vincenza Aloisi, Josephine du Brusle (Paris); Ann Natanson (Rome) Valuable assistance was also provided by: Jeanne Buys (Amsterdam); Hans-Heinrich Wellmann (Hamburg); Lesle Coleman (London); Bona Schmid (Milan); Carolyn T. Chubet, Christina Lieberman (New York); Michèle le Baube (Paris); Mimi Murphy (Rome).

CONTENTS

Making Fare of Fowl

Poultry," wrote the 19th Century French gastronome Jean Anthelme Brillat-Savarin, "is for the cook what canvas is to the painter. It is served to us boiled, roasted, fried, hot or cold, whole or in pieces, with or without sauce, boned, skinned, stuffed, and always with equal success."

This volume explores all these possibilities. The first half of the book presents various techniques for preparing poultry as the main course of a meal. It aims at nothing less than teaching all the skills necessary to make a first-class poultry cook.

Some of these techniques, such as cutting a bird into serving pieces or trussing it whole, are so basic you will resort to them regularly. Others, such as boning a bird without breaking the skin, are more unusual and you will probably save them for special occasions.

To complement the techniques, the second half of this book offers a unique anthology of published recipes—for chicken, turkey, duck, goose, Rock Cornish game hen, squab and guinea hen—drawn from around the world and across the centuries. Used together, the two sections will not only give you access to a complete repertoire of poultry dishes, they will also inspire you with the confidence to experiment with different combinations of ingredients and devise your own recipes.

The universal chicken

The bird that lends itself to the greatest number of cooking variations is the chicken. It would be a pardonable exaggeration to say that this bird was created especially for the table. Descended from the red jungle fowl of Southeast Asia, and domesticated as early as 2500 B.C. in the Indus Valley, the easy-to-raise, egg-producing chicken has by now become an established part of almost every cuisine. And in every country where chicken has been eaten for centuries, it has inspired dozens of recipes, prepared with the locally available ingredients. The Italians, for example, sauté chicken with tomatoes, mushrooms and wine to make *pollo alla cacciatora;* the Japanese deep fry chicken pieces that have been marinated in ginger, soy sauce and rice wine to produce *toriniku no tatsuta-age;* Indians make *tandoori murg,* a roasted or broiled dish seasoned with yogurt and hot spices. Such dishes were once the specialty of the cooks of a particular country; now they are enjoyed the world over.

Chickens—understandably the most popular of birds—are marketed under different names according to age and weight. A broiler or fryer is 7 to 9 weeks old and weighs 2 to 4 pounds [1 to 2 kg.]. These tender birds are best broiled, sautéed or roasted—

they will become stringy and dry if stewed. Broilers are so named because, while they make excellent sautés, broiling is perhaps the ideal way to bring out all their flavor. If the bird is first marinated in a piquant blend of herbs and oil, then carefully broiled under a constant and direct heat, or better still, over a glowing bed of charcoal, the flesh will remain moist and tender while its flavor develops.

A roast chicken, cooked until the skin is crisp and golden and then served with a simple sauce made from the juices left in the roasting pan, represents the best in home cooking. The primary candidates for this splendid result are, of course, roasters—birds 3 to 5 months old, weighing 4 to 7 pounds [2 to 3 kg.]—and capons. The latter, martyrs to the cause of cooking, are castrated male chickens 4 to 5 months old; they weigh 6 to 9 pounds [3 to 4 kg.]. Caponizing was invented in ancient Greece, but the practice became widespread in classical Rome after a law was passed forbidding the consumption of fattened hens, which were considered a delicacy, but were too valuable as egg layers to be recklessly slaughtered. With a simple surgical procedure, Roman poultry breeders not only circumvented the ban, but produced a bird that grew to twice the size of a chicken while retaining all the tenderness of a young bird. Unlike ordinary chickens, the capon has a thick layer of fat just under the skin, a result of the caponizing. The fat melts during cooking, producing an extraordinarily succulent roast.

Another good roasting bird is a special hybrid—the tiny Rock Cornish game hen. It weighs 1 to 2 pounds [½ to 1 kg.], and is slaughtered at the age of 5 to 6 weeks. Like the roasters, it also is a suitable candidate for sautéing in butter or oil, or for deep frying in sizzling fat.

A roasting bird may be cooked with no more than a basting of butter and a sprinkling of salt and pepper; or, as is more often the case, with a moist stuffing that will heighten the flavor of the meat as it cooks. The stuffing may range from the forthright to the intricate, from a simple bread-crumb mixture to a robust blend of minced veal with chopped vegetables, or to an exotic marriage of nuts, fruits and spices.

Today, most roasts are prepared in ovens. But in medieval Europe, a bird was impaled on a spit and roasted in front of an open fire—a method that was used until the end of the 19th Century and still has its enthusiastic adherents. To prevent the bird from cooking unevenly, it was rotated on the spit—either by a servant, by a wound-up spring device or, in some households, by a dog hitched to a treadwheel connected to the spit. As the bird turned, it was basted with the juices that dripped into a pan beneath it.

Roasting will not suit the oldest and toughest bird available on the market, a stewing chicken. This bird is more than a year old and weighs 3 to 7 pounds [1½ to 3 kg.]—but it is not to be scorned. It has a rich flavor that is emphasized when the bird is poached in water or stock—and longer periods of poaching make the bird as tender as one half its age. And, of course, a stewing chicken is excellent in a slow-cooking braise such as the French coq au vin (pages 54-57).

The festive turkey

The "true, original native" fowl that Benjamin Franklin proposed as the official United States bird—he thought it more respectable than the bald eagle—had been roaming the Americas for two million years before the 16th Century Spanish conquistadors discovered in Mexico a version domesticated by the Aztecs. The conquistadors introduced it to Europe, where it soon became immensely popular; Brillat-Savarin described it as "one of the finest gifts given to the Old World by the New." The English dubbed the newcomer the turkey, apparently confusing it with the peacock, then popularly called the turkey. (How the peacock got the name is uncertain, but there are two possible explanations. The bird originated in India but arrived in Europe via Asia Minor, which was generally known as Turkey. Alternatively, the word may derive from the Tamil word "toka," meaning trailing skirt, which would have been appropriate for the gaudy peacock.)

The important things to remember about turkey are not to overcook it—this is far too frequently done—and to baste it often to prevent dryness. Nowadays, small fryer-roaster turkeys weighing 5 to 9 pounds [2½ to 4 kg.] are available, as are turkey pieces. But the traditional bird for holiday gatherings is a large hen or tom ranging in weight from 12 to 25 pounds [5 to 11 kg.] and in age from 4 to 6 months. Bulging with chestnut, sausage, corn-bread or oyster stuffing and accompanied by cranberry sauce, the roast bird crowns the Thanksgiving table, a continuing reminder of the four wild turkeys served at the Pilgrims' harvest feast in 1621. In England, the turkey, served with currant jelly and bread sauce, is a symbol of Christmas joy.

Duck and goose

Of the several breeds of duck raised for the table, the one almost inevitably found in American markets is the White Pekin or Long Island duck, which is raised commercially not only in New

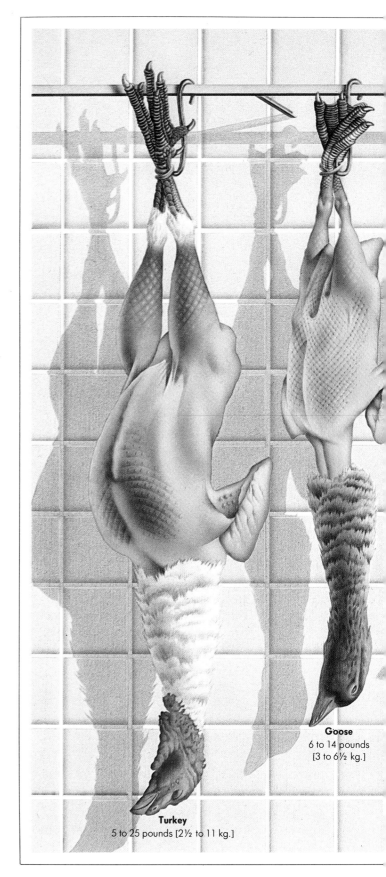

Goose
6 to 14 pounds
[3 to 6½ kg.]

Turkey
5 to 25 pounds [2½ to 11 kg.]

An array of poultry. The scene at right would be familiar to turn-of-the-century cooks, whose poulterers marketed fresh birds "New York dressed"—with the heads and feet left on so as to be identifiable. This painting includes today's birds, however, and indicates the range of weights at which they are customarily sold. When buying poultry, allow about ¾ pound [⅓ kg.] for each serving of squab, Rock Cornish game hen or chicken and a little less for turkey or capon. Allow up to 1¼ pounds [⅔ kg.] for goose or duck; they may lose 35 per cent of their weight in cooking.

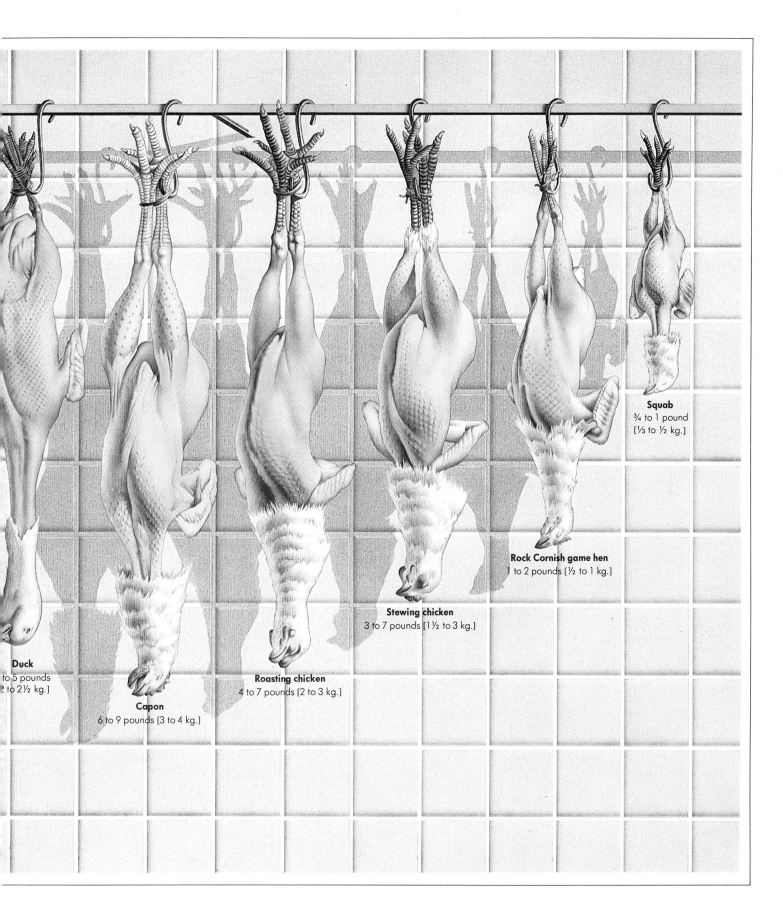

Squab
¾ to 1 pound
[⅓ to ½ kg.]

Rock Cornish game hen
1 to 2 pounds [½ to 1 kg.]

Stewing chicken
3 to 7 pounds [1½ to 3 kg.]

Roasting chicken
4 to 7 pounds [2 to 3 kg.]

Capon
6 to 9 pounds [3 to 4 kg.]

Duck
to 5 pounds
2 to 2½ kg.]

York but also in seven other states. It traces its lineage to nine white ducks brought from China to Long Island in 1873 by a clipper-ship captain. Ducks have been domesticated in China for at least 2,000 years. The Chinese, in fact, have a special reverence for the duck, which in times past they regarded as a symbol of fidelity. Their cooks are masters at making the most of the rich, succulent flesh that is the duck's greatest virtue while minimizing its major disadvantage—the relatively large proportion of bone and fat that inspired the Western saying: "A duck is too much for one, but not enough for two." One way to solve that problem is to remove the skeleton and fill the boned bird with a savory stuffing *(pages 62-65)*. Prepared this way, the duck will serve six generously.

Strictly speaking, the word "duck" applies only to birds more than 10 weeks old and weighing more than 5 pounds [2½ kg.]. Most of the birds sold are actually ducklings, 7 to 8 weeks old and weighing 4 to 5 pounds [2 to 2½ kg.]. A duckling has a fine flavor that is tasted to advantage if the bird is simply roasted, without stuffing or elaborate garnishes. It also is complemented by sauces made of tart fruit—cherries, apples or oranges.

The English cooking authority Elizabeth David suggests that a duck is one of the most difficult birds to roast properly, since the legs remain underdone when the breast is cooked to perfection—with a hint of pink left in the meat. A solution to this particular culinary problem is to serve the roasted duck breast alone for one course and then broil the legs for another 10 to 15 minutes and serve them—accompanied by a simple salad—as another course.

Before the introduction of the turkey to Europe, goose was the bird for festive occasions: "Christmas is coming; the goose is getting fat," runs an old English rhyme, evoking Dickensian scenes of feast and plenty. In Germany—where geese were domesticated as early as 1500 B.C.—and in Scandinavia as well as Central Europe, roast goose is still traditional Christmas fare. There, the stuffings chosen for goose are based on fruits and vegetables: apples and prunes, potatoes and cabbage.

Most geese are sent to the market at 4 to 6 months; their weights range from 6 to 14 pounds [3 to 6½ kg.]. Older, larger birds become too tough for roasting. With Gallic initiative, the French rejuvenate such a bird by braising it with vegetables, pork rinds and calf's feet for many hours in a tightly sealed pot *(pages 60-61)* until the meat is completely tender. The French, in fact, make particularly enterprising use of almost all parts of the goose. Enlarged livers, or foie gras, from force-fed geese are prized as a delicacy; the goose giblets are incorporated in sausages (wrapped in the skin of the bird's neck); and the abundant internal fat is used for cooking and for preserving salted goose flesh *(pages 84-85)*. Goose fat is to the cooks of southwestern provincial France what butter is to Norman ones or olive oil to those of Provence.

Squab and guinea hen

The several breeds of squab or domesticated pigeon are not to be confused with their wild relatives, which have dark meat and a gamy flavor. The domestic bird's meat is pale and has a much milder taste. In medieval times, manorial dovecotes provided a welcome supply of fresh meat in early spring. Now young bir[ds] weighing ¾ to 1 pound [⅓ to ½ kg.] are bred and killed all yea[r] round when they are about 4 weeks old and barely fledge[d]. (Once pigeons have been on the wing for a while, their muscl[es] toughen.) Squabs usually are sold frozen. The birds are sautée[d,] roasted or split and broiled; slightly older ones should be braise[d] or pot roasted, or incorporated into a pie. Squab is not served [as] often in the United States as it is in Europe, but this mild, swe[et] fowl is definitely worth a try.

Another bird more commonly found in European marke[ts] than in American ones is guinea hen. Sold at 16 to 18 weeks an[d] weighing 2 to 3 pounds [1 to 1½ kg.], it is smaller than a roastin[g] chicken; its flavor is delicate, with a faint suggestion of gam[e.] Since its meat tends to be dry, it should be covered with a laye[r] of fresh or salt pork slices during cooking, or stuffed under th[e] skin with moistening ingredients, as shown on page 37.

Selecting poultry

The very best tasting birds are fresh-killed young ones th[at] were raised on a farm where they were allowed exercise and [a] varied diet. Their youth—and therefore their tenderness— [is] not difficult to gauge: on a young and tender bird, the beak an[d] tip of the breastbone are flexible to the touch, but on older bir[ds] they are rigid.

However, very few people today are fortunate enough to g[et] barnyard-reared, fresh-killed poultry; instead they must bu[y] their birds in butcher shops and supermarkets. Almost all the[se] birds are the products of intensive, scientific crossbreeding an[d] rigidly controlled environments. They are fed special grain mi[x]tures that give their skin a healthy glow and fatten them u[p] quickly, and they are prevented from exercising so that the[ir] muscles do not toughen. They are killed at specific ages an[d] weights, determined by the kind of cooking they are intende[d] for. Young, small birds are guaranteed to be plump, tender an[d] lightly flavored; they are best for roasting, broiling and saut[é]ing—rapid cooking methods that seal in flavor and preserv[e] succulence. Older, larger birds have tougher flesh, but they al[so] have a depth of flavor rarely found in commercially reare[d] young birds. Their flesh can tolerate the long cooking that [is] necessary to tenderize it.

Tenderness and flavor are much affected by the treatment [of] a bird before it gets to the butcher or supermarket and after [it] arrives. When buying a bird, keep in mind the general rule: th[e] fresher the better. If you are able to select live birds and hav[e] them killed and cleaned, by all means do so. Otherwise, whe[n] you can, buy freshly killed poultry that has never been froze[n.] Sometimes this is not possible—most ducks, geese and Roc[k] Cornish game hens are sold only frozen, for example—and i[n] that case you must find a reliable butcher who takes good ca[re] of his poultry. Freezing always affects a bird's texture an[d] sometimes its taste. The damaging effects of freezing can b[e] minimized by careful handling, but this is not always don[e.] Poultry must be quick-frozen and its temperature rigorousl[y] maintained at 0° F. [-18° C.] if it is to remain tender. Unfort[u]nately, in transportation and in supermarkets, the birds ofte[n] become partially defrosted, and are then refrozen.

If you must buy frozen poultry, inspect it carefully. Check for the same signs of quality you expect in a fresh bird: the skin should look smooth and there should be no discolorations. Then examine the wrapping. It should be completely sealed; otherwise the flesh will dry out, an effect known as freezer burn. If there is pinkish ice around the meat, do not buy it; it is a sign that the bird has been defrosted and refrozen, and will be stringy and tasteless.

You may certainly freeze the fresh poultry you yourself buy, as long as you have a freezer that maintains a temperature of 0° F. [-18° C.], and as long as you wrap the birds—or pieces of birds—in airtight plastic or special freezer wrap. Poultry will keep up to six months stored this way; the giblets—the neck, liver, heart and gizzard that come with a whole bird—deteriorate more rapidly than the meat and should be separately wrapped and used within three months.

Preparing a bird for cooking

Thoroughly defrost any frozen bird before you cook it—otherwise the meat will cook unevenly. The best method is to leave the frozen bird in its wrapping and let it thaw in the refrigerator, allowing 3 to 4 hours' defrosting time per pound. This will help retain its juice and flavor. Once defrosted, use the bird, as you would a fresh one, within two days. Refrigerated poultry does not keep longer than that.

Before cooking a fresh or defrosted bird, check to see that it has been properly prepared. Some birds have a few small feathers, especially around the vent and wings. These feathers can easily be removed by hand or with tweezers. If there are any hairs on the flesh, carefully pass the bird over a low flame to singe them, then brush them away. The neck and breast cavity should be clean. Sometimes, however, the kidneys are left in place and occasionally shreds of lung tissue remain attached to the inside of the backbone. You can remove them if you wish, although it is not strictly necessary, as they will not affect the flavor of the cooked bird. Sometimes, too, you will purchase a duck or goose that still has its oil glands—two small nodules on the upper side of the tail that help keep the bird's plumage waterproof. Contrary to widespread belief, the oil glands of most birds are innocuous and are removed only for esthetic reasons. However, if you should happen to have a Muscovy duck—or any wild duck—you must remove the glands; they will give the flesh a musky taste. You can cut out the glands easily with the tip of a sharp knife.

In general, however, this is not necessary. Most birds require only a check for interior tissue, perhaps a plucking of extra feathers and a singeing of hairs, and a brief rinse and thorough drying on paper towels before they are ready for any of the cooking techniques suitable to poultry.

Many of the recipes for chicken, turkey, goose and duck in the recipe anthology (pages 87-169) are interchangeable. Once you understand the basic principles of cooking poultry, experimentation with ingredients is well worthwhile. In the words of Louis Diat, a distinguished French chef and author: "The end result of learning the basic cookery methods . . . is that you develop versatility and flexibility obtainable in no other way. You come to understand recipes far more quickly and easily—the very reading of them can be a pleasure—and you become, also, less dependent on them. And this kind of assurance is, I believe, a test of a good cook."

Serving Wine with Poultry

There is a popular fallacy that white wines are the logical choice for serving with poultry. In fact, suitable wines may be either white or red, and can run the gamut from light bodied and simple to full bodied and complex, from rough and rustic to restrained and elegant, from direct and fruity to intricately bouqueted. Each type of bird has its own distinctive taste and therefore a natural affinity with certain types of wines.

The full flavor of goose and duck is usually complemented by a correspondingly full-bodied red wine, such as a mature Bordeaux or Burgundy, although a well-aged Sauternes can marry surprisingly well with goose. Guinea hen, retaining the subtle gamy flavor of its wild relatives, is best appreciated with a relatively young Bordeaux, a red Burgundy or a dryish white wine, such as a Graves. When simply roasted or casseroled, chicken and turkey are equally at home with any wine of quality—whether it be a brittle six-month-old white, a young Zinfandel from California, a venerable Bordeaux, or a perfumed Gewürztraminer from Alsace.

If you are serving a poultry dish as the main course of a menu, your choice of wine may be affected by the wines that you plan to serve with the preceding and following courses. As a rough guide, it is logical to work from white wines to red, young to old, light bodied to full bodied. Another consideration will be the other ingredients used in preparing the poultry dish. If a bird's natural flavor has been elaborated upon by a marinade or sauce, the accompanying wine should be selected accordingly so that it does not compete with the sauce. Marinades may detract from a mature red wine, but a dry white has enough natural acidity to counter their sharpness. Sauces thickened with egg yolk, as used in chicken fricassee (page 58), go best with a fine white or light red wine. The depth and vigor of a red wine sauce deserve to be matched by a red wine for drinking—perhaps a wine that is less robust, but more intricately flavored than the wine used in the cooking.

Like the methods of cooking poultry described in this book, these suggestions for the use of wine are not meant to be cast-iron rules; they represent merely a framework of principles formed by experience and tempered by common sense. Taste, however, is an individual thing; and once the basic principles are understood and mastered, the cook is free to use imagination and improvisation—in the preparation of a chicken for the table or in the selection of a wine to accompany it.

Vegetable Garnishes that Marry Poultry Flavors

Some garnishes—a sprinkling of raw parsley, for example—are mere visual embellishments; others, such as the separately cooked vegetable garnishes that surround a roast, are arranged on the platter as edible decorations.

In poultry cooking, however, garnish vegetables can be much more than merely decorative. By adding them to the bird while it cooks, you invite the flavors of the vegetables to mingle with those of the bird. Such a garnish thus becomes an integral part of the finished dish while

still giving it color and contrast. Both the braising *(pages 52-65)* and poaching *(pages 66-71)* methods rely on the group of vegetables known as aromatics: carrots, turnips and onions, for example, whose robust flavors are drawn out during long cooking to enhance the bird and its sauce. In sautéing, *(pages 18-27),* prepared vegetables are added only a few minutes before the end of the cooking time. This gives the cook an opportunity to use delicately textured and flavored types, such as new peas or cucumbers,

which would lose their shape, color a essences during longer cooking.

For any method of cooking, most fres vegetables need to be cleaned, peele shelled, trimmed or otherwise readied f the pot or pan. A few, including the s shown in the small photographs belov require some special preparation.

Many garnishes used in sautés also r quire brief precooking. Trimmed fenn and celery are usually halved or qua tered and parboiled, as are such ro vegetables as turnips, carrots and pot

Stringing snow peas. Break off the stem end of each pod and pull away the fibrous strings from each edge *(above).*

Cleaning leeks. Insert a knife tip at the top of the white portion and slice through the trimmed leaves. Rotate the leek a quarter turn and repeat *(above).* Rinse well.

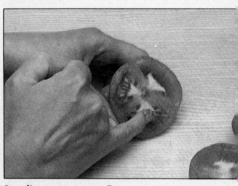

Seeding tomatoes. Dip a tomato into boiling water for 30 seconds, peel it, halve it, then force out the seeds and juice.

Trimmed artichoke

Fennel

Leek

Peeled tomatoes

Shelled peas

Mushrooms

Broad beans

Snow peas

Peeled turnip

es. Most broad or lima beans, snow peas d shelled peas should be parboiled, but ly for about a minute. Scallions and der small beans and peas may be scat-ed raw on the nearly ready sauté.

To prepare an artichoke, pull back the ugh outer leaves until they break off, ap off the stem, slice off the upper ugh part of the remaining leaves and, iral-fashion, peel the outer part of the ugh green base. If the artichoke is ung and tender, dig down into its cen-r with a spoon to remove the prickly choke that covers the fleshy bottom; if it is old, parboil it before removing the choke. Halve or quarter the artichoke and stew the segments in butter for 10 to 15 minutes. Then add them to the sauté and cook them for a few minutes more.

Mushrooms need only be tossed quick-ly in butter over high heat and incorpo-rated into the sauté just before serving. Okra, too, should be cooked briefly in butter before being added to the sauté. Prepare okra for cooking by cutting off the thick stem ends; do not pierce the hol-low pod. Leeks and peeled boiling onions can be stewed in butter until tender. Cu-cumbers can be parboiled in salted water and also stewed in butter. Eggplants may be peeled or not and, like zucchini, sliced or cubed, and sprinkled with salt to draw out the bitter juices. After 30 minutes the vegetables are rinsed if salty, patted dry, then added raw or partly cooked in oil.

Properly prepared, any of the vegeta-bles shown here will complement your sauté. By making your own combina-tions, you can invent distinctive dishes.

moving carrot cores. Halve old rrots lengthwise, loosen the centers with a ife, and pry out the woody cores *(above)*.

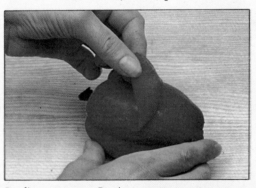

Peeling peppers. Broil a pepper, turning it to char the skin, which then will peel off easily. Halve it and remove the seeds and ribs.

Removing cucumber seeds. Halve each cucumber lengthwise and scoop out the seeds with a melon baller or a spoon.

Zucchini

Carrots

Pepper

Seeded cucumber

Trimmed celery

Boiling onions

Eggplant

Okra

Scallions

Peeled potatoes

Soy sauce

White wine vinegar with tarragon

Lemon

Red wine vinegar

Orange peel

Tarragon

Chives

Chervil

Rosemary

Thyme

Flat-leafed parsley

Flavoring and Tenderizing with Marinades

Alone, or in different combinations, all of the liquids, fruits, vegetables, spices and herbs shown here enhance the taste of poultry. To get the most from these flavorings, put your selections together as a marinade and allow them to penetrate the meat of a bird before you cook it.

Originally a brine for pickling fish, a marinade now is made with a range of seasonings and its primary purpose is to flavor food—not preserve it. The most familiar poultry marinade is a so-called "wet" one, in which herbs and spices are

mixed with enough liquid to immerse the bird at least partially. Generally, a wet marinade is used uncooked, although for a smooth blend it may be cooked and cooled before it is poured over the bird. The liquid for the marinade is usually an acid, such as lemon juice or wine, that tenderizes the bird; it often contains also an oil to lubricate the flesh and sometimes a flavorful sauce, such as soy. Unless the bird can be wholly immersed, turn it from time to time so that all sides absorb the marinade.

Less familiar are the so-called "dry" marinades. Blends of herbs and spices moistened usually with oil, they are simply rubbed into the skin of poultry.

With both wet and dry marinades, be sure to allow time for the ingredients to act. Let the bird marinate at room temperature for 2 to 4 hours, or in the refrigerator for up to 48 hours. Before cooking wipe the bird dry so that it will brown evenly; save leftover marinade or the juice from the bird that dampens the dry marinade and use it for basting.

Juniper berries

Nutmeg

Cinnamon sticks

Mixed dried herbs

Mace

Cardamom pods

Coriander seeds

Olive oil

Garlic

Red wine

White wine

Onion

Sherry

Ginger root

Basil

Marjoram

Bay leaves

Winter savory

Lovage

Rosemary and a dry marinade perfume a split, flat bird.

Cayenne pepper and onions sharpen wine marinade.

Paprika

Cayenne pepper

Black peppercorns

White peppercorns

Cumin seeds

Saffron threads

Whole cloves

Allspice

A Waste-free Way of Disjointing

Poultry pieces purchased from a butcher or supermarket are sometimes poorly trimmed and, pound for pound, are usually more expensive than a whole bird. By learning how to cut up poultry at home, you can save money and also provide neater looking, more appetizing portions. There is a bonus, too, in the giblets that come with a whole bird.

The process is simpler than it looks. Approached with confidence, it can be accomplished in only a few minutes. All you need are a chopping board, a heavy, sharp-edged chef's knife and educated hands. Learn to locate the joints by feel so that, when you bear down on the knife, you avoid the bones and cut through the less resistant tendons and cartilage.

On these pages, a chicken is used to demonstrate the technique but, since all birds have the same basic anatomy, you can adapt the steps to cut up duck, turkey and other poultry.

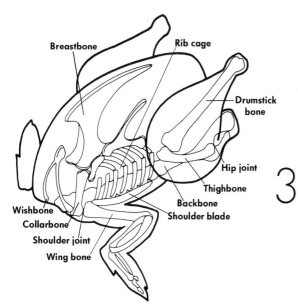

The bones of a bird. The first bone you will feel in a bird's breast is the wishbone; cartilage joins its apex to the breastbone and its tips to the collarbones on either side. Cartilage also connects the collarbones and shoulder blades. The rib cage, backbone and breastbone form the body. Ball-and-socket joints link legs to body, and the wings to the collarbones and shoulder blades.

1 **Removing the legs.** Place the chicken, breast side up, on a board. Pull one leg away from the body and cut through the skin between the body and both sides of the thigh. Now bend the whole leg firmly away from the body until the ball of the thighbone pops from the hip socket. Cut between the ball and socket, and the leg will come away. Repeat with the other leg.

2 **Dividing the legs.** Place each whole chicken leg in turn on the board, skin side down, and cut firmly down through the joint between the drumstick and thigh to separate the two pieces. If the bird is a very small one, you may omit this step.

3 **Removing wings.** Press the top bone of one wing against the bird's body so that you can feel the shoulder ball-and-socket joint. Make an incision between the ball and socket, then pull the wing away from the body (right) and cut down through the skin at the base of the wing. A thin slice of the breast meat will come away with the wing. Take off the other wing the same way.

Halving the carcass. Put the knife blade into the cavity of the bird from the tail end and pierce the thin area bounded by the shoulder joint, collarbone and rib cage *(diagram, opposite page)*. Cutting carefully toward yourself and parallel to the backbone, slit the bones of the rib cage. Repeat the same cut on the opposite side of the bird's backbone.

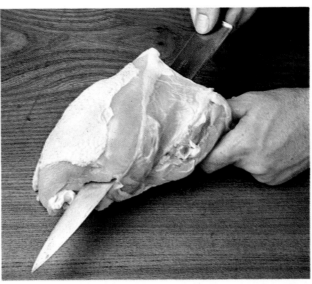

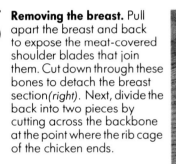

Removing the breast. Pull apart the breast and back to expose the meat-covered shoulder blades that join them. Cut down through these bones to detach the breast section *(right)*. Next, divide the back into two pieces by cutting across the backbone at the point where the rib cage of the chicken ends.

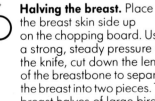

Halving the breast. Place the breast skin side up on the chopping board. Using a strong, steady pressure on the knife, cut down the length of the breastbone to separate the breast into two pieces. The breast halves of large birds, such as turkeys or geese, can be cut across to yield four to six breast portions.

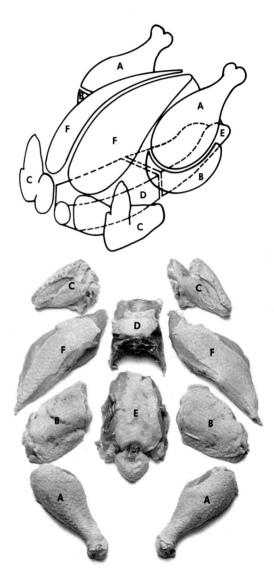

Pieces for every purpose. The quick, efficient way to disjoint a bird produces the 10 pieces shown above. The diagram identifies the location of each piece on the bird. Drumsticks (A) and thighs (B) provide four sections; the wings (C) two. The back (D and E), cut crosswise and the breast (F), divided lengthwise, will produce four more. The meaty breast, thighs and drumsticks are choice pieces for broiling, frying and braising. The bony wings may also be broiled or fried and, like the back, make excellent material for stocks, or may be added to a braise.

Equal Portions and How to Obtain Them

The quick and economical method for cutting up poultry shown on the previous pages produces both meaty serving portions and large pieces that serve as a basis for a stock. Professional chefs who want to use as much of the bird as possible for serving portions cut it up by the slightly different technique demonstrated here, which produces five attractive portions, each with roughly the same amount of meat.

In this method, the preliminary removal of the wing tips, neck skin and bone, and excess fat ensures neatness. The legs are not divided into thighs and drumsticks; instead, each leg makes one serving, which includes an "oyster"—the succulent button of dark meat on each side of the bird's back that usually disappears into the stock pot with the carcass. The wings are cut so that each piece includes some tender breast meat. The breast itself is left whole. The back—along with the wing tips, neck bone and any oddments trimmed off in the process of shaping the bird for cooking—is reserved for stock or soup.

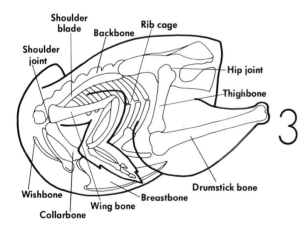

Using the skeleton as a guide. This view of a bird's bone structure will help you to make the cuts shown on these pages. Each shoulder blade is separated from the backbone. Each wing is then cut off with a diagonal stroke that starts at a point where the collarbone meets the breastbone and ends just below the shoulder blade. Above each hip joint against the backbone is a disc of meat, the oyster, that remains with the leg portion.

1 Cutting the back. Lay the chicken on its breast and locate the ends of the shoulder blades with your fingers. Cut a shallow slit across the back below the shoulder blades. From the midpoint of this slit, cut down the backbone to slightly below the hip joints. Do not slice through the bone. These cuts outline the area that contains the morsels known as oysters.

2 Freeing the oysters. Each oyster nestles snugly in a small hollow on each side of the backbone. Use the point of the knife to free each oyster from the bone, leaving the oyster attached to the skin.

3 Removing the legs. Lay the chicken on its back. Cut through the skin where one thigh joins the body. Bend the leg outward to pop the bone from its hip joint. Cut through the socket, but not through the skin on the back lest you sever the oyster. Turn the bird on its side and finish cutting, removing the leg and the oyster. Repeat with the other leg. Trim off the bony drumstick knobs.

Freeing shoulders. Turn the chicken over, breast side down. Starting at the neck, slice down into the cavity between the backbone and one shoulder blade until you arrive at the end of the shoulder blade; leave the wing attached to the breast. Repeat this step on the other side of the backbone. Then pull back the freed section of backbone and, when it cracks, twist it off.

Removing the back. Insert the knife from the rear into the bird's cavity, so that the tip of the blade protrudes from the space that was created by removing the section of backbone. Next, cut carefully toward yourself, slitting diagonally through the rib cage away from the backbone. Repeat on the other side of the bird. The back will now pull away.

Removing wings. Turn the whole breast, with wings attached, skin side up and press down firmly on the breast to crack the bone, producing a flat piece of meat. Sever the wing portions by cutting firmly through the skin and flesh at the points where each collarbone meets the breastbone. Make the cuts diagonally so that some of the breast meat is included in each wing portion.

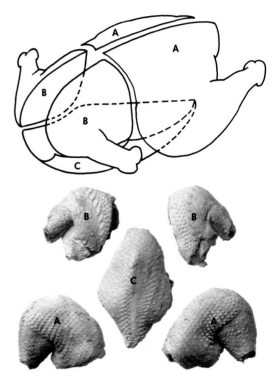

Equally handsome portions. When cut along the lines shown on the diagram at top, the average roasting or broiling chicken will yield five pieces of equal size for pan frying, deep frying, broiling or braising. The leg cuts (A) include part of the back, the wing cuts (B) part of the breast. And most of the meat from the rest of the carcass is included in the breast cut (C). The breast of a larger bird, such as a capon, a goose or a turkey, can be further divided into two or more pieces. The bones left behind have very little flesh on them, but can, of course, be used for stock.

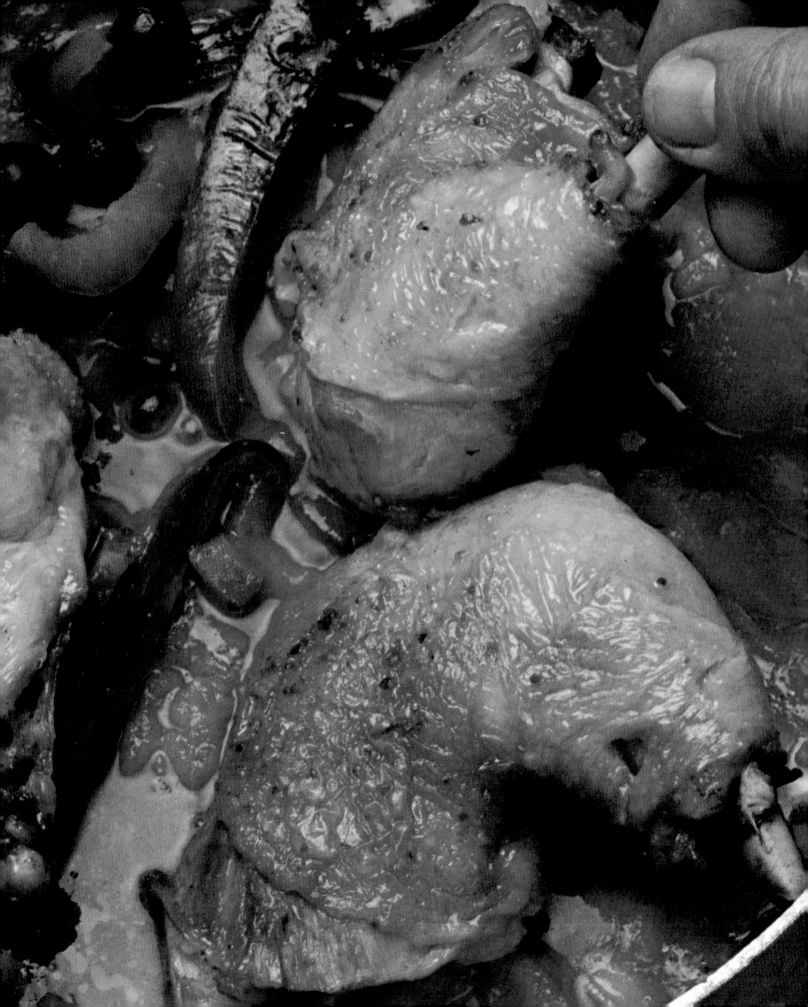

1

Pan Frying
Guaranteeing Succulence

the final assembly of an eye-
catching sauté with a Provençal flavor,
tender pan-fried chicken pieces
are combined with a wine sauce and a
colorful garnish of green peppers,
seeded tomatoes and black olives.

To be savored at its best, young poultry should be cooked by a method that preserves its natural succulence and tenderness. Pan frying, particularly appropriate for chicken pieces, ensures such a result.

The simplest of pan-frying methods is called sautéing—from the French *sauter*, "to jump." Strictly speaking, the term is applied to the technique of tossing small chunks of meat or vegetables in a pan set over high heat; making the pieces "jump" promotes even cooking and prevents sticking. Chinese stir frying is a variation on this basic method; morsels of food are sautéed by being rapidly lifted, turned and stirred as they fry in a large, curved pan, or wok.

In the more common application of sautéing, the pieces are turned over, rather than tossed. Usually the poultry pieces are first browned over the initial high heat and then, with the heat reduced, cooked until done. The pan—coated inside with just enough oil or fat to keep the chicken from adhering to it—transmits heat directly to the meat, searing its surfaces and turning it golden brown. In a variation of this technique the poultry is sautéed at a constant low heat to keep the surfaces lightly colored. All you need for either version is a sauté pan or skillet of highly conductive metal: tin-lined copper is an excellent choice, but you can achieve good results with a less expensive pan made of cast iron or heavy aluminum (be sure, though, that your recipe does not include wine, eggs or such vegetables as artichokes, whose flavor or color may be affected by the metal).

A second method of pan frying calls for dipping the poultry pieces in seasoned flour at the outset. The oil or fat does not come directly into contact with the meat, but transforms the layer of flour into a crisp, golden crust that locks in the poultry juices. Unlike sautéing, in which a minimum of oil or fat is used, this method calls for up to ½ inch [1 cm.] of oil or fat—a layer deep enough to immerse the poultry partway and seal the crust quickly, first on one side, then on the other.

These two methods of pan frying are the foundation of a limitless number of poultry dishes. Sautéing, in particular, is so easy to master that it invites improvisation. In addition, sautéing is a preliminary step in the preparation of braises and casseroles. Its vital role in these dishes makes it one of the most important of all culinary techniques.

Step by Step to a Perfect Sauté

In the three-stage pan-frying procedure called sautéing, the poultry pieces are first browned in an open pan. Then the pan is covered with a lid and the pieces are cooked through gently. Finally, when they are done, the pieces are removed, and the juices and coagulated bits of protein at the bottom of the pan are put to use as the base of a sauce.

Ideally, the pan for sautéing should be just wide enough to hold the chicken pieces side by side. If they overlap, the moisture they exude will not evaporate readily and the pieces will start to stew instead of browning. On the other hand, too much space between pieces will allow the oil or fat to overheat and burn.

Butter enriches the taste of poultry, and many sauté recipes call for it—usually in combination with oil to prevent the butter from burning. Olive oil and poultry fat can be safely used alone and also contribute special flavor.

A vegetable garnish may be added to the poultry during the gentle-cooking stage to enhance the finished dish. The vegetables should always be introduced after the poultry has browned, lest their moisture interfere with the process.

The range of garnishes is boundless (see the box on this page and the detailed instructions for preparing garnishes on pages 10-11). The vegetables can be raw or partly cooked before they are added to the pan. In the cooking sequence illustrated here, the chicken pieces are garnished with parboiled and sautéed cu cumber chunks. In the version recorded by the French gastronome Curnonsky, the cucumber chunks are poached until they are tender and then finished in the sauté juices *(recipe, page 88)*.

When the meat and garnish are done, the excess fats are poured off and a liquid is used to loosen the brown flecks adhering to the bottom of the pan. This process is called deglazing and it is the first step in making the sauce. In this demonstration, white wine is used to deglaze the pan, but stock or water will do.

1 Browning the chicken. In a sauté pan, heat enough oil or fat to coat the bottom. Dry the chicken pieces and arrange them in the pan, skin side down. Fry the pieces over high heat, turning them with tongs until they are golden brown. This will take 10 minutes or so.

2 The gentle-cooking stage. Reduce the heat and cover the sauté pan. The breasts will be done after about 8 to minutes. You can test for doneness by pressing a breast with a finger; when t meat feels springy to the touch, it is don Remove the breasts to a warm dish, replace the lid and cook the other piec of chicken for 10 minutes more.

Elaborating with vegetables and herbs

Peppers and tomatoes add coloring.

Mushrooms and leeks provide texture.

By adding various garnishes to sautéed poultry pieces and finishing the sauce in different ways, a surprising number of original dishes can be created. A small bundle of fresh herbs, for example, contributes an aromatic presence that eliminates the need for any additional garnish; just put the herbs in the pan at the start of the gentle-cooking stage and remove them when cooking is complete. You can prepare a sauce in the pan by bringing wine to a boil and simmering it until it is reduced to half its original volume.

For a dish in the tradition of Provençal cookery, garnish the poultry as it cooks with tomatoes, green peppers, black olives, garlic and parsley *(above, left)*. Or create a medley of flavors by adding mushrooms and leeks *(above, right)* that have been briefly sautéed in butter. Finish the dish with white wine and butter, as here, or with a velouté sauce *(recipe, page 168)*.

3 **Adding the garnish.** After the breasts have been removed, add a vegetable garnish if you want one. The exact moment for adding it depends on the ingredient *(recipes, pages 88-94)*. Here, chunks of cucumber that have first been parboiled in salted water and drained, then sautéed in butter, constitute the garnish.

4 **Pouring off.** The juices exuded by chicken complement the flesh, but the fat is unpalatable. Put the remaining chicken pieces and the garnish in the dish with the breasts. Pour off and discard the fat, but stop pouring before the dark meat juices in the pan run out. Skim off any remaining fat with a spoon.

5 **Deglazing.** Add a generous dash of liquid — in this case, white wine — to the pan. Over high heat, stir and scrape briskly with a wooden spoon until the coagulated meat juices sticking to the sauté pan have been loosened and incorporated into the liquid. Boil the enriched liquid briskly for a few minutes to reduce and concentrate it.

6 **Finishing the sauce.** Sauces for sautéed poultry are usually completed by introducing an element that enhances both flavor and consistency. Here, heavy cream is added to the pan liquid and stirred constantly over high heat until the sauce thickens lightly. Taste the sauce for seasoning, and add salt and pepper if needed.

7 **Assembling the sauté.** Reduce the heat to low, then return the chicken pieces and the garnish to the sauté pan. Stir to coat them evenly with the sauce, cover, and warm the poultry and vegetables through before serving.

Boning Chicken Breasts for Elegant Suprêmes

Chicken breasts that have been skinned, boned and halved are known in culinary parlance as suprêmes. Rapidly sautéed and coated with a vinegar-and-butter sauce *(opposite page)* or with a delicate wine-and-almond sauce, as in the recipe on page 88, suprêmes are perfect for a luncheon or light supper. Each suprême makes an elegant single serving.

To prepare the meat, start out with a whole breast from the butcher or one produced at home by disjointing a chicken as shown on pages 14-15. The bones and cartilage all have well-defined forms: if you use your fingers and a small, sharp knife, it is short work to separate them from the flesh and remove them after you pull off the breast skin.

1 **Freeing the breastbone.** Place the breast skinned side down and slit along the membrane covering the breastbone. Grasp the breast at the collarbones and twist back the breastbone to snap it free.

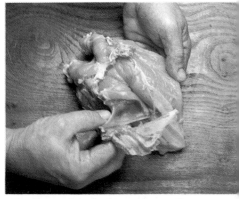

2 **Removing the breastbone.** Snap the breastbone from the white cartilage attached to the narrow end of the breast. Gently pry out the breastbone. The ribs *(foreground)* may come away with it, as here.

3 **Removing the ribs.** Any ribs left attached to the breast can be pulled away with your fingers or cut away with the knife. Trim the tips of the ribs from the sides of the breast *(above)*.

4 **Removing the cartilage.** Push your thumbs underneath the thin, flat piece of cartilage that is attached to the narrow end of the chicken breast and pry the cartilage free.

5 **Removing the collarbones.** Use the knife tip to cut through the flesh that covers the collarbones, carefully following the contours of the bones. When the bones are attached only at their two ends, pull or cut them free.

6 **Removing the wishbone.** Feel the shape of the wishbone beneath the flesh and carefully cut away the surrounding flesh with the knife tip. When the wishbone is uncovered, firmly grasp its prongs and pull it out.

7 **Trimming the breast.** Halve the breast along the cleft that contained the breastbone. Carefully trim off any fat or membrane to shape each piece of meat into a neat-looking fillet.

8 **Cooking the suprêmes.** Melt butter in a small sauté pan or skillet. Sauté the breast halves for 6 to 8 minutes or until they feel springy. Remove the breasts and cover them to keep them warm while you make a pan sauce

A Piquant Vinegar-and-Butter Sauce

A good sauce highlights the qualities of the food it accompanies without disguising its taste. The delicate texture and taste of sautéed chicken is enhanced by a light sauce with just a hint of sharpness to lend vigor to the dish. The sauce prepared here, which pairs well with sautéed chicken, is flavored with red wine vinegar and chopped shallots *(recipe, page 88)*.

The vinegar is reduced, to concentrate its flavor and give it more body. To finish, butter that has been cut up into small pieces is stirred into the sauce to bind it and give it a velvety texture. When the butter is absorbed in the hot—not boiling—vinegar, it goes into suspension. But the sauce will separate if heated further, so as soon as the butter and vinegar have blended, pour the sauce over the chicken pieces and serve.

1 **Deglazing with vinegar.** Pour off any excess fat from frying the chicken and use the same pan to sauté finely chopped shallots. Stir over low heat until the shallots are lightly colored. Add the vinegar and deglaze the pan.

2 **Transferring to a saucepan.** Pour the vinegar and shallots into a small saucepan. The smaller diameter of the pan will make it easier to control the rate at which the liquid reduces.

3 **Reducing the liquid.** Boil the vinegar over brisk heat until it has reduced to the consistency of a light syrup. While the liquid is reducing, test its consistency frequently with a wire whisk *(above)*.

4 **Enriching with butter.** After cutting the butter into small chunks, take the pan off the heat and add the butter all at once. Whisk *(left)* until the butter blends into the vinegar. Season with salt and pepper to taste, then pour the sauce onto the chicken *(below)*.

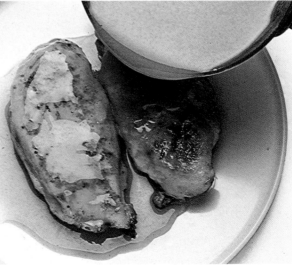

The Chinese Technique of Stir Frying

Using this centuries-old Chinese technique, you can fry morsels of meat and vegetables in minutes by tossing them briskly against the side of an intensely hot but well-oiled pan. Because the cooking time is so short, flavor and juices do not have time to escape. Meat stays moist and tender; vegetables come out crisp.

Before chicken—or, as a substitute, turkey—is stir fried *(recipes, pages 95 and 96)*, the raw meat is coated to seal the pieces for cooking and to give the outside of each piece a smooth texture. After the poultry is done, it is removed from the pan, and vegetables and seasonings are stir fried in the same oil. Finally, the poultry pieces are stirred back into the pan and—in most cases—lightly glazed before serving.

Although a Chinese cleaver, a wok and a Chinese spatula are used in this demonstration, the meat may be sliced with any firm-bladed knife, stir fried in any metal skillet that heats up quickly and evenly, then tossed about with any wood or metal spatula.

1 **Preparing a breast.** Skin, bone and halve a chicken breast *(page 22)*. Place each half on a cutting board with the skinned side down so that the tubular fillet, along the outer edge of each breast half, faces up. Grasp a half in one hand and its fillet in the other. Pull gently until they come apart.

2 **Removing the tendon.** Use the tip of your blade to scrape the fillet away from the tough white tendon that attaches it to the rest of the breast. Pull the tendon from the underside of the fillet with one hand and cut with the othe

5 **Oiling the wok.** Heat a wok until you feel warmth radiating from the sides when you hold your hands close to it. Slowly pour in enough oil to coat the pan, dribbling it around the rim *(above)* so that it runs down to cover the sides evenly. If necessary, spread the oil over bare spots with a spatula.

6 **Cooking the meat.** Drop the slices into the hot wok and toss them about lightly with the spatula. Keep the slices in continuous motion so that they will not stick to the pan and burn. As soon as the meat turns white, transfer it to a platter. Immediately stir fry any other ingredients your recipe calls for.

Cutting Slices into Shreds

3 **Slicing the breast and fillet.** Hold the blade horizontally with the cutting edge parallel to the grain of the meat. Keep the meat firmly flattened with your fingers. Use a sawing motion to slice pieces about ⅛ inch [3 mm.] thick. Then cut the larger slices in half so that all the pieces of meat will be about the same size and shape.

4 **Coating the slices.** Prepare the coating mixture — in this recipe, water, cornstarch and salt — and drop in the poultry slices. Work the coating into the slices with your fingers. Refrigerate the slices for about half an hour to set the coating, then let the meat stand at room temperature for 10 minutes or so before you begin to cook it.

Forming matchsticks. After cutting the breast into slices ⅛ inch [3 mm.] thick (Step 3 at left), stack the slices with the grain running lengthwise, overlapping them like stairs. Then hold the stack flat with your fingertips, but curve your fingers so that your knuckles can guide the knife blade. Cut straight down along the grain to get shreds the shape and size of matchsticks. Partially freezing the breast slices beforehand makes the meat easier to shred.

7 **Adding the glaze.** Return the meat to the wok when the other ingredients have finished cooking — here, parboiled carrots, raw zucchini and mushrooms cut to the same size as the chicken. Stir in a few spoonfuls of a cornstarch glaze. In less than half a minute, the glaze will lightly envelop the chicken and vegetables, and the dish will be ready to put on the table.

Fried Chicken in a Crisp Coating

Fried chicken is one of the world's great basic dishes. In America it ranks as a national institution—albeit one subject to infinite variations from region to region and cook to cook.

Some people insist that the chicken be fried in the fat from smoked bacon; others swear by lard, still others by peanut oil. Inventive cooks test their ingenuity by devising original and sometimes exotic coating mixtures. Although the dish demonstrated here uses ordinary white flour *(recipe, page 96),* some cooks supplement it or replace it with buckwheat, rye or whole-meal flours; others add ground-up nuts and cereals flavored with different combinations of fresh or dried herbs and spices.

In some parts of the world, chicken is marinated before being coated for frying, as in the Greek recipe on page 102—a process that both flavors the flesh and increases its tenderness.

The cooking method, too, can be subject to variations: although chicken is normally pan fried until done, an alternative is to give the pieces an initial browning in the frying pan and finish by baking them in a moderate oven.

However frying is done or the coating prepared, there are two keys to accomplishing a perfect finished dish. Do not wipe the chicken pieces dry first, as you would for sautés; a slight moistness helps the coating to adhere. Flour the pieces an hour or so before frying them; this allows time for the coating to stick firmly, making it less likely that bits of flour will become detached during the cooking period and burn.

Unlike the more elaborate sautés, with their garnishes and sauces, simple fried chicken tastes as good cold as it does hot. If it is prepared a day in advance, it makes excellent picnic fare.

1 **Coating the chicken.** An hour or so before frying, salt and pepper the chicken pieces on all sides. Spread flour on a plate and roll each piece in the flour until it is evenly coated *(above).* Or if you prefer, put flour in a paper or plastic bag, add a few chicken pieces at a time, close the bag tightly and shake it vigorously to coat them.

2 **Firming the coating.** As you flour the chicken pieces, place them on a wire rack so that air can circulate around them. Leave them there until you are ready to fry; doing so gives the flour a chance to blot up the surface moisture and then dry, so that the coating will cling to the pieces while they cook.

3 **Frying the chicken.** Fill a heavy frying pan with oil or fat to a level of ¼ to ½ inch [½ to 1 cm.]. Heat the oil until it is hot but not smoking. Using your hand to protect the flour coating, place the chicken in the pan, skin side down. Do not crowd the pan. As the skin begins to color, flip the pieces with tongs.

An Easy-to-Make Pan Gravy

While cooks may argue about the relative merits of different coatings for pan-fried chicken, most would agree that milk gravy is a worthy accompaniment to the dish. The gravy is made by first browning flour in a little of the fat left in the pan, and then deglazing the pan scrapings with milk. The resulting smooth sauce provides a nice contrast to the crisply fried chicken.

You can improve on this basic sauce by substituting cream for the milk, as in the recipes on pages 98 and 99. Or try replacing some of the milk with chicken stock. You can soften finely diced bits of green pepper or onion in the fat before stirring in the flour. Or add separately fried chopped giblets or a sprinkling of herbs along with the milk. Whatever gravy you make, you can serve it either poured over the chicken or on the side in a gravy boat.

4 **Cooking until done.** Turn the chicken pieces occasionally so they cook evenly. After about 20 minutes, the breasts will be cooked through; place them on a platter in a warm oven. After another 10 minutes remove the pieces of dark meat, add them to the platter with the breasts, and serve.

Making a roux. After frying the chicken, pour from the pan all but a few tablespoons of fat. Return the pan to a low heat and sprinkle flour into the fat. With a wooden spoon, briskly stir fat and flour together until they begin to bubble. This mixture — the thickening agent of many sauces — is called a roux.

2 **Adding the liquid.** Slowly pour milk, light cream or stock into the pan; stir and scrape rapidly to blend the liquid with the fat, flour and pan scrapings. Add salt and pepper to taste.

3 **Finishing the gravy.** Simmer the gravy gently for 15 minutes to remove any hint of a floury taste and reduce the gravy to a consistency that coats the spoon. Stir the gravy from time to time to keep it from sticking to the pan.

2

Deep Frying
A Sizzling Way to Ensure Crispness

In his book *The Physiology of Taste*, Brillat-Savarin expounded an accurate, if somewhat eccentric, theory of deep frying. "The whole merit of deep frying," he wrote, "comes from the surprise"—a term he used to describe the instantaneous sealing of a piece of food when it is immersed in hot oil or fat. "By means of this surprise," Brillat-Savarin explained, "a sort of shell is formed around the food, which prevents the fat from penetrating and seals in the food's juices."

Brillat-Savarin noted that the success of deep frying depends on the high temperature to which the cooking medium is heated. "The boiling liquid," he stressed, "must be hot enough to make its action rapid and immediate; but it cannot arrive at this point unless it has been exposed for a considerable time to a high and lively fire." In precise terms, "hot enough" means that the oil or fat must reach a temperature of at least 350° F. [180° C.]; for most deep frying of poultry the perfect temperature will be 365° F. [185° C.].

A simple way to gauge the temperature of the oil or fat is to drop into it a small piece of bread; if the bread turns golden brown in about a minute, the liquid has reached 365° F. When you deep fry poultry pieces coated with batter, you can use a drop of the batter to test the temperature *(overleaf)*. Many cooks prefer to take the temperature of the oil more accurately with deep-frying thermometers clipped conveniently to the side of the pan; others do away with testing by using thermostatically controlled deep-frying pans.

The initial heating of the cooking medium is only the first step. When you put in poultry pieces, the temperature of the liquid will fall, and the heat under the pan must be raised to compensate. Thereafter you must regulate the heat so that the food cooks evenly and without excessive browning. Chicken pieces with the bones in will cook through in 10 to 15 minutes, depending on size and type—breasts and wings take less time than thighs and drumsticks. Bearing these timing figures in mind, lower the heat if the food is browning too quickly; raise the heat if the food is not coloring fast enough. A word of caution: large pieces of poultry, such as turkey legs, will burn on the outside before being cooked within and are therefore not suitable for deep frying; duck and goose are too fatty to be cooked by this method.

butter-stuffed chicken cutlet fried
olden brown in sizzling oil is ready to be
ted out with a wire scoop. Such a
:oop will not damage the bread-crumb
oating or pierce the flesh of the
utlet, yet it lets excess oil drain quickly.

Marinated Fried Chicken with a Crunchy Crust

The variety of poultry dishes that may be created by deep frying depends mostly on precooking preparations. Chicken can be cut into pieces *(pages 14-17)* or Rock Cornish game hens can be split in half *(pages 48-49)* and cooked with the bones left in. Turkey can be carved into large chunks—boneless and skinless, if you like. The raw meat can be seasoned imaginatively with spices or a marinade before deep frying. The most tempting variations, though, are those achieved by coating marinated pieces in a batter, such as the one shown here, that cooks to a light, golden crispness.

When cooking with the deep-frying method, you should observe a few simple safety measures. To avoid spillage, use a high-sided pan designed for deep frying; when you fill the pan with 3 inches [8 cm.] or so of oil or melted fat, it should be only half full. Dry all utensils thoroughly before you use them; water coming into contact with very hot oil vaporizes instantly and makes the oil splatter. If you regulate the heat properly, there is little chance of the oil or fat catching fire; but as a precaution, keep a tight-fitting lid near the deep-frying pan so that flames can be quickly smothered.

1 **Marinating the chicken.** Cut up a chicken into five or 10 pieces. Season the pieces or flavor them with a marinade—in this case, chopped scallions, herbs, lemon juice and white wine. (Instructions for preparing marinades appear on pages 12-13.)

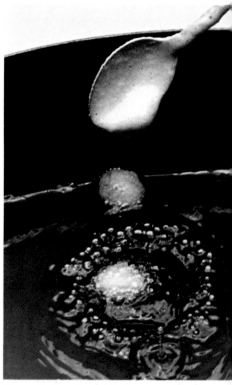

2 **Heating the oil or fat.** Fill a deep-frying pan with oil or melted fat to a depth of 3 to 4 inches [8 to 10 cm.], and place it over a high heat. Drop a dab of batter into the oil to test the temperature; if it sizzles instantly the oil has reached 365° F. [185° C.].

The Secret of Light, Puffy Batter

Batter for coating deep-fried poultry should be prepared at least an hour in advance. If it is used immediately, the batter will be too elastic to cling properly to the poultry pieces, and the coating will shrink and split when it comes into contact with the hot fat. An hour's rest before the coating process enables the batter literally to relax.

A simple batter can be made by beating together water, flour, oil and whole eggs. You may substitute milk or wine for the water to achieve more flavor.

To make a fluffier coating, substitute beer for the water and separate the eggs; fold the beaten whites into the batter just before frying the poultry *(recipe, page 169)*. The beer will cause the mixture to ferment slightly and, together with the egg whites, will give the finished batter a light, airy texture.

1 **Mixing the batter.** Put flour, salt and oil into a mixing bowl. Separate the eggs, add the yolks to the bowl and reserve the whites. Slowly pour in the beer, beating the ingredients together with a wire whisk. Cover the bowl and set aside for 1 hour at room temperature.

2 **Folding in the whites.** In a separate bowl, beat the egg whites until they form peaks. With a wooden spoon or spatula, gently fold the beaten whites into the batter mixture.

3 **Coating the pieces.** Remove the chicken pieces from the marinade and pat them dry. Hold each piece by a corner, dip it into the batter, then use tongs to grip the piece and slip it into the pan. Be careful to avoid wiping off the batter. Do not crowd the pan — even if you must fry several batches and keep the fried pieces warm in a low oven.

4 **Cooking the pieces.** Adjust the heat so that the batter does not brown before the meat is done. The poultry pieces will float in the fat; turn them occasionally so they cook evenly. After 10 to 15 minutes, remove the pieces with a scoop or skimmer and pierce a thigh with a small skewer. The juices should run clear; if they are pink, fry the chicken for a few more minutes. Place the pieces on a towel to drain.

Boneless Chicken Breasts with a Surprise Inside

Presented in different guises, boned and stuffed chicken breasts are featured in many cuisines. The most celebrated example is the Russian dish called chicken Kiev *(recipe, page 101)*, which requires a flattened breast rolled around a finger of butter, dipped in flour and beaten egg, coated with bread crumbs and then deep fried in hot oil or fat. Italian versions substitute slices of prosciutto ham or Fontina cheese—or both—for the butter.

Classically—as here—one joint of the wing is left attached, but this refinement is unnecessary if you buy already-boned breasts. The dish demonstrated is like traditional chicken Kiev, but instead of being rolled around the filling, the breast is slit to make a "purse" or pocket in which the butter stuffing—or other suitable filling—can be lodged. This convenient method was favored by Escoffier.

1 **Breaking the breastbone from the collarbones.** If you start with whole chickens, cut them up by the method shown on pages 14-15, but do not remove the wings. The wing will give each halved breast portion a neat cutlet shape. Skin the breast, turn it skinned side down and cut off the outer joint of each wing. Slit the membrane that covers the breastbone and the attached cartilage. Grasp the breast by its wide end and bend back the breastbone to snap it from the collarbones *(above)*.

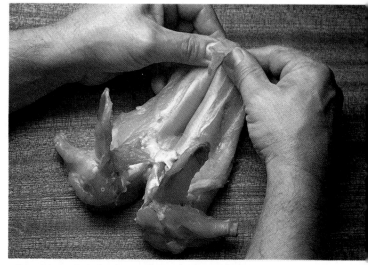

2 **Removing the breastbone and cartilage.** Snap the breastbone from the piece of white cartilage embedded in the narrow end of the breast. With your fingers, pry the breastbone from the flesh. Press the tips of your thumbs underneath the cartilage and ease it out of the flesh *(above)*. With a sharp knife carefully trim away the ribs that remain attached to the breast.

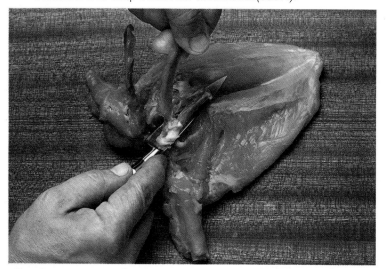

3 **Removing the collarbones.** Twist back one wing to expose the shoulder joint. Cut through the connecting tendons. With the knife tip, cut through the flesh that covers the collarbone to expose the joint it shares with the shoulder blade and wishbone. Sever the joint to free the collarbone and shoulder blade *(above)*; remove these bones. Repeat with the other wing.

4 **Removing the wishbone.** Turn the breast over. Feel the wishbone, and slit the surrounding flesh with the knife tip *(above)*. Grasp the wishbone where the prongs meet and pull it out. Turn the breast over again and halve it along the cleft that contained the breastbone. Pare the flesh away from the outer tip of the remaining wing bone. Each portion will now resemble a cutlet.

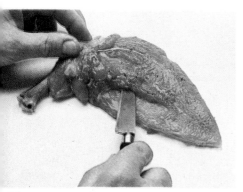

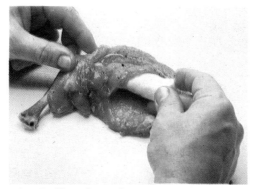

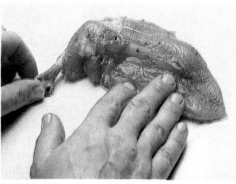

5 Cutting pockets. With the knife tip, make a deep slit along the thick edge of each cutlet. Be careful not to slit so deeply that you penetrate as far as the opposite side of the cutlet.

6 Stuffing the cutlets. Carve two pieces of plain or seasoned butter into finger shapes that can be slipped neatly into the pockets. It will be easier to shape the butter if you put it in the freezer for an hour or so beforehand.

7 Sealing the stuffed cutlets. With your finger tips, press the edges of the pockets together. You will find that the two surfaces of raw flesh cling together; no skewers are necessary.

8 Coating with crumbs. Place one cutlet at a time on a plate covered with flour; sprinkle additional flour over the cutlet *(far left)* to coat it completely. Dip both sides of the cutlet in beaten egg *(center)*. Place the cutlet in a mound of bread crumbs and sprinkle the top with crumbs. Refrigerate the cutlets for at least an hour to set the coating. Bring them to room temperature just before frying.

9 Deep frying the cutlets. To avoid damaging the bread-crumb coating, use tongs to hold each cutlet by the wing bone and slip it into a pan of hot oil or fat. The meat will be done and the butter inside melted in 8 to 10 minutes depending on the size of the cutlets. Serve the cutlets immediately, but remember to cut into them cautiously. The butter can spurt surprisingly high.

3

Roasting and Grilling
Juicy Meat from Dry Heat

Roast poultry seems made for feasting. Served golden brown and glistening, a plump bird turns the simplest meal into a celebration.

Roasting is a method of cooking by indirect, dry heat. When the air of a warmed oven heats poultry, the skin and outermost flesh are quickly cooked. Then, beneath this protective layer, the meat's own juices spread the heat inward to finish the cooking. Broiling or grilling is a kindred process, but the dry heat is direct and generally it emanates only from above or below the meat, so that only one side at a time of the poultry sears and cooks. Spit roasting utilizes indirect heat if the spit is mounted in an oven or rotisserie; as the spit rotates, the bird bastes itself with more even results than could be achieved by ladling fat over it. When the spit is mounted over the coals of a barbecue grill, the roasting is done by direct heat and the bird browns with exceptional uniformity.

In the days when open fires were the only source of heat in the kitchen, all roasting was accomplished by securing poultry to a spit that could be rotated. All grilling was done on a rack over the coals in the hearth. Often cooks burned fragrant woods or added herbs to the fire to perfume the meat as it cooked. But few kitchens today can accommodate an open fire and a modern oven has so many conveniences—most notably safety, ease of operation, efficient insulation, automatic ventilation and regulated temperatures—that modern cooks rarely use coals except outdoors. Roasting, grilling or spit roasting in a stove, however, has limitations. The heat source does not contribute flavor and steam evaporating from the meat may prevent the surfaces from searing perfectly.

Any form of roasting or broiling demands fine timing, as anyone knows who has chewed the dried-out meat of an overroasted bird or the charred skin of a carelessly broiled one. Choice of poultry is also important: only young birds should be roasted or broiled. Old fowl will become desiccated long before the cooking has had time to tenderize them. The techniques demonstrated in this chapter—such as stuffing, trussing and basting roasters or splitting and flattening broilers—are designed to preserve the juiciness of young poultry as well as to enhance its flavor and appearance. Imaginatively applied, the techniques will make it possible to get good results when you roast or grill any bird, be it a majestic turkey for 10, a family chicken or a diminutive squab to serve one.

plump turkey, basted with pan
ces, develops an appetizing brown
aze outside. And inside, the meat
neath this protective shield of crisp skin
ains its natural moisture and flavor
ile it cooks to succulence.

Easy Ways to Fill a Bird with Goodness

Any bird can, of course, be roasted unstuffed, but one of the simplest ways to vary menus that feature poultry is by using different stuffings. Some stuffings— whole onions or apples, for example— are tucked into the cavity only as a means of flavoring the meat and are discarded before the bird is brought to the table. Most stuffings, however, should be served with the bird; the five panels on the right sketch different approaches to their creation.

Plain bread is the foundation for many stuffings, and the results you get depend as much on how the bread is prepared as on your choice of accompanying ingredients. One kind of stuffing is based on dry bread cubes that have been baked or fried in butter until crisp (first panel). Although no moisture is added ahead of time, this rough-textured stuffing is anything but dry after roasting; it absorbs enough meat juices to become moist and flavorful, yet retains its crispness.

A softer, more even-textured version can be made by combining bread and other ingredients with a liquid (second panel). To give the stuffing extra flavor, make a simple stock by simmering in water for half an hour the bird's neck, gizzard and heart, together with a carrot and a small bunch of parsley. Skim and strain the stock before mixing as much of it as you need into the stuffing.

Vegetable stuffings offer an interesting change. Prepare the vegetable (third panel) and mix it with white curd cheese, such as Italian ricotta, then add bread crumbs and egg to bind the mixture together. Use the stuffing recipe for the split, stuffed baked chicken on page 106 as a guide to quantities. That recipe will produce about 2 cups [½ liter] of stuffing—enough for a 4-pound [2-kg.] bird. Adjust the amounts as needed, allowing ½ cup [125 ml.] stuffing for each pound [½ kg.] of your bird's weight.

Whatever stuffing you make, it can be enriched economically with the bird's liver, heart and gizzard (fourth panel), but sauté the giblets before adding them.

Chicken and turkey will always benefit from being smeared with butter or oil before roasting; but you can also stuff additional butter—and flavorings—beneath the skin of the breast (fifth panel).

A Dry Bread Stuffing

Make croutons from firm, unsliced bread about two days old. Choose other ingredients that will complement poultry: here, chopped celery, parsley and mixed herbs are combined to complete the roast turkey stuffing used in the demonstration on pages 38-39.

1 **Browning the croutons.** Cut the bread into chunks and fry in butter over low heat, adding more butter as it is absorbed, until the bread is browned. Or spread the chunks in a buttered pan and bake, turning occasionally, for half an hour in a moderate oven.

2 **Mixing the stuffing.** Place the croutons with the other ingredients in a bowl. The best way to mix any kind of stuffing is with your hands: this method combines all of the elements thoroughly while producing a light, airy mixture.

A Moist Bread Stuffing

Although you can season a moist bread stuffing in many ways, one of the oldest flavor combinations is sage and onion (recipe, page 166). The pungency of the herb and the sweetness of the precooked onion give the stuffing an appetizing perfume that improves with roasting.

1 **Preparing ingredients.** Parboil an onion for about 10 minutes. Chop it coarsely. Finely chop fresh sage leaves (above right) if obtainable; if not, with your fingers crumble ½ teaspoon [2 ml.] of the dried herb.

2 **Moistening and mixing.** In a bowl, combine the onion and sage with fresh, coarse bread crumbs, chopped parsley and giblets, salt, pepper, butter and an egg yolk. Add liquid—here, giblet stock—to moisten the combination. Mix all together gently but thoroughly.

Precooking Vegetables

For use in a vegetable-based stuffing, summer squash, turnip or rutabaga should be shredded, salted and squeezed dry, then precooked before it is combined with other ingredients. Spinach and other greens are parboiled, squeezed as dry as possible and then chopped.

1 **Removing moisture.** Coarsely shred the vegetable — here zucchini. In a bowl, arrange the shreds in 1-inch [2½-cm.] layers, salting each one. After 30 minutes, squeeze out the water *(above)*. Taste; if the vegetable is too salty, rinse it and squeeze it dry again.

2 **Cooking the vegetable.** Sauté the vegetable shreds in butter for 7 to 8 minutes over moderately high heat. Toss them regularly *(above)* or stir with a wooden spoon so that they cook evenly. When they are dry and lightly colored, take the pan off the heat. Cool the vegetable shreds before mixing the stuffing.

Preparing Giblets

Reserve the bird's gizzard, heart and liver for addition to the bread-based stuffing. (Goose giblets are used here.) Wash them in cold water to rinse away any blood before you cut them up. Pat them dry and remove any white connective tissue from the giblets.

1 **Cutting up the giblets.** Use a small, sharp knife to pare away the dark red flesh from the thick, hard membranes that separate the lobes of the gizzard. Slice up the gizzard, heart and liver.

2 **Cooking the giblets.** Melt butter in a saucepan and add the giblet pieces. Sauté them briefly over moderate heat. When they have changed color from red to a pinkish gray, add them to the other stuffing ingredients; they will cook through as the bird roasts.

Buttering under the Skin

Flavorings and a generous quantity of butter placed under the breast skin will keep the meat of a roasting bird moist. Anchovies and almonds are used below, but you can substitute other combinations such as pistachios and slivers of broiled, peeled sweet pepper.

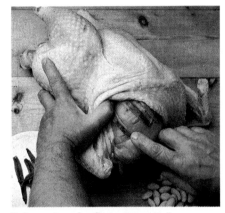

1 **Inserting the flavorings.** Pull back the skin at one side of the neck to expose half the breast flesh. Holding back the skin, cut little slits all over the breast; insert an almond into each slit. Lay anchovy fillets on the surface of the flesh *(above)*. Repeat on the other side.

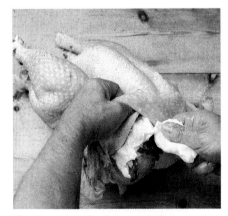

2 **Buttering the breast.** Soften the butter to room temperature. With your hand, spread the butter over the breast meat, generously covering the anchovies and almonds. Repeat the same process on the other half of the breast, then pat the skin back into place.

Removing the Wishbone and Trussing the Bird

Oven roasting is a straightforward cooking method: put the bird in the oven (see page 41 for temperatures and timing), baste and turn it periodically so it browns evenly, take it out ready to eat. But a few preliminaries will improve the dish.

Removing the wishbone from the uncooked bird *(right)* will enable you to carve the breast easily, and neatly, after roasting. If the bird—here a turkey—has a high-arched breast that might color too quickly, thump the ridge of the breast with your fist to flatten it a little.

Stuffing, of course, adds flavor and texture, and it helps keep the meat moist. (See pages 36-37 for the preparation of stuffings; pages 165-167 for recipes.) Be wary, though, about how much stuffing you pack in; it will expand as it cooks and an overstuffed bird may split.

Trussing not only gives any poultry a compact shape by holding the legs and wings close to the body, it also simplifies turning the bird during roasting and prevents the skin from splitting at joints.

Generously smearing the skin of a lean bird with butter *(page 40)*, or barding it—covering it with strips of fresh pork fat—protects against the dry heat.

For the correct way to roast a fatty bird such as duck or goose, see page 44.

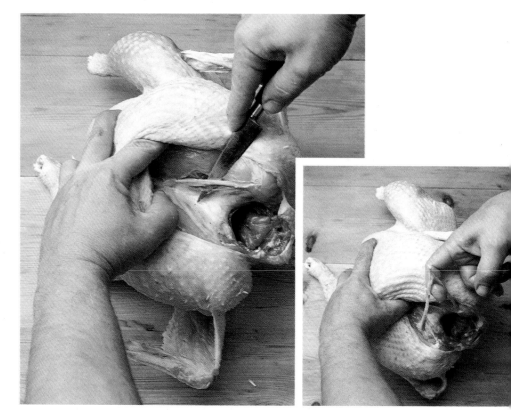

1 Removing the wishbone. Turn the bird breast up and pull back the neck skin until you are able to locate the wishbone with your fingers. With the tip of a small knife, cut through the flesh—along the visible contours of the bone on both sides—just deeply enough to free the wishbone *(above, left)*. When it is attached only at the ends, hook a finger under the bone *(inset)* and pull it out.

3 Closing the tail vent. Thread a trussing needle with butcher's twine or thin cotton string. Leaving a tail of string about 4 inches [10 cm.] long, sew up the vent by loosely stitching back and forth through both edges of the flesh. Cut off the string, leaving a 4-inch [10-cm.] length hanging loose.

4 Securing the wings. After again threading the trussing needle—2 feet [60 cm.] is a convenient length—fold the wing tips and the neck skin flap onto the back as shown. Push the needle in through one wing, the shoulder and neck flap, then out the other wing. Do not unthread the needle.

5 Securing the drumsticks. Turn the bird breast uppermost. Using the same string as in Step 4, push the needle through the upper part of the nearer drumstick and into the body, then out the body and through the same point in the opposite drumstick.

2 **Stuffing the bird.** Fill the turkey partly through its tail vent *(above)* and partly through its neck opening. If there is no skin flap at the neck, stuff only through the tail vent — and sew up the neck with thin, uncoated cotton string.

Tying with a Single Length of String

Although a long trussing needle is essential for dealing with a large, bulky bird such as turkey and goose, a small bird can be trussed effectively by using just one long piece of string, as shown here. You will need at least twice as much string as would be necessary to encircle the bird lengthwise; a generous length is easier to pull tight and the excess can be cut off when the job is completed. Before you begin to truss the bird, pull down the flap of neck skin and fold it over the back to close the neck opening. If the bird has been stuffed, handle it carefully so that the stuffing does not spill out.

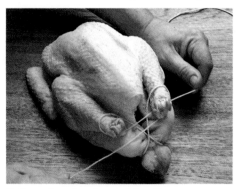

1 **Securing the drumsticks.** Place the bird on its back with the string underneath its tail. Cross the string ends and loop each end over and around the opposite drumstick. Pull both ends away from the bird *(above)* to draw the drumsticks and tail tightly together over the vent.

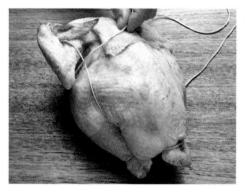

2 **Completing the trussing.** Turn the bird on its breast. Leaving one string end loose, bring the other end across the thigh, loop it around the upper wing and pull it firmly across the neck flap *(above).* Loop the string around the other wing, tie it securely to the loose end of string and cut off the excess.

6 **Tying the first knot.** Pull the needle off the string. Turn the bird on its side, with the loose ends of string from the leg and wing on top. Pull the string tight, tie a knot close to the wing *(above)* and cut off the excess string.

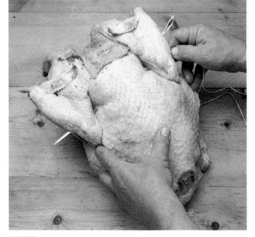

7 **Securing the wing joints.** Thread the needle with another 2-foot [60-cm.] length of twine or string. Turn the bird breast side down. Insert the needle through the wing near the middle joint, push it into the body and out the other wing. Leave string at the first wing and do not unthread the needle.

8 **Securing the drumstick ends.** Turn the bird breast up. Push the needle through the lower part of a drumstick, into the body and out through the opposite drumstick *(above).* Remove the needle. With the bird on its side, pull the string tight, tie a knot at the wing and cut off the excess lengths. ▶

9 **Buttering the bird.** To ensure that the skin browns crisply, smear the bird all over with vegetable oil or butter *(above)*. Set it on a rack or directly on the bottom of a roasting pan big enough to let you turn the bird and baste it easily.

10 **Testing for doneness.** Push a skewer deeply into the thickest part of a thigh or, if the bird is not stuffed, grasp it with a towel and tip it up on its tail. If the juices that run out are clear, the bird is done; if not, roast it 10 minutes more.

11 **Removing the strings.** Take the roasted bird out of the pan. Before carving it, let the bird rest in a warm place so that the meat will become firm enough to carve easily. (Allow 20 minutes for a turkey, less resting time for a smaller bird.) Cut each trussing string on one side of the knot *(left)*; grasp the knot and pull out the string. See pages 42-43 for carving instructions.

A Guide to Oven Temperatures and Roasting Times

The chart below gives the temperatures and approximate times needed to roast whole, unstuffed birds that are removed from the refrigerator about an hour ahead of time; for stuffed birds simply add 20 to 30 minutes.

The chart presents both the quick and the slow roasting methods. For quick roasting, a bird is started in an oven preheated to 425° F. [220° C.]. After 15 to 30 minutes, depending on size, the temperature may be reduced to moderate until the bird is done. The initial period of high heat is essential for drawing off excess fat from ducks and geese, and it will be enough to cook completely Rock Cornish game hens and squabs. Chickens, capons and turkeys may be roasted either by the quick method or by the slow method in an oven set at a constant temperature of 325° F. [160° C.].

Whichever method you follow, roast the bird until the juices run clear when you pierce a thigh with a skewer or—in the case of a large bird—until a meat thermometer inserted into the thigh before roasting registers 180° F. [80° C.]. The bird will brown more evenly if you turn it—start it on one side, turn it to the other side, then place it breast up. A turkey of more than 15 pounds [7 kg.] is cumbersome to turn and can be roasted breast up, but when done its underside will not be as brown as the breast.

To keep the flesh from drying and to help the skin brown, baste the bird regularly: about every 15 to 20 minutes for large fowl, every 5 to 10 minutes for small ones. If you are not using a rack, use a towel to lift the bird off the bottom of the pan when you baste so that the juices can get underneath to keep the skin from sticking to the metal. Use the drippings in the pan for basting.

If you find that the breast is brown before the bird is cooked through, shield the breast by covering it with a loose sheet of aluminum foil.

| TYPE OF BIRD | SIZE OF BIRD | | QUICK ROASTING | | SLOW ROASTING |
	Pounds	Kilograms	Cooking time at 425° F. [220° C.]	Cooking time at 350° F. [180° C.]	Cooking time at 325° F. [160° C.]
CHICKEN 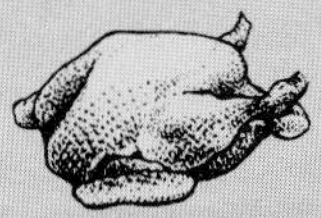	2-4	1-2	¼ hour	¾-1 hour	1-1½ hours
	4-7	2-3	¼ hour	1-1½ hours	1½-2 hours
CAPON 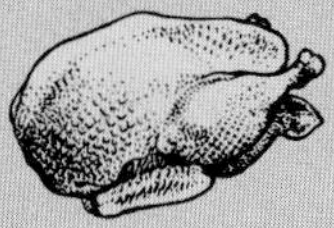	6-9	3-4	¼ hour	1¼-2 hours	2-3 hours
TURKEY 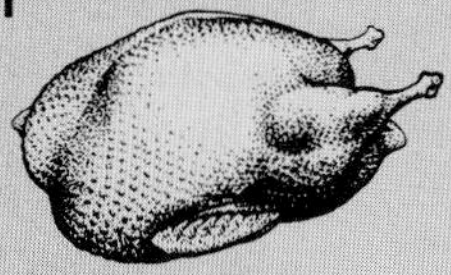	5-12	2½-5	½ hour	1-1½ hours	2-3 hours
	12-18	5-8	½ hour	1½-2½ hours	3-4 hours
	18-25	8-11	½ hour	2½-4 hours	4-5 hours
DUCK 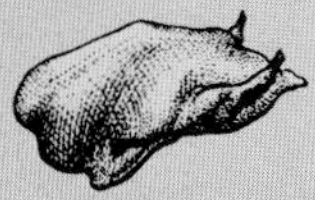	4-5	2-2½	½ hour	¾-1½ hours	
GOOSE 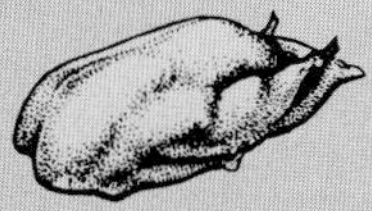	6-10	3-4½	½ hour	¾-1½ hours	
	10-14	4½-6½	½ hour	1½-2½ hours	
ROCK CORNISH GAME HEN 	1-2	½-1	½ to ¾ hour		
SQUAB 	¾-1	⅓-½	½ hour		

Learning to Carve with Skill and Confidence

Carving a turkey is easy, provided you use the right tools. Pick a pointed knife with a very sharp edge and a long, flexible blade that can cut straight through a joint, yet bend enough to follow the contours of the bird. And choose a large two-tined fork to hold the bird while you cut.

Carve the leg, wing and breast from one side of the turkey before you cut into the other side. Work with the back of the fork on the first side so that the tines do not pierce the skin and flesh. Then stick the fork firmly into the carcass to hold it steady while you slice the other side. Carve only as much as you will serve at once so that the rest stays hot and moist. If there is stuffing, spoon it out through the neck and vent.

Chickens and capons are handled like turkeys, but game hens *(box, below)* are merely halved and squabs are usually served whole. To carve a duck or goose, see the demonstration on page 44.

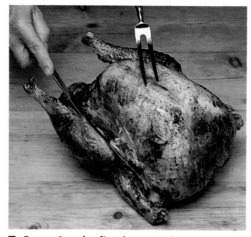

1 **Removing the first leg.** Lay the turkey breast up on a carving board or a large platter. Steady the bird with the carving fork. Cut the skin between the thigh and breast. Bend the thigh outward to locate the hip joint and slice down through the joint *(above)* to remove the whole leg.

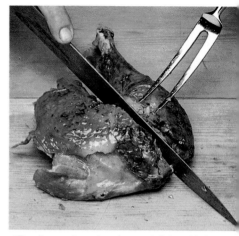

2 **Removing the drumstick.** Hold the knife so that it bisects the angle between the thigh and drumstick bone and cut down firmly through the joint to sever the leg into two portions.

Carving Methods for Small Birds

Roast chicken can be carved with the same long, flexible knife used for turkey—and by the same method, except for its legs. If the chicken is large, separate the drumstick from the thigh and serve each half separately (but do not slice the meat off the bones). With small chickens, serve thigh and drumstick in one piece.

Carving Rock Cornish game hens requires a long but rigid knife and a different, far simpler, method. Half a hen is just the right amount for one serving. All you need do is split the bird in two by cutting straight down along the center of the breastbone and backbone.

A heavy, rigid blade halves a game hen neatly.

A slender, flexible blade can curve to cut across a chicken breast.

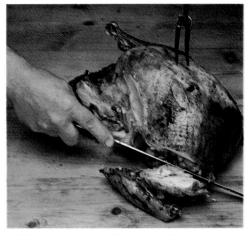

3 **Slicing the drumstick.** Cut a thick slice of meat and skin from one side of the drumstick, parallel and close to the bone *(above)*. Rolling the leg over, cut three more slices in the same way, one from each side of the bone.

4 **Slicing the thigh.** Lay the thigh flat on the cutting board; then, keeping the knife blade parallel to the bone and steadying the meat with the back of the fork, slice the thigh *(above)* into pieces.

5 **Removing the first wing.** Slice diagonally down through the corner of the breast toward the wing. Move the wing to find the shoulder joint; cut through the joint *(above)*. Remove the wing with the piece of breast attached. The wing will yield one serving.

6 **Carving the breast.** Hold the back of the carving fork against the side of the breastbone on the half that you are going to carve, and slice down diagonally through the meat. Lift off each slice between the fork and the knife *(left)*. If you removed the wishbone before roasting *(page 38)*, you can cut the breast into unbroken slices.

Techniques for Roasting and Serving Goose and Duck

Because the thick skin of goose and duck conceals a great deal of fat, these birds should not be roasted in the same way as lean poultry, such as turkey or chicken. There is no need to protect the breast by barding or smearing it with fat; on the contrary, fat must be drawn off during roasting so that the cooked bird—a goose in this instance—will not be greasy.

To start this process, lightly pierce the skin all over with a trussing needle (or a similar, sharp-pointed instrument) before the stuffed-and-trussed bird is put in a hot oven. During cooking, baste the bird every 15 to 20 minutes with its own drippings, thus melting out more fat and helping the skin to crisp. Discard the excess drippings as they accumulate.

Carving, too, requires a different technique. The body of a goose or duck is narrower than those of other birds, and their leg and wing ligaments are tighter and tougher. A heavy, rigid chef's knife is needed to cut the close-set, sinewy structures, although the tender breast meat should be carved with the same slender, flexible carving knife used for lean birds.

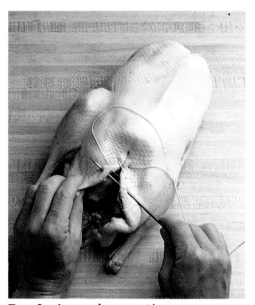

1 **Sewing up the vent.** After removing the wishbone, as demonstrated on page 38, fill the goose loosely with a suitable stuffing—here apples and onions. Sew up the vent and truss the goose. Use a needle to pierce all skin surfaces, without puncturing the flesh underneath.

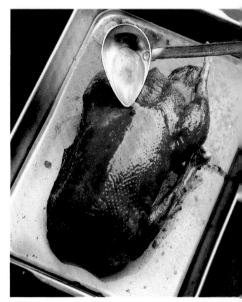

2 **Roasting the goose.** Place the goose on its side in a shallow pan in a hot oven, using a rack to hold the bird if desired. Pour a little water into the pan to keep the fat from burning while the bird roasts (for times and temperatures, see page 41). Baste with the drippings as soon as the flow. Turn the bird on its other side and finally, breast up—basting all the while.

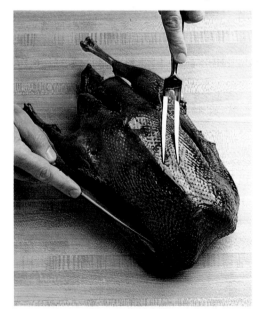

3 **Removing the wing.** After letting the roasted goose rest on a cutting board for 15 minutes, remove the trussing strings. Locate the shoulder joint by gently moving the wing bone. Using a heavy-bladed knife, cut down firmly through the joint, severing the strong tendons (above) to free the wing.

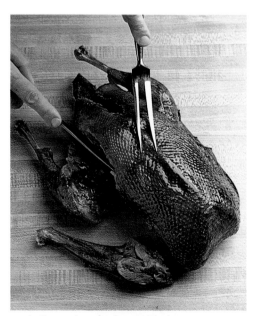

4 **Removing the leg.** With the same knife, cut through the skin in an arc around the leg. Press the knife down between the thigh and the body. The leg will fall away from the body (above) and the joint will be exposed. Cut through the joint to free the leg. Separate it into thigh and drumstick.

5 **Carving the breast.** Using a long knife with a slender blade, carve the breast into slices (above). Work from the front of the bird, with the blade at a slight diagonal to the breastbone. Lift the slices by holding them between the knife and fork to avoid piercing the meat.

uffing, traditionally confined to the dy cavity of a bird, can turn a plain ast into elegant party fare if it is insert- instead between the skin and flesh. iis unorthodox method is shown here th a chicken and a moist stuffing of cchini and ricotta cheese *(demonstra- n, page 37; recipe, page 106)*, but the chnique can be used with a large vari- y of stuffings and applied to game hen d capon, as well.

Supple and strong, the skin of a chick- is firmly attached to the body in four aces: the backbone, the end of each umstick and the crest of the breast-bone. Elsewhere, only thin membranes join skin to flesh, and these membranes can be detached easily by working your fingers under the skin. If the bird's skeletal structure is first collapsed by splitting it along the backbone and then flattening it with a sharp blow *(below)*, the pockets between the skin and the flesh will hold a thick layer of filling—up to 2 inches [5 cm.] in a fair-sized chicken.

If the skin has been torn—either by the butcher or while being loosened and stuffed—use a large sewing needle and uncoated cotton thread to make good the damage. Even a small tear may enlarge drastically during the roasting process.

Although the technique may look fanciful at first, it has several very practical advantages. The tender breast meat is protected from drying out by a thick coat of stuffing that keeps it moist while the whole bird cooks through. And the skin, loose and flexible, can conceal an unusually generous amount of stuffing. When the stuffing swells during cooking, the skin expands smoothly to accommodate it. Basted from the outside by the cook and from the inside by the stuffing, the bird turns a rich, crisp brown.

At table, the promise of the exterior is more than fulfilled when the bird is finally carved to reveal an unexpected and delicious interior.

Cutting through the backbone. Place the chicken on its breast and cut off the wing tips if the butcher has not done so. Using poultry shears, cut along the entire length of the backbone, as near as possible to the center of the bone so that the skin will stay firmly attached to each side of the back. If you work without shears, lay the bird on its back, insert the blade of a long, heavy knife through the body cavity and press down hard with a rocking motion to cut through the backbone.

2 **Flattening the bird.** Open the bird out as much as possible and place it on a flat surface with the breast uppermost and the legs turned inward. Using the heel of your hand or the flat side of a wooden mallet, strike the bird firmly on the breast. Do not be gentle; the object is to break the breastbone, the collarbones, the rib cage and the wishbone. There will be more room inside the skin if the underlying bone structure is not rigid. ▶

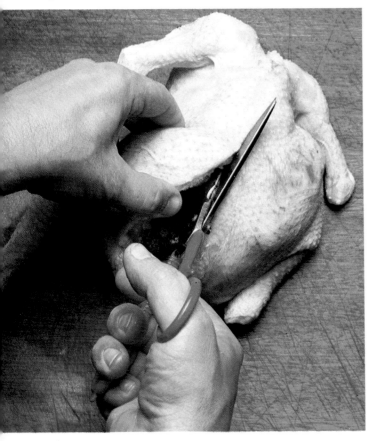

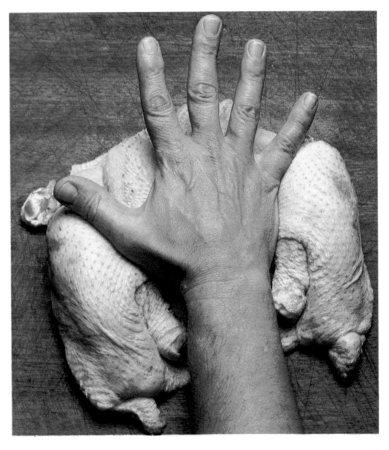

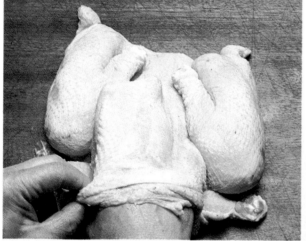

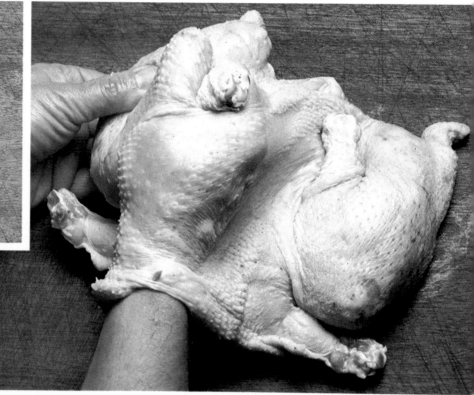

 3 Loosening the skin. Starting at the neck, slip your fingers between the skin and flesh, and work them toward the tail to loosen the skin over one side of the breast *(above)*. With your entire hand underneath, free the skin from the leg, leaving the skin attached only at the tip of the drumstick *(right)*. Do the same to the other side of the breast.

4 Stuffing the bird. From the neck, push the filling under the skin with one hand, using the other hand to settle the stuffing into place from the outside *(right)*. After stuffing the drumsticks and thighs, push a thick coating over the breast. Finally, pull the neck flap over the opening and tuck it under the bird. If there is no flap, spread the stuffing only partway to the neck cavity so that the breast skin around the edge will cover — and seal — the opening.

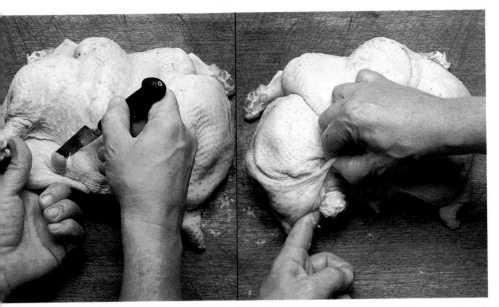

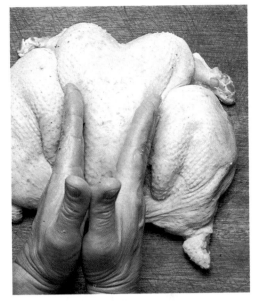

Pinning the drumsticks. To keep the drumsticks from spreading outward during cooking, pin them under a flap of skin. Make a small slit with the point of a knife between the thigh and the breast *(above, left)*. Push the end of the leg through the slit *(above, right)*: the knob of bone on the drumstick will hold it in place. Follow the same procedure with the other drumstick.

Shaping the stuffing. Using both hands, smooth the skin to make the stuffing layer conform evenly to the bird's natural shape. Place the bird in a roasting pan and set it in a hot oven. Lower the heat after 10 minutes and baste the bird frequently with the pan juices after another 30 minutes.

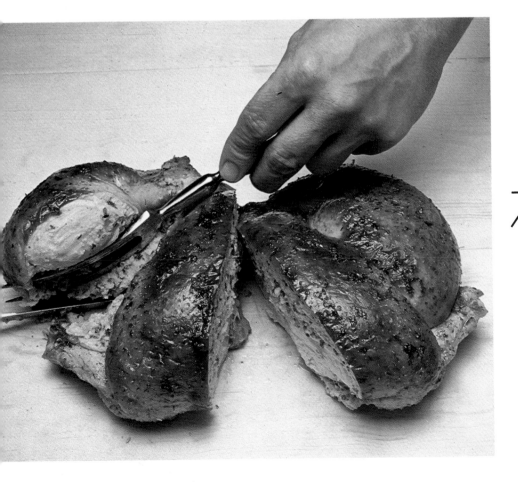

Carving the bird. The chicken will cook in 50 to 60 minutes. Remove it from the pan and let it rest 10 to 15 minutes. Split the bird in two, using a very sharp knife and cutting gently through skin and stuffing. Because you broke bones to flatten the bird, you will meet with little resistance as you slice through the breast. To remove the legs, cut between the thighs and the body, using the curved creases as guidelines *(left)*.

Quick Searing for Brown Skin and Juicy Meat

In broiling, food is exposed to intense dry heat, one side at a time *(recipes, pages 108-111, 154, 157)*. Whether the heat radiates from above in oven broiling, as shown on these pages, or rises from below a metal grid, as in barbecuing *(pages 50-51)*, it quickly sears the surface of the meat so that the interior stays moist.

Ducks and game hens can be split down the back and flattened for broiling by the method shown on page 45 *(Steps 1 and 2)* and page 47 *(Step 5)*, or halved and flattened as demonstrated here with a chicken; turkeys need to be cut into smaller pieces. Lean birds are usually basted with oil or butter during the broiling to keep them from drying out. Ducks need no such coddling; they are fatty enough to baste themselves. But any kind of poultry can be marinated before cooking to heighten, or add to, its flavor.

When an oven has only one setting for broiling, the heat will be very high—approximately 550° F. [290° C.]—and the bird must be watched constantly lest it burn or dry out. Ranges that have thermostatically controlled broilers should be set at 350° to 400° F. [180° to 200° C.] for poultry; even so, the cooking process should be carefully monitored.

To encourage air flow and prevent the build-up of heat inside the oven, leave the door of an electric oven open a crack during broiling. Because gas ovens have built-in ventilation systems, there is no need to leave the door open.

To ensure that your halved birds will turn crisp and brown without burning, and will cook through evenly, broil them 4 inches [10 cm.] or so from the heat. Always remove the wing tips and flatten the birds before cooking them so that protruding wings and legs will not char during the time it takes the breast to brown.

1 Removing the backbone. With the bird on its back and the legs pointing toward you, insert a large, heavy knife into the breast cavity. Draw it down along one side of the backbone, severing the hip joint *(diagram, page 14)*. Open the bird and cut along the other side of the backbone to free it *(above)*.

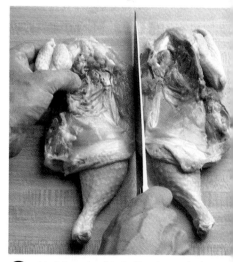

2 Halving the bird. Cut through the white membrane along both sides of the breastbone. Turn the bird over. Grasp the top of the breast on each side of the breastbone and bend the breast backward until the breastbone snaps. Pull out the bone and attached cartilage. Then sever the halves *(above)*.

Finishing Touches for an Oven-broiled Bird

A cheese topping will crisp in the broiler.

Pan drippings provide a base for sauce.

To turn simple broiled poultry into a more finished dish, spread on a top coating of grated cheese *(above, left)* or bread crumbs. Do so before taking the bird from the broiler, and let the topping toast. Or stir up a sauce from the pan drippings *(above, right)*.

The crusty topping is a mixture of finely grated Parmesan and creamed butter. You can improvise with various kinds of cheese and bread or cracker crumbs, and such flavorings as garlic, lemon peel and fresh or dried herbs—

adding creamed or melted butter or a little oil to moisten them.

To create a delicate sauce, put the bird on a heated platter, place the broiler pan on top of the stove, lift off the rack and spoon off any liquid fat. Heat the remaining juices. Loosen the brown particles with a wooden spoon. Stir in a handful of chopped onions; when they wilt, add a cup or so of wine or chicken stock, then boil the mixture to reduce it to half its original quantity. Season the sauce and serve it.

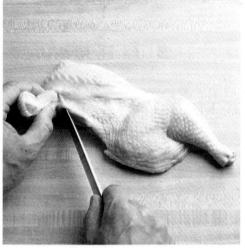

3 **Opening up the leg joint.** With each half flesh side up, make a nick in the flesh of the thigh at the point where it meets the drumstick. This small incision will expose a greater area of the leg's flesh to the heat; as a result, the thicker thigh will finish cooking at the same time as the breast.

4 **Cutting the wing tendon.** Slip the point of a knife under the skin at the shoulder joint *(diagram, page 14)* and sever the tendon on top of the joint. Cutting this tendon will prevent it from contracting and pulling the wing up closer toward the heat source.

5 **Cooking the bird.** After removing the pan and rack, preheat the broiler. Put the bird on the rack in the pan bone side up, season and baste *(above)* with oil or melted butter. Slide the pan underneath the broiler so that the surface of the bird will be about 4 inches [10 cm.] away from the source of heat.

6 **Turning the meat.** Cook the bird for 12 to 15 minutes or until the meat is golden brown. Turn the halves over, using long-handled tongs so you do not pierce the flesh unnecessarily and let the juices run out. Baste the meat again.

7 **Testing for doneness.** The meat is done when the skin has cooked to a deep golden brown and the juices run pale yellow when you stab a skewer or knife tip into the thickest part of the thigh. If the juices look pink, put the bird back under the broiler for a minute or two more. Before serving, you may want to cut the halves into quarters. Season the bird with salt and pepper.

Getting the Most out of Outdoor Cooking

There are many options in cooking poultry outdoors, each with advantages. Using a rack lets you barbecue flattened halves *(pages 48-49)*, quarters or cut-up pieces that grill quickly. A rotating spit, on the other hand, enables you to roast whole birds—at a slower rate.

Both racks and spits can have as a heat source either an outdoor gas or electric grill or a fire. A gas or electric grill lets you adjust the cooking temperature with control knobs. A charcoal or log fire—particularly of fruit wood—gives poultry a subtly smoky taste; adjusting the heat of the coals, however, calls for finesse. Fires react to weather—wind, for example, acts like a bellows to intensify them. And, of course, the cooking heat changes as you add or remove fuel, adjust dampers, or raise or lower the rack.

You should allow 20 to 40 minutes for the coals to reach a temperature that is hot enough for grilling. You can test the temperature of the fire by placing the palm of your hand above the coals at the height at which the food will broil—4 to 6 inches [10 to 15 cm.] for poultry. If you are able to hold your hand steady for four seconds, the fire is medium hot and ready for grilling.

Although all poultry cooks best over moderate heat, timing varies widely. On a rack, turkey quarters need about 45 minutes to a side; chicken halves will take less than half as long to cook. Roasting time for a whole bird on a spit is longer. You can figure about 45 minutes altogether for birds that weigh up to 1½ pounds [¾ kg.], but allow 20 to 30 minutes a pound [½ kg.] for larger birds.

You may shorten the time on the spit for large birds and prevent fatty ones from dangerously spattering grease onto hot coals by partially precooking them. An hour in a moderate oven will draw out most of the ¼- to ½-inch [6-mm. to 1-cm.] layer of fat under the skin of a duck or goose, and the rest of the fat can be caught in a foil pan underneath the spit *(Step 3, bottom row)*.

For safety, however, keep a squirt gun or spray bottle filled with water at your side to douse gouts of flame; and use long-handled utensils and fireproof mitts.

The Right Way to Barbecue

1 Preparing the coals. Pile charcoal in a mound and start the fire. After about 30 minutes, when all the coals are covered with white ash, use a long-handled implement to spread them out evenly over the bottom of the firebox. Set the grill rack 4 to 6 inches [10 to 15 cm.] above the coals, let it heat for five minutes, then grease it with an oil-soaked cloth or pieces of fat.

2 Grilling the birds. Put the oiled grill rack 4 to 6 inches [10 to 15 cm.] above the coals. If you have marinated the poultry halves, wipe them dry to keep the marinade from dripping. Place the halves on the rack, bone side down; the bones diffuse the heat evenly through the meat. Grill until the meat is brown. Turn the pieces and grill until the skin side browns.

Roasting Whole Birds on a Spit

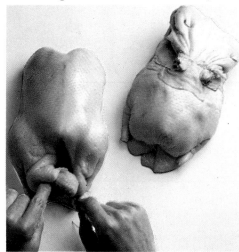

1 Trussing. Always tie up each bird—in this case, each duck. Skewer the neck flap to the back. Clip off the wing tips, tie a string to each wing and knot the strings under the bird. Tuck in the skin at the tail and tie the legs together.

2 Spitting. Push the spit blade, from tail to neck, through the cavity of the bird—here partly cooked duck. Press the prongs of the first fork into the thighs. Add a second bird if desired. Slide the second fork into the bird's breast.

Saucing the birds. When sauce is to be used, grill the poultry only until the skin side is a light-gold color, then slather the sauce — here a spicy tomato mixture *(recipe, page 165)* — onto the bone side and turn the halves. Allow the sauce to set, then sauce the skin side and turn the pieces. Continue turning and saucing until the bird is done.

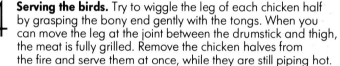

4 **Serving the birds.** Try to wiggle the leg of each chicken half by grasping the bony end gently with the tongs. When you can move the leg at the joint between the drumstick and thigh, the meat is fully grilled. Remove the chicken halves from the fire and serve them at once, while they are still piping hot.

Spit roasting. Mound the preheated coals *(Step 1, above left)* behind a drip pan placed under the spit. The fat should fall into the pan, not on the coals. Start the spit and let the birds turn until the skin is golden brown, basting them with sauce — here an orange mixture *(recipe, page 157)* — during the last 15 minutes or so. When done, the legs will move easily in response to pressure.

Lining Up Small Birds

Prepare small birds—here, game hens—by clipping off two joints of each wing and tying together the third joints beneath the bird. Cross the legs and tie them. The forks will hold a brace of birds snugly, spitted neck to tail. With more than two birds, spit them sideways *(below)*, alternating the direction in which the legs point; but the forks must pierce the innermost birds.

Game hens gleam with herb butter.

4

Braising
Creating an Assemblage of Flavors

Like many cooking terms, "braise" is French in origin: it comes from the word for a bed of live coals. The earliest use of braise in cookery referred to the ancient practice of embedding a tightly closed food vessel in the hot ashes of a fireplace overnight to achieve a long, slow stewing process. Old cooking pans often had a depression in their lids to accommodate hot coals; in that way food was cooked by heat from above as well as below.

Today, the equipment is simpler and the time required is almost always shorter. Braising now is a term for a cooking process in which meats or vegetables or both are combined with a relatively small amount of liquid, enclosed in a tightly covered pan or casserole and simmered very gently in a slow oven or over a burner at the lowest possible heat. Stews, daubes, and ragouts are all braises; and although their preparation may vary in detail, the basic techniques are common to all of them.

In its typical form, poultry braising starts by sautéing the bird—whole or cut into pieces—in fat or oil until it is golden. While it colors, the bird exudes juices that leave dark residues in the bottom of the pan. Aromatic vegetables—usually onions and carrots—may be browned in the same pan, before or after the bird is sautéed. Next, a small amount of water, stock or wine is stirred in to incorporate all the rich pan deposits; then more liquid may be added before the pan is covered. With the surface of the liquid barely trembling, the poultry is simmered until it is tender. The liquid should not be allowed to boil: too high a temperature dries out the flesh without shortening the cooking time, while the turbulence of boiling liquid interferes with the delicate merging of flavors.

The cook's work is not over when the poultry is done. The sauce in the pan or casserole will contain an emulsion, suspended in the liquid, of cooked fats that would be difficult to digest and would give the food a muddy taste. The emulsion must be broken down and the fat allowed to float to the surface where it can be removed by a careful process of skimming *(page 57)* to leave the braising juices lightened and purified. After cleansing, it may still be necessary to concentrate the flavor and improve the body of the braising liquid. One way to do this is simply to boil the liquid vigorously to reduce it. But straining it through a sieve and returning a purée of some of the braising vegetables to the liquid will reward the cook with a finished dish of richer flavor.

h veal stock is added to sautéed
icken pieces, carrots, onions and red
ne for a classic French braise: coq
vin. With the lid in place, the dish will
allowed to simmer gently; long
oking makes the chicken fork-tender.

Composing a Classic Chicken Braise

Chicken that is braised in wine is a classic dish—or, rather, many classic dishes. Scores of recipes develop the theme with variations that depend on the country of origin and the imagination of the creator. One of the most celebrated is coq au vin *(recipe, page 112)*, a specialty of the Burgundy region of France, which combines chicken with the full-bodied red wine of that province. Cooked with care and attention, the dish is not only a superb example of French provincial cuisine; it is also a model of braising techniques.

Given the choice, a Burgundy cook will prepare coq au vin with a farmyard rooster about one year old. Such a bird, too tough for roasting or frying, has more flavor than its young relations, and its meat, sinews and bones yield gelatin to enrich the braising liquid. Since, in all probability, you will be using a commercially raised bird, choose a large roasting chicken. Give extra body to the sauce by supplementing the wine with veal stock *(box, below right)*.

Like many fine braises, coq au vin is an assembly of ingredients that are first prepared individually to bring out their flavors. Different recipes may call for variations in the choice of ingredients and the order of working, but coq au vin is usually started by frying pieces of salt pork to partially render their fat and to color them, cooking aromatic vegetables in the fat, then browning the chicken pieces in the same pan. Then the braising liquid is added and the pan covered.

While the chicken is simmering on the stove or in the oven, the garnish vegetables—in this case, small white boiling onions and whole mushrooms—are partly cooked and set aside.

When the chicken is done, it is removed from the pan and the braising liquid is cleansed of fat and impurities to produce a rich, yet pure and digestible sauce. Then, at last, the chicken and garnish vegetables are combined with the sauce for the final minutes of cooking.

Preparing the aromatics. Parboil pieces of salt pork to rid them of excess salt, then pat them dry. Melt down the pieces by frying them in a little oil. When the pieces are golden brown, remove and set them aside on paper towels to drain; they will form part of the garnish for the finished dish. In the same pan, gently fry coarsely chopped onions and carrot pieces *(above, right)*. Cook the onions and carrots for about 20 minutes, stirring to prevent them from burning. Remove them from the pan and reserve.

The Multiple Blessings of Veal Stock

A good stock forms the basis of thousands of dishes, from delicate sauces to hearty stews. Such dishes can only be as good as their foundation and there is no substitute for a stock made from fresh, natural ingredients.

Since stock should contribute body and flavor to a dish without overwhelming the taste of the other ingredients, chicken or veal stock—which are rich yet mild in flavor—are the best choices, suitable for all poultry dishes.

To make the veal stock demonstrated here *(recipe, page 168)*, you will need a cracked veal knuckle to furnish gelatin and some inexpensive cuts of veal—rib tips or a shank bone with plenty of meat left on—for flavor. To prepare chicken stock *(recipe, page 169)*, use the carcasses and giblets. Simmer these gently with such aromatic vegetables as carrots, onions, leeks, garlic and celery— plus a bouquet garni—for about 4 hours for the veal, 2 hours for the chicken. Strain the liquid and, when it cools, remove every last bit of the surface fat.

Although the veal bones require the full cooking time to give up their gelatin, the meat will have surrendered much of its goodness after half that time. If you remove it at this point you can cut up the meat to take advantage of the flavor that remains; if you leave it in the pot, you will have to discard it. Left to cool and served with coarse salt, pickles and a salad, the veal pieces can make a meal in themselves.

Because veal or chicken stock needs such lengthy cooking, it is best to prepare a large quantity at one time. The finished stock will keep for a few days in the refrigerator. Better still, since the stock loses none of its flavor by being frozen, it can be divided into convenient 1-pint [½-liter] batches and stored in a freezer for later use.

2 **Coloring the chicken.** Season the chicken pieces with salt. Add more fat or oil to the pan if necessary and cook the pieces over moderately high heat, turning them until they are lightly browned all over. Sprinkle flour on the chicken *(above, right)* and turn the pieces until the flour is lightly colored. The flour will help thicken the braising liquid. Return the onions and carrots to the pan.

3 **Flaming with brandy.** Brandy is not essential, but it can be added even when recipes do not specify it. Flaming burns off most of the alcohol but leaves most of the brandy flavor. Pour over a little warm brandy (too much will drown the other flavors), carefully set it alight and stir the contents of the pan gently until all of the flames die. ▶

Skimming the liquid. Put the veal bones and meat in a pot and add cold water to cover. Heat very slowly, letting the water take about an hour to reach a simmer, so that the finished stock will be clear. As soon as scum rises to the surface, remove it with a spoon. Keep skimming, adding a dash of cold water occasionally to help bring up scum, until no more scum forms. .

2 **Adding the vegetables.** Add whole carrots, onions (one of them stuck with two or three cloves) and a bouquet garni. If you like, include a whole, unpeeled bulb of garlic; peeled garlic cloves would cook to a purée that could not be removed. Reduce the heat, if necessary, to keep the liquid gently simmering.

3 **Straining the stock.** After the stock has simmered for 4 hours, strain it carefully by pouring the contents of the pot through a colander or sieve into a large bowl or a clean pot. Discard the bones and the vegetables. After the stock has cooled, spoon off any fat that has risen to the surface.

4 **Deglazing with wine.** Pour the wine (perhaps the same wine that you plan to serve with the meal, but any good red wine will do) into the pan. As you bring it to a boil, scrape the bottom of the pan *(above, right)* with a wooden spoon to loosen all of the residues — they are important flavoring elements. The next stage — the slow braising — can be done in the same pan or in an earthenware or metal casserole. (Earthenware can be used on top of the stove if protected from direct heat by a fireproof pad.)

5 **Adding stock.** Pour in sufficient hot veal stock to cover the chicken. Add a bouquet garni *(page 68)*. Bring the liquid to a boil, then regulate the heat so the liquid barely trembles and cover the pan tightly. If the bird is old, simmer for at least 1½ hours; a roasting chicken may cook in 45 minutes or so.

6 **Preparing the garnish.** While the chicken is cooking, peel small boiling onions. Drop the onions into butter, cover the pan, turn the heat down and cook for 20 to 30 minutes. Stir or shake the onions frequently to color them evenly. Clean the mushrooms and trim their stems. When the onions feel almost tender when pressed lightly with a spoon, remove and set them aside. Using the same pan, toss the mushrooms in butter for a few minutes — over high heat so that the moisture they exude evaporates quickly *(above, right)*, thus preventing the mushrooms from stewing.

7 **Straining the braising liquid.** When the chicken pieces are tender, remove them. Pour the braising liquid through a strainer into a saucepan. Discard the bouquet garni, but return the carrots along with the chicken to the braising vessel, covering it to keep them warm. The chopped onions, unlike the carrots, will have lost most of their texture, but do not discard them: press them through the strainer into the sauce with a pestle *(above, right)* or a wooden spoon to give the sauce more body. Skim off the surface fat, using first a spoon and then absorbent paper.

Cleansing the sauce. Bring the sauce to a boil, then reduce the heat and place the pan half off the burner so that only one side continues to boil. On the still side, a skin of fat and impurities will form; when the skin is thick enough, remove it with a spoon. Repeat for half an hour or so, until the skin that forms is free of fat and the sauce has reduced to a consistency that will coat a spoon.

Assembling the dish. Add the whole onions and mushrooms, and the pieces of pork to the chicken and carrots, then pour in the sauce. Simmer, covered, for 15 to 20 minutes.

Finishing the dish. Gently fry cubes of bread in butter until they are golden-brown croutons. Use slightly stale bread with the crusts removed, and plenty of butter, or butter mixed with a little oil. Sprinkle the croutons with a little chopped parsley or with a *persillade*, made by mixing chopped parsley and crushed raw garlic *(above)*. Cook the parsley or *persillade* with croutons for a minute or so, then scatter the garnish over the finished dish *(right)* and serve directly from the braising vessel.

Changing a Braise into a Fricassee

When beaten egg yolks—often blended with fresh cream as shown here—are added to warm braising liquid, they serve as an emulsifier that thickens the liquid and transforms it into a smooth, rich sauce. Finishing a chicken braise with such a sauce turns the dish into a chicken fricassee *(recipes, page 118)*.

Up to the point when the yolks, or yolks and cream, are added, the preparation could be almost identical to that of the coq au vin shown on the preceding pages. To prevent masking the delicate flavor of the sauce, however, it is best to sauté the chicken and vegetables in butter rather than pork fat, and to braise them with white wine in place of red.

The secret of successful sauce making lies in preventing the egg yolks from cooking rapidly. Too much heat applied too fast will cause the proteins in the yolks to coagulate before they combine with the liquid, thus curdling the sauce. After the cream has been blended with the yolks, the mixture should be diluted with warm braising juices before it is poured into the pan. Thereafter, you have to guard against overheating the sauce lest the emulsion break down and the sauce separate. An egg-yolk sauce should be only warmed —never allow it to reach even a light simmer—if it is to remain thick and smooth.

1 **The initial blending.** In a bowl, combine the egg yolks with the cream. Beat lightly with a fork until the mixture is smooth and both ingredients are thoroughly amalgamated.

2 **Diluting the mixture.** Pour some of the warm — but not boiling—liquid from the braised chicken into the blended yolk-and-cream mixture, stirring the mixture as you pour.

3 **Thickening the sauce.** Set the pan containing the chicken over very low heat. Stir the diluted yolk-and-cream mixture into the braising liquid left in the pan, moving the chicken pieces around to blend liquid and sauce. Lift the pan off the heat or dip its base in cold water if the sauce shows signs of bubbling to a boil. Stir until the sauce thickens and coats the spoon.

Wines and Spirits in the Kitchen

Wine is not only a perfect accompaniment to good food, it is also a valuable cooking ingredient in countless dishes. Used in a marinade *(pages 12-13)*, it will flavor young poultry and help tenderize older fowl. In a braise, red or white wine can provide all or part of the cooking liquid. And a little wine, added to a pan after sautéing, will dissolve the meaty residues and furnish the liquid for a quick and convenient sauce.

But wine in cooking should be regarded as a raw material and, like other raw materials, it must be cooked. Wine contains acids, tannin and complex organic compounds that, uncooked, would give a sauce an overpowering and unpleasant taste. Moreover, alcohol that is perfectly acceptable in a drink is harsh and aggressive in food. Pure alcohol, however, evaporates at only 172° F. [78° C.], well below the boiling point of water: thus, even the slow simmer of a braise will dispose of most of the alcohol eventually. But in preparations where the cooking time is less than 30 minutes or so, the wine must be boiled vigorously to eliminate the alcohol and smooth the rough edges of its other constituents. After boiling, only the essences of the wine remain to flavor the finished dish.

It is a wise rule to use only wine that is fine enough to drink. So-called cooking wines contain salt—in a quantity the cook can only guess at—that will upset the balance of a carefully developed recipe. On the other hand, the finest drinking wines lose far more of their unique qualities through heating than they will contribute to the food; opening a great wine for cooking is, therefore, wasteful. A neat solution: save up what is left in bottles that you have served, then use the contents in the kitchen. The remnants of wine can be mixed as long as they are of the same color and the same degree of dryness or sweetness. But be sure to decant the wines into a bottle you can cork tightly. The bottle should be full, to minimize contact with air and keep the wine from turning to vinegar.

Whether you choose red or white wine for cooking is largely a matter of personal preference. Red wine gives a deeper color to a sauce; white wine is usually more acid and more delicately flavored.

Flaming brandy. Ladle warmed brandy over the food cooking in the pan — here sautéed chicken breasts — and ignite the brandy with a long match. Stir gently until the flames die.

Poultry is usually cooked with white wine—but there are many exceptions, the most famous of which is Burgundian coq au vin, shown on pages 54-57.

Because of their powerful flavors, fortified wines such as sherry, port and Madeira have comparatively few uses in poultry cooking: to enhance an aspic for glazing cold birds *(page 86)*, for example. But duck, more than other birds, is complemented by the sweetness and heaviness of port, which is used for marinades and braises in recipes such as duck with figs *(recipe, page 160)*.

Spirits—whiskey, rum, gin, brandy and liqueurs—may be even more concentrated in flavor. Most spirits can be used with poultry, but brandy is by far the most common choice. Because brandy—or any other spirit—has a strong taste and high alcohol content, few recipes call for more than half a glass.

As with wine, only good-quality brandy should be used in cooking. Brandy is usually added early in the cooking process and set alight to eliminate the alcohol. Flaming is not strictly necessary, since most of the alcohol will evaporate anyway, but many cooks believe that flaming sears the flavor of the brandy into every part of the food.

The safest way to flame brandy is to warm the required portion in a heat-proof cup by setting the cup in a pan and pouring hot water around it. If you have an exhaust fan above the stove, turn it off before igniting the brandy, otherwise the fan may draw up the flames. Pour or ladle the warmed brandy into the cooking pot carefully, lest the brandy ignite spontaneously. Finally, pass a long kitchen match gingerly above the liquid. But keep your head out of the way; alcohol flames can shoot up high.

Beer and hard cider also have much to offer an enterprising cook. Like wine, they are products of complex fermentation, and they are rich with the taste and aroma of hops and barley or apple. Naturally brewed, light-bodied beers are often chosen for cooking poultry, although in some cases dark beer is called for *(recipe, page 114)*. Hard cider (flat, noncarbonated is best) makes an excellent braising liquid, with a delicate flavor well suited to chicken.

A Slow-cooking Braise for Goose and Turkey

An old farmhouse braising method that develops a meltingly delicious flavor is cooking *en daube:* simmering meat and vegetables with a little liquid in a covered vessel for several hours. Duck, stewing chicken, turkey and goose *(recipes, pages 147 and 161)* are especially suitable for this treatment, since they can tolerate long, slow cooking without losing their flavor and texture. Goose is used in the daube shown on these pages.

Any daube benefits from the addition of fresh pork rinds. These butchers' trimmings are a generous source of natural gelatin and the long cooking time allows them to contribute their inimitable richness to the sauce. For extra body, add two calf's feet *(Step 2, below)* as well as rinds.

To make a daube, the poultry pieces, the rinds, the calf's feet and a mixture of chopped vegetables are arranged in la[yers]; the vegetable juices provide most [of] the liquid. Traditionally, the dish is pr[e]pared in the deep, bulbous *daubière* use[d] here. This earthenware vessel has a na[r]row neck that cuts down on evaporatio[n] and allows the fat to collect in a thi[ck] layer for easy removal. But any pot de[ep] enough to hold all of the ingredients [in] several layers will be equally suitable.

1 **Preparing the bird.** Cut up the goose, or other suitable bird, by the method illustrated on pages 14-15. If you use goose or turkey, divide the breast — as is being done here — into six pieces. To draw out excess fat from goose or duck, broil the pieces skin side up for 20 minutes on a rack set 6 or 7 inches [15 or 18 cm.] from the heat.

2 **Preparing feet and rind.** Split the calf's feet lengthwise so that they will render their gelatin readily. Cut the pork rind into pieces 2 to 4 inches [5 to 10 cm.] square. To rid the feet and rind of impurities that would muddy the cooking liquid, put them in a pan of cold water and bring the water to a boil. After 5 minutes, drain and rinse in cold water.

3 **Packing the daubière.** Finely chop a mixture of vegetables: onions, shallots and carrots are obvious choices, while tomatoes and mushrooms may also be included, as here. Line the bottom of the *daubière* with some of the pork rinds and the calf's feet. Add goose pieces, then vegetables and additional pork rinds in alternate layers, sprinkling each layer lightly with salt. When the pot is half full, add a large bouquet garni that includes a twist of dried orange peel *(above).* Continue layering the remaining ingredients, finishing with vegetables and pork rinds.

4 **Adding wine.** Add enough wine to cover the ingredients. Cover the *daubière* and simmer in a slow oven or on a stove top — protecting the earthenware pot with a fireproof pad. Cook goose at low heat for 5 hours. Duck, turkey or stewing chicken will require from 2 to 4 hours, depending on the age and size of the bird.

5 **Removing fat.** If you wish to serve the daube at once, the fat can be spooned off while it is still liquid. But if the dish is left to cool overnight in the refrigerator, the fat will solidify and be easier to remove. Cooling and reheating the daube has another advantage: it improves the flavor of the dish.

6 **A perfect daube.** If you are serving the daube at once, check the juices. If they are too thin, drain them into a small saucepan, then reduce and skim before returning them to the pot. Present the finished dish in the *daubière*. When you reheat a daube that has been refrigerated in its covered pot, use very gentle heat or a slow oven to prevent the meat from disintegrating; 1½ hours is about right. Check the juices and reduce them if necessary.

An Ingenious Method for Boning Birds Whole

Filled with savory stuffing, a boned bird is an impressive demonstration of the cook's art—and an economy as well. With the bones taken out, stuffed poultry can be served in slices *(page 65)*, a simple carving method that wastes no meat. The technique is especially useful for duck *(shown here):* a single duck usually provides only two or three portions; boned and stuffed, it can serve six. And the extracted bones can be made into a rich stock for cooking the bird.

The apparently intricate boning technique can easily be mastered by any cook who can cut up a chicken *(pages 14-17);* as with disjointing, the boning technique is identical for all poultry. All you need are a small, sharp knife and patience. At first the process may take an hour; later, it will go more quickly.

The boning technique keeps the bird's skin intact, with no slits except the openings where the butcher cleaned the bird. First, the structure comprising the wishbone, collarbones and shoulder blades is removed. The flesh can then be carefully peeled back from the carcass, leaving a limp meaty sack *(above)*. The main wing and leg bones are left in place, so that the bird—after it has been stuffed, trussed and cooked—will have a natural appearance. Carving then reveals the surprise within.

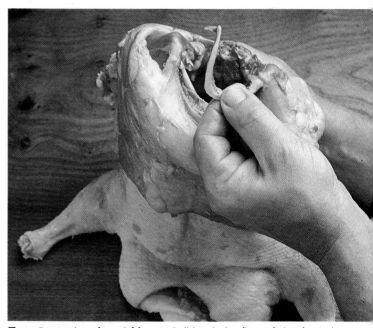

1 Removing the wishbone. Pull back the flap of skin from the duck's neck and then over the shoulders, turning it inside out until your fingers can locate the wishbone — the first bone in the cavity. Use a knife to slit just deep enough into the surrounding fles to expose the wishbone fully. Snap the wishbone from its attachment at the shoulder joints *(above)* at the point where it mee the collarbones, shoulder blades and wing bones.

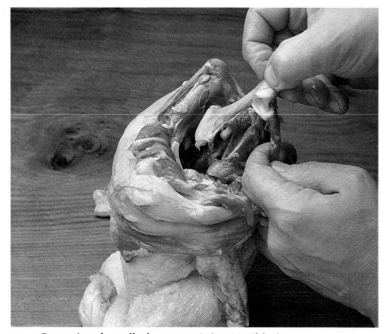

4 Removing the collarbones and shoulder blades. Each collarbone is now attached only by a connecting joint to a shoulder blade — a thin strut whose other end is embedded in the flesh. Pare back the flesh around one joint to expose it fully. Then remove both bones by pulling steadily on the joint *(above)*. If the bone breaks, cut out any remaining pieces with the knife. Repeat the procedure with the other collarbone and shoulder blade.

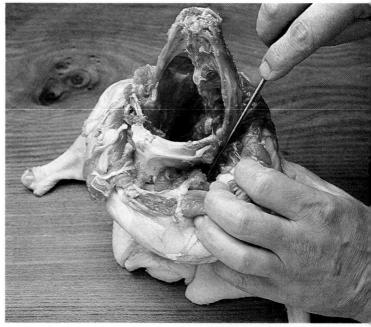
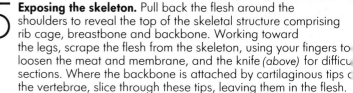

5 Exposing the skeleton. Pull back the flesh around the shoulders to reveal the top of the skeletal structure comprising rib cage, breastbone and backbone. Working toward the legs, scrape the flesh from the skeleton, using your fingers to loosen the meat and membrane, and the knife *(above)* for difficu sections. Where the backbone is attached by cartilaginous tips the vertebrae, slice through these tips, leaving them in the flesh.

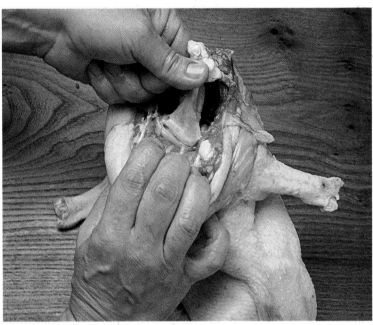

Freeing the wings. Pull back one wing, as shown above, and pull the flesh away from the shoulder until you have exposed the tough white bands of sinew that hold the wing bone to the collarbone and the shoulder blade. Cut through these sinews to free the wing, but do not pull out the wing bone. Repeat the procedure of pulling back and cutting to free the other wing.

3 **Snapping the collarbones from the breastbone.** One end of each collarbone is attached to the corresponding shoulder blade; the other end is joined to the breastbone by a weak and easily broken seam of cartilage. First, clear away the flesh around the collarbones with your fingers, scraping with the knife where necessary; then, snap each one free from the breastbone *(above)*.

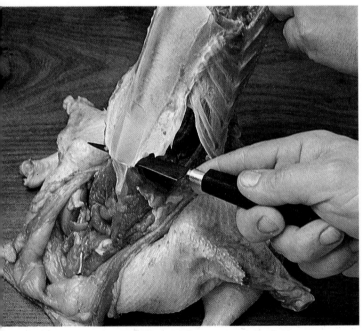

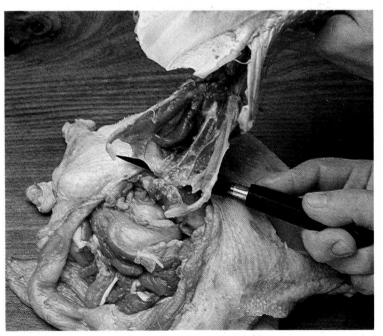

Separating the breastbone. When you have freed the skeleton as far as the legs, pop the thighbones from the ball-and-socket hip joints where they join the backbone and cut through the tough connecting cartilage. Leave both leg bones in place. Continue peeling back the flesh until you reach the end of the breastbone: a thin strip of cartilage connects it to the body. Cut through this strip *(above)* to free the breastbone.

7 **Removing the skeleton.** The flesh will now be almost completely peeled away from the skeleton. Lift up the skeleton and cut through the backbone at the tail *(above)*, leaving behind the last three or four vertebrae—the tail's bone structure. If the lower ribs, which are not firmly attached to the rest of the skeleton, remain in the flesh, cut them out. The boned duck is now ready for stuffing, trussing and cooking *(pages 64-65)*.

Boneless Duck, Plumply Stuffed

The wonderful flavor of duck has been appreciated by generations of diners, but finding a way to extend the number of servings is a problem. Duck is seldom inexpensive and its long body holds proportionately less flesh and more bone than do most other types of poultry.

One solution is to bone the duck *(pages 62-63)* and substitute a stuffing for the skeleton. Prepared this way, the stuffing itself becomes a major part of the finished dish, and a bird that would normally feed two now provides six generous portions. With its bones removed, the duck can be sliced as neatly as a loaf—which makes serving and carving it at the table both elegant and impressive.

It is important to choose a stuffing that marries well with the rich taste of the duck. A chopped-meat stuffing might be too heavy, a bread or rice stuffing too bland. A stuffing based on vegetables—such as zucchini, chard or spinach—mixed with ricotta cheese should be just right. (See the stuffing recipe for split, stuffed baked chicken, page 106, but double the quantities to provide enough to fill the enlarged cavity.) The clean, simple flavor of this combination will not be overwhelmed. The ricotta gives the stuffing a creamy texture. Egg binds the cheese with the vegetables and ensures that the cooked bird can be sliced cleanly, without crumbling the stuffing.

After the duck has been boned and stuffed, it can either be braised or roasted—or cooked by a combination of the two methods, as demonstrated here. Partial roasting draws off fat and turns the skin an appetizing brown; subsequent braising moistens the meat in a stock made with the bones that have been removed. Simmered for several hours in veal stock *(pages 54-55)* or in water to which flavoring vegetables have been added, the bones surrender flavor and gelatin to furnish a braising liquid that can be reduced to a sumptuous sauce. The stock, however, must be prepared in advance—so be sure to leave plenty of time.

Although this is a complex dish that requires care and planning, not one of the techniques used—boning, stuffing, trussing—is difficult in itself. Only the combination is novel—one of the enormous number of possible variations on simple themes that makes cooking such an inexhaustible source of pleasure.

Basting in Cramped Quarters

A handy gadget. With a bulb baster, which uses suction to draw up the pan juices, you can simplify the chore of basting a bird—especially if the bird is in a close-fitting pan. Just squeeze and release the bulb to pull the juices into the tube of the baster; squeeze the bulb again to expel the juices.

1 Stuffing the duck. Fill the boned duck until it has regained its normal shape and is about two thirds of its former size. During cooking, the bird will shrink slightly, while the stuffing will expand; if the duck is packed too full of stuffing, the skin will split.

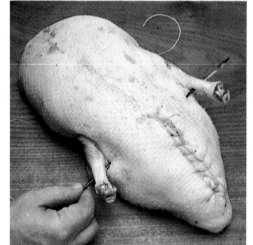

2 Trussing the duck. So that the duck retains its shape during cooking, use a trussing needle to tie the bird by the method demonstrated with a turkey on pages 38-39. Make sure you secure the neck flap to prevent the stuffing from escaping.

3 Preparing for roasting. Pierce the skin lightly all over the bird to allow the release of fat. Place the duck on its side a pan and roast it at 425° F. [220° C.] for about 15 minutes. Turn the bird to th other side and, after 15 minutes, place it breast uppermost to finish roasting f a total of 45 minutes. Basting with hot f will draw more fat from the bird.

4 **Braising in stock.** Remove the bird from the roasting pan and pour off the excess fat. Deglaze the pan with a little wine. Place the bird in a heavy, close-fitting vessel and fill the vessel with hot stock to a depth of about 3 inches [8 cm.]. Add the deglazed roasting juices, cover the vessel and put it back inside the oven. Braise for 20 minutes, basting often. Uncover and continue basting for about 30 minutes *(left)*; as the stock reduces, the basting juices will glaze the skin of the bird.

5 **Carving the duck.** Pour or ladle the braising liquid into a small saucepan, cover the braising vessel to keep the duck warm and set it aside. Prepare a sauce by reducing the braising liquid and cleansing it *(page 57)*. Transfer the bird to a platter or cutting board and remove the trussing strings. If you carve at the table your guests will be astonished by the ease with which you slice through the stuffed, boned duck.

5

Poaching
Simple and Delicious

At the beginning of the 17th Century, when chicken was such a luxury that its presence on the table was a symbol of prosperity, King Henry IV of France declared: "I want there to be no peasant in my kingdom so poor that he cannot have a chicken in his pot every Sunday." The king meant a poached chicken—*poule au pot (overleaf)*—made by cooking a fowl in water with fresh vegetables. The dish is still popular—deservedly so, for it exemplifies the virtues of the poaching method: simplicity, economy and flavorful results.

Poaching differs from braising in degree rather than in principle. In braising, the bird, which is browned in fat beforehand, simmers in relatively little liquid in a covered pot. A poached bird is never browned. In poaching, a greater amount of liquid is used than in braising and the liquid is rarely more extravagant than plain water or stock. It is seldom reduced, as braising liquid is; a portion can be set aside and thickened with a flour-and-butter roux to make a simple sauce. In addition, any leftover broth provides a stock that can be used in preparing other meals or frozen for future cooking.

Most poaching recipes call for chicken—stuffed and cooked whole—and vegetables such as carrots, onions and turnips, either left whole or cut into pieces large enough to retain their texture during the long cooking process. Other types of poultry may be used, however, including capon, duck and—provided you have a large enough pot—goose *(recipe, page 163)* or turkey. You can also vary the choice of vegetables used according to your personal preference and what is available in the neighborhood grocery stores or your garden.

Whatever combination of poultry and vegetables you choose, and whatever the poaching liquid, the art of successful poaching lies in regulating the temperature of the liquid throughout the cooking process. The bird should be immersed in a pot of cold or warm water and brought slowly to a boil; if it were put directly into boiling liquid, the skin might split. During cooking, the poaching liquid should be kept just below the boiling point to prevent the bird from drying out and becoming stringy. The great French chef Escoffier considered this so important that he was moved to write: "However nonsensical it may sound, the best possible definition of a poaching is a boiling that does not boil."

lump chicken is lifted from its bath
oaching liquid. Having flavored the
th, the vegetables bobbing on the
ace may also serve as an
ompaniment to the cooked bird.

A Whole Meal from a Single Dish

The cooking method originally evolved to prepare a tough old hen for a peasant's table—poaching the bird with vegetables *(recipes, pages 129 and 132)*—produces a complete meal. The poaching liquid becomes a broth to serve as a first course, and the chicken and vegetables make a main course. If you use a roasting bird rather than a stewing chicken, the dish will be ready in about half the time (one hour instead of two) and the meat will be more tender; but the broth will not be as savory as that produced by the older bird's rich flesh.

Old or young, the bird's flavor will be improved by a stuffing *(recipe, page 167)*. Remember to sew up the vent of a stuffed bird as you truss it; this keeps liquid from seeping in or stuffing from creeping out.

Put the trussed bird in the pot with water to cover, bring the liquid slowly to a boil, then skim it. Now add vegetables and flavorings—here, leeks, carrots, onions, a bouquet garni and garlic. If your bird is a stewing chicken, the vegetables will be limp and tasteless after the two hours of cooking. For a garnish, they should be replaced with fresh vegetables 30 minutes before the chicken is done.

1 **Immersing the chicken.** Place the bird, stuffed and trussed as for roasting *(pages 38-39)*, in a pot containing enough water to cover it. Add salt and bring slowly to a boil, spooning off any scum that comes to the surface.

2 **Adding vegetables.** When no more scum forms, reduce the heat so that the liquid barely trembles. Add vegetables and a bouquet garni *(box, below)* — and, if you like, a whole bulb of garlic. If you add leeks, as sho[w]n here, trim off the tough leaves and clean the leeks, then tie them in a bun[dle] to prevent them from falling apart.

A Neat Bundle of Seasonings

A bouquet garni is simply a bunch of mixed herbs that flavors stocks, soups and braises during cooking and is discarded at the end of the process. The commercial version, which is a spoonful of dried herbs in a little muslin bag, is usually stale and expensive. The real thing is cheap, easy to make and much more flavorful. The basis of a classic bouquet garni is the triple alliance of fresh or dried bay leaf, fresh parsley (including the stems, and the roots, if you can get them) and fresh or dried thyme. The herbs are wrapped with a celery rib or leek green—or both, as here—and tied with string. There are no unbreakable rules about the composition of a bouquet garni. Bay leaf, parsley and thyme are nearly always present, but other herbs and vegetables—and even orange or lemon peel—can be added.

1 **Assembling the bouquet.** Wash a large rib of celery and place in it your chosen flavorings: shown here are fresh flat-leafed parsley, dried thyme leaves, a bay leaf, celery tops and leek greens. Fold the celery rib and leek greens around the bundle of herbs.

2 **Tying with string.** Holding the bouquet together, tie enough kitchen string tightly around it to make a secure package. Leave a loop of string hanging free to remove the herb bundle when cooking is completed.

3 Poaching the chicken. Regulate the heat so that hardly a bubble breaks the surface of the liquid. Test a roasting bird for doneness after about an hour of cooking by pushing a skewer into the thickest part of a thigh; if the juices run clear, the bird is cooked. A stewing chicken will show clear juices after the same cooking time but needs at least 1 hour more to reach tenderness.

4 Serving the broth. When the bird is done, skim off any surface fat from the broth. Put a slice of bread in each soup plate, garnish with a slice of cooked carrot and ladle the broth on top. Grate Parmesan cheese over the soup. Leave a little broth in the pot with the chicken and vegetables to keep them moist. Keep the pot covered.

5 Serving the chicken. Remove the bird from the pot and cut the trussing strings as shown on page 40. Arrange the vegetables on a warm serving platter. Carve the chicken (page 42) and place it on the platter. Traditionally, *poule au pot* is accompanied by pickles, coarse salt and fresh creamed horseradish.

Keeping a Young Chicken from Falling Apart in the Pot

A young roaster or broiler poached in chicken or veal stock will absorb flavor from the cooking liquid and emerge almost as rich tasting as a stewing chicken. And the young chicken, unlike the older bird, will be meltingly tender.

The poaching liquid is not served as a soup; instead it is turned into a velouté (velvety) sauce *(recipe, page 168)*. For rich flavor, use a minimum of stock. A close-fitting poaching vessel helps to limit the liquid needed. To keep the chicken's flesh from falling away from the bones as it cooks, truss the bird and wrap it in cloth. Cheesecloth is traditional, but stockinet offers a more convenient, if unconventional, way to protect the bird. Tubular cotton gauze similar to the stockinet shown here is sold at medical-supply dealers or drug stores. Although the tube is only 1½ inches [4 cm.] wide, it stretches to fit snugly around a bird.

Finishing the poached chicken wi[t] sauce may be as simple as combining th[e] poaching stock with a butter-and-flou[r] roux. Adding cream to the mixture tran[s]forms it into a *sauce suprême (Step* ,[ ]*right);* for an even more sumptuous r[e]sult, add both cream and egg yolks *(re[c]ipe, page 133).* Two other intriguing var[i]ations on the velouté sauce are presente[d] in the box on the opposite page.

1 **Preparing the chicken.** Loosely stuff the cavity *(recipes, pages 165-167)*, sew up the vent and truss the bird *(pages 38-39)*. To keep the skin white during cooking, rub the bird all over with the freshly cut side of a lemon half.

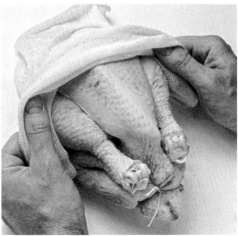

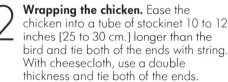

2 **Wrapping the chicken.** Ease the chicken into a tube of stockinet 10 to 12 inches [25 to 30 cm.] longer than the bird and tie both of the ends with string. With cheesecloth, use a double thickness and tie both of the ends.

3 **Cooking in stock.** Place the chicken breast up in a close-fitting vessel and add cold stock until the bird is almost submerged. Slowly heat the stock, skimming off the scum that rises. When the stock bubbles, reduce the heat to maintain a very gentle simmer and partially cover the vessel. Cook for about an hour or until the juices run clear when you prick the chicken thigh with a skewer.

4 **Making a velouté.** Remove several cupfuls of the poaching stock and cover the vessel to keep the bird warm. Make a roux by mixing butter and flour over low heat. Add all the stock *(above)*, whisking until it boils. Position the pan half off the heat and simmer for at least 30 minutes to eliminate the taste of flour from the sauce.

5 **Completing the sauce.** As the velouté simmers, a skin containing fat and impurities will form at the side of the pan that is off the heat. Skim it off at intervals, until the sauce is free of fat. You can serve the sauce at this point or transform it into a *sauce suprême* by adding heavy cream *(above)*.

6 **Coating with sauce.** Use the tied ends of the wrapper to lift the chicken from the poaching vessel to a deep platter. Cut off the wrapper and then the trussing strings. Place the bird on a warmed platter and, to mask any marks on the skin, spoon the sauce over it. Serve the rest of the sauce from a sauceboat, with the carved bird.

Variations on a Basic Sauce

The basic velouté is the foundation for a variety of sauces, all of which are excellent with poached chicken. To make a sorrel sauce *(near right)*, stem the sorrel leaves and, if they are not young and tender, blanch them quickly in boiling water. Drain the leaves, then squeeze them thoroughly dry. Next stew the leaves gently in butter until they are soft (about 5 minutes), then purée them through a food mill or a sieve. Whisk the purée into the velouté and add cream. (Caution: cook sorrel in an enamelware or tinned-copper or stainless-steel pan; the plant reacts with aluminum and cast iron, and in so doing would spoil the flavor and color of the sauce.)

For another variation on the basic velouté add peeled, seeded and chopped tomatoes, reduced to purée consistency after about 30 minutes of simmering in a small pan. Stirred into a velouté sauce together with cream, the tomato purée forms a *sauce aurore (far right)* that is named after its warm, rosy hue.

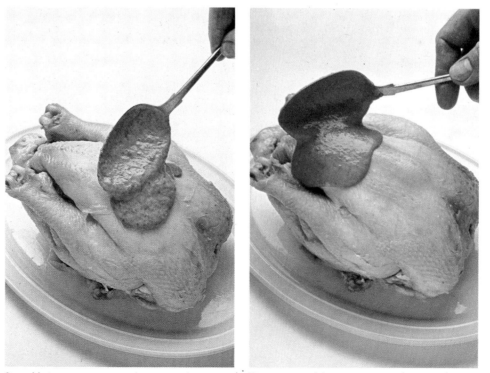

Sorrel brings tartness and green color.　　　Tomatoes add sweetness and rosy color.

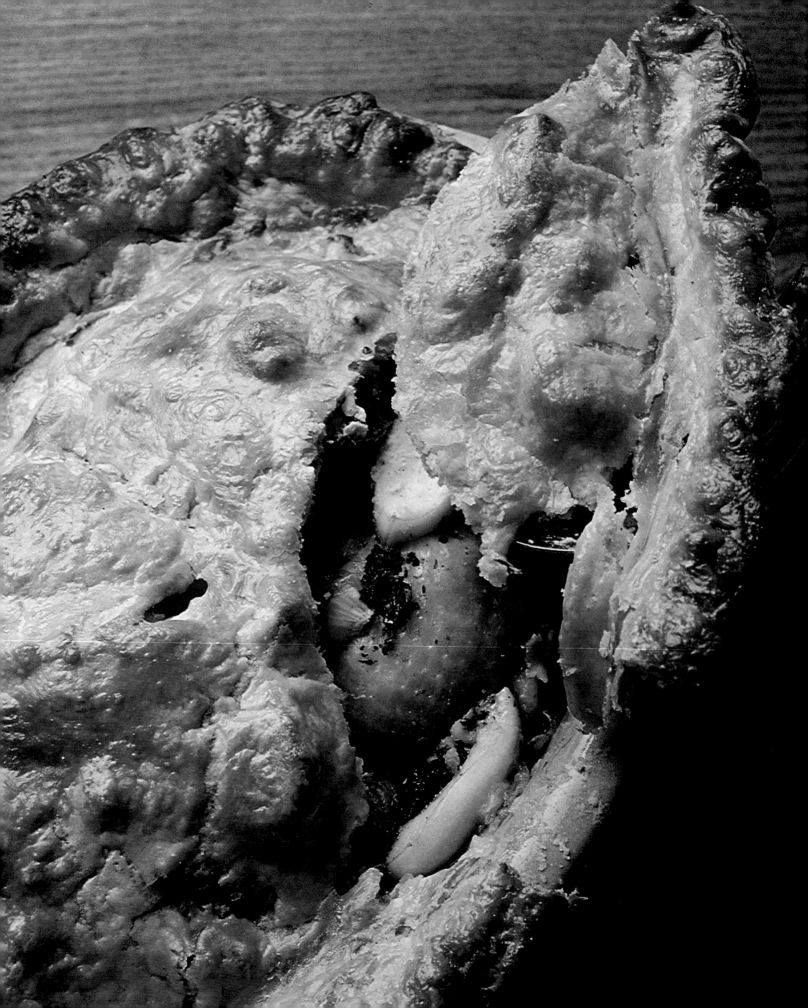

6

A Medley
of Methods

In addition to the general methods of cooking poultry—roasting, frying, braising and poaching—there are many specialized techniques that can be used to produce a range of attractive dishes not only from raw fowl but also with leftovers. You can, for example, bake any whole lean bird with your choice of vegetables and only a small amount of liquid in a tightly covered vessel, a process called casseroling. The liquid used in casseroling may well be water, but you can also enrich the mixture by substituting wine or stock. It is possible, too, to cook a bird without adding any liquid at all by encasing it in a clay pot that has been previously soaked in water; as a result, the pot releases steam during cooking *(pages 76-77)*. Both these methods rely on tightly closed cooking vessels that seal the fowl from the drying air, ensuring a moist finished dish.

Alternatively, you can seal out the air with the bird's own rendered fat and preserve fatty birds for months by the time-tested technique shown on pages 84-85. Or you can take any whole bird that is already cooked and serve it handsomely coated with an aspic *(page 86)* that not only is a sort of sealant but also serves as a substitute for sauce. The leftover aspic can be chilled and then chopped or cut into cubes for use as an attractive garnish to the platter.

Cut-up poultry, raw or leftover, tends to dry out, as every cook knows. This problem can be prevented by cooking or heating such poultry in stock with aromatic vegetables such as onions and carrots, and covering it all with a delicious rough puff pastry crust *(pages 78-79)* that turns the dish into the pie shown at left.

Sauces—such as the velouté described on page 71, which is based on stock, or the basic white sauce on page 80, which is based on milk—furnish another means of moistening dry pieces of cooked fowl. Sauces lend themselves to infinite variations in presentation as well as flavoring. Chicken pieces and vegetables covered in sauce can, if you like, be topped with crumbs and cheese, then heated in the oven or under the broiler to form a delicious, golden-crusted gratin *(page 81)*. Or the same ingredients can be presented as a filling for rolled, paper-thin crepes or tidy, boxlike bread cases (the techniques for making them are shown on pages 82-83). Such finished dishes are so good that you may decide it is worth cooking a fowl especially to make them.

spoon breaks through the golden
ust of a chicken pie into a delectable
erior: chicken pieces baked with
uartered artichokes and onions, and
oistened by rich veal stock. Pie
ings may include any type of poultry
d a variety of fresh vegetables.

Letting a Bird Baste Itself

When packed into a covered casserole with aromatic vegetables, a whole chicken requires little additional liquid as it simmers on top of the stove or in the oven. As the ingredients cook, they release moisture, which turns into steam that "bastes" the bird. After the chicken is done, the vegetables—typically a mixture that includes onions and carrots—become a hearty side dish.

Casseroling may appear to resemble braising, but it is in fact a different technique using steam, not liquid, as the moistening agent. While a fowl cooked this way often is called "casseroled chicken," it may appear on menus as *"poulet en cocotte"* or even "pot roasted chicken." But the last term is misleading; dry, searing heat—the prerequisite of true roasting—plays no part in the cooking. The roasted appearance of the finished chicken is due mainly to a preliminary browning in oil or fat, which also helps color and enrich the juices in the pot. In the simple casserole demonstrated here, bacon pieces also add flavor to the dish.

When cooking is complete, the concentrated liquid that remains in the casserole may be served as a sauce without further reduction or embellishment. Or the liquid may be combined with cream or other ingredients, as some recipes suggest. Other ways to vary the casserole include introducing different vegetables, filling the bird with one of a variety of stuffings, and using wine or stock as the moistening agent, instead of the water shown here *(recipes, pages 111-114).*

As to the choice of a vessel for the casserole, earthenware is perhaps the best material: it absorbs heat evenly and well, and usually looks attractive enough to be brought to the dinner table. Protected by a fireproof pad, such a pot can safely be used on top of the stove. Whatever the material, select a vessel that will hold the chicken and vegetables snugly and that has a tight-fitting lid that ensures a moist cooking atmosphere.

1 Preparing the bacon. In a pan with a little butter, brown a few strips of thick bacon that have been diced, blanched for 12 minutes in boiling water, drained and patted dry. Cook over medium heat, stirring frequently. Remove the bacon, set it aside and reserve the fat for browning the bird.

2 Browning the chicken. Wipe the chicken dry with paper towels, salt and pepper it, and place a bouquet garni in the cavity. Or fill the cavity with a stuffing made from the recipes on pages 165-167. Truss the bird *(pages 38-39)* and brown it on all sides in the bacon fat over low heat *(below).*

3 **Rendering excess fat.** Transfer the chicken to the casserole and place it, covered, in a hot oven. After 10 minutes, remove the casserole from the oven. Pour off any fat that has collected in the casserole *(above)* or use a bulb baster to draw up the fat.

4 **Adding liquid.** Surround the chicken with the bacon and the vegetables — here new potatoes, small onions and carrots — that have been lightly colored in fat. Add just a few tablespoons of liquid — water in this case *(above)*.

5 **Completing the dish.** Cook the chicken in the covered casserole in a moderate oven for about 1 hour, turning the bird occasionally; or cook it on top of the stove over low heat, protecting the pot if necessary with a fireproof pad. Test for doneness by the method shown in Step 10, page 40. Transfer the chicken to a platter, surround it with the vegetables and spoon the juices over it. Serve the vegetables before you carve the bird.

Cooking with the Bird's Own Juices

Baking chicken or other lean poultry in a sealed covering is an effective and ancient way of achieving moist, tender results without basting the bird or otherwise adding any liquid *(box, opposite)*. In Spain, for example, cooks encase a bird in wet clay and bury it in the embers of a fire. The clay hardens into a brittle shell; when the cooking is done, the clay is cracked open and pulled off.

A simplified version of this method makes use of a clay "brick"—a lidded pot designed to accommodate the shape of a bird *(right)*. Before the poultry is added, the pot is soaked in water; the porous clay absorbs the water then releases it as steam during cooking to keep the bird from drying out. As cooking proceeds, the bird's own juices provide extra moisture.

Another way to cook lean poultry is to wrap it in aluminum foil and steam it in the oven. To prevent juices from spilling, the foil should be folded carefully *(below, right)*, but not so snugly that steam cannot circulate around the bird. When you use foil wrapping, you can cook poultry at a higher temperature and for a shorter time than you otherwise would. If you want to brown the skin, however, you have to open the wrapping 20 to 30 minutes before the cooking time elapses.

How to Season Unglazed Clay

Food that is cooked in any new unglazed clay vessel will acquire an earthy taste and its own flavors will permeate the clay. If the inside of the vessel is glazed, or partially glazed, the manufacturer's instructions will tell you how to season it to prevent any transfer of flavor; if it is unglazed, use the traditional seasoning method to eliminate the clay taste: fill the vessel with water and add celery leaves, onion skins, leek greens and a few chopped carrots. Set the vessel on a fireproof pad and simmer the mixture slowly on top of the stove for at least 2 hours. Obviously, a vessel treated in this way should be used only for savory dishes; the seasoning flavors would permeate more delicate foods.

Baking in a Moisturizing Clay Vessel

1 **Preparing for the oven.** Immerse the clay vessel in water for as long as the manufacturer recommends. Season the bird's cavity with salt and pepper, and stuff it if you wish. Or insert a bouquet garni, some coarsely chopped onion and chopped garlic. Truss the bird and rub it with lemon, olive oil, salt, pepper and garlic as here. Drain the vessel, put in the bird and set the lid on top. For added flavor, make a bed of lemon slices for the chicken *(above, left)* and arrange olives around it *(above, right)*.

Baking in Sealed Aluminum Foil

1 **Preparing the bird.** Lay a doubled sheet of aluminum foil lengthwise in a roasting pan or an ovenproof dish. Place on it a trussed chicken that has been rubbed with butter or oil. Add a little water to produce steam and, if you like, cover the breast of the bird with chopped and sautéed carrots, onions and celery.

2 **Wrapping the bird.** Draw the two long sides of the foil together across the top of the bird. Fold back each side to make neat edges. Hold the two edges together, fold them over and then fold again in the same direction. Pinch the lengths of the double fold together.

2 **Cooking and serving.** Place the vessel in the oven before you turn on the heat to 450° F. [230° C.]; clay pots may crack if they are put directly into hot ovens. It will take about ¾ hour of baking time after the oven temperature reaches 450° F. to produce the finished bird shown here.

3 **Completing the parcel.** At each end of the sheet, repeat the folding technique to make a fairly loose parcel. Since the foil protects the bird from the drying oven heat, you can cook it at a temperature 125° F. [50° C.] higher than the slow-roasting temperatures shown on page 41; reduce the cooking time by about a third.

4 **Unwrapping after cooking.** Make a slit along the length of the foil package to allow the steam to escape. Then pull the foil apart and test for doneness before lifting out the bird; if necessary, continue roasting the chicken in the opened package. Place the bird on a platter, remove the trussing string and spoon the cooking juices over it.

A World of Cooking Wrappers

Foil and clay are just two of the many wrappings that are used for cooking lean poultry. The Chinese bake chicken encased in soft pastry that seals in moisture and is then served with the finished dish. In the Caribbean, birds for roasting are wrapped in banana leaves; in Senegal, baobab leaves are used.

One turn-of-the-century English chef recommended roasting birds in special paper bags; but a modern, heat-resistant nylon bag is safer. Moisture trapped inside it bastes the bird and the cooking time is shorter than it is in conventional roasting. Caution: Nylon bags must be pierced to allow some steam to escape and thereby prevent explosions during cooking.

Creating a Light, Flaky Crust

Making rich, flaky pastry to cover a pie *(opposite)* requires only the flour, butter and water mixture used for a standard short-crust dough *(recipe, page 167)*. But the dough must be repeatedly folded and rolled to create many thin, buttery layers. Then, as the pastry bakes, steam released by the butter and water will puff up those layers.

Cold is the key to light, successful puffing: the butter should be chilled and so should the dough, before and after each rolling; a marble pastry slab, if you have one, will help keep everything cool. Because this pastry calls for so much time-consuming chilling and rolling, it is a good idea to make it in large quantities; it freezes well for later use.

1 **Combining butter and flour.** In a chilled bowl, rapidly mix salted flour and chilled, ½-inch [1-cm.] pieces of unsalted butter. Cut the ingredients together with two table knives; your warm fingers would soften the butter.

2 **Binding the dough.** When the butter pieces are the size of large beans and well coated with flour, stir in enough ice water to bind the mixture. Use a fork and work quickly and carefully so that you do not mash the butter.

3 **Molding the dough.** Gather the dough quickly into a firm ball. Cover the ball with plastic wrap to keep it moist and chill it in the refrigerator for 2 to 3 hours, or in the freezer for 20 minutes.

4 **Flattening the dough.** Place the chilled ball on a cool, floured surface and strike it with a rolling pin, until it is a thick, workable pancake shape. Turn it over and flour it on both sides.

5 **Rolling the dough.** Pressing lightly and always in one direction, roll the dough into a long rectangle ¼ inch [6 mm.] thick. To prevent sticking, turn over the rectangle of dough often so that both sides are lightly floured.

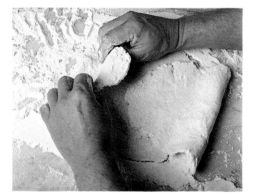

6 **Making the first fold.** Fold both ends of the rectangle toward the center; they should meet or overlap by an inch or two [2½ to 5 cm.]. Brush off the top surface before you fold; excess flour tends to toughen the dough.

7 **Making the second fold.** Fold the dough in half so that the first two folded edges are aligned lengthwise, one above the other. You now have a rectangle four layers thick. Cover it and chill in the refrigerator for 30 minutes.

8 **Rolling the layers.** Keeping the narrow, open end of the rectangle facing you, roll and fold the dough as described in Steps 5 through 7. Repeat the procedure two or three times, chilling the dough after each repetition.

Morsels Baked in a Pie

pie offers a golden opportunity to com-
ne poultry with a very wide range of
gredients, even including other meats.
re, pieces of chicken are cooked in a
stry crust with prosciutto, quartered
tichokes that have been steamed in
tter, hard-boiled eggs and veal stock.
her combinations appear in the recipes
pages 140-141, and of course you can
ate pies with whatever you have on
nd that melds well with poultry.

The poultry in the pie can be precooked
raw, boned or unboned. If you choose
w, unboned chicken, use the disjoint-
g method shown on pages 14-15 to cut it
o small pieces that will fit snugly into
e pie dish without wasting space. Be
nerous with the filling—a few bulges
der the crust will not hurt—so that
e pastry will not sag as it cooks.

The crust itself may be made from any
stry, but the rough puff pastry shown
re (box, opposite) is particularly light
d crisp. The time it takes the crust
puff and brown—usually a total of 45
nutes—determines the cooking time
en you use precooked meat. If your
ling is raw, unboned fowl, allow a long-
cooking time and cover the crust with
l if it begins to brown too much.

1 Packing the dish. Line the buttered sides and bottom of the
pie dish with ham slices, fit in the chicken pieces, and use quartered
artichokes and hard-boiled eggs to fill the gaps. Add only a little
stock (above) — or wine or even water — since the ingredients yield
their own moisture. The liquid must not touch the crust; that
would make it soggy. Sprinkle salt, chopped onion, mixed herbs
and freshly chopped parsley over the ingredients.

2 Covering the dish. On a floured
work surface, roll out enough chilled
dough to form a pie top that overlaps
the rim of the dish by at least an inch [2½
cm.]. The dough should be about ¼
inch [6 mm.] thick. Moisten the rim of the
dish, roll the dough loosely around the
pin and unroll it over the dish.

3 Sealing the crust. Fold under the
dough to make a double thickness all
around the edge. Press it firmly
against the moist rim and, with floured
thumbs, crimp it. Cut a few small slits
in the top to allow steam to escape. To
glaze the pastry, brush the top with
beaten egg mixed with a little water.

4 Baking the pie. Cook the pie in a
hot oven for 10 to 15 minutes until the
crust is puffy and crisp. Reduce the
heat and continue cooking until
the poultry is done. If the bird is
precooked, follow the same procedure
but serve the pie as soon as the crust
has turned golden brown.

A Gratin Sauce with Varied Uses

A white sauce made from butter, flour and milk *(recipe, page 168)* is a versatile ally when you want to reheat leftover poultry. The version shown here may appear in many dishes—from a creamy gratin *(opposite)* to a smooth filling for a crepe or a bread case *(pages 82-83)*.

Every white sauce starts out with a roux—a mixture of butter and flour that is gently cooked for a few minutes in a heavy, nonaluminum pan (aluminum may discolor the sauce). When milk is added, the flour thickens the mixture slightly. It does not matter whether the milk is added warm or cold, away from the heat or over it. The simplest method is to add the milk cold, all at once, while the pan is on the stove. If you whisk briskly, the sauce will be free of lumps. If lumps should form, simply strain the sauce through a sieve.

After the milk is added, the sauce is gently simmered for at least 40 minutes to reduce it to the desired consistency and to eliminate the taste of the flour. It is possible to produce a white sauce more quickly by increasing the quantity of flour, but that sauce will have neither the refined texture nor the purity of flavor of a sauce that has been only lightly bound with flour, and then thoroughly cooked.

To make enough white sauce for a gratin of chicken, add about 2 cups [½ liter] of milk to a roux made from 2 tablespoons [30 ml.] of butter and 2 tablespoons [30 ml.] of flour. If the sauce thickens too much, correct it by stirring in a little more milk. And if you find it necessary to keep the sauce warm before you are ready to use it, place a large pat of butter on the surface to prevent a skin from forming; stir in the butter before using the sauce.

1 Making a roux. Melt the butter in a heavy saucepan over low heat. Add the flour and cook gently, stirring constantly, for 2 to 5 minutes—until the mixture separates slightly and assumes a granular look. The brief cooking ensures a delicately pale sauce; longer cooking would darken it.

2 Adding the milk. With the pan still on gentle heat, pour the milk all at once into the roux, whisking briskly to blend the mixture smoothly. Raise the heat and continue whisking steadily while the sauce is coming to a boil.

3 Simmering the sauce. When the sauce boils, turn the heat very low and simmer gently for at least 40 minutes, stirring occasionally. Test the consistency: the sauce is thick enough for a gratin when it thickly coats a spoon. Season with salt, pepper and, if you like, with nutmeg. Add the pepper only at the last minute to retain its fragrance.

tting a Golden Crust on a Smooth Sauce

of the simplest ways to dress up
es of chicken—or any lean poultry—
y cloaking them in a smooth white
:e *(opposite)*, adding freshly cooked
etables and then crisping the top of
mixture to a golden brown gratin, or

crust, under the broiler or in the oven.
The resulting dish flatters both the texture and flavor of the fowl. Many cooks
associate the term gratin with melted
cheese and bread-crumb toppings. But,
while cheese and crumbs often are added
to help firm the surface, they are not necessary. If the sauce is rich and thick, a

thin brown crust will form flawlessly on
its own. To ensure that the top of the
sauce browns evenly—instead of burning in patches—arrange the mixture in a
flat baking dish so that it presents a rea-
sonably smooth surface to the heat.

:ubing the meat. Skin and bone
oth the white and dark pieces of the
oultry. Slice the meat about 1 inch
2½ cm.] thick, cut the slices into long
rips *(above)* about 1 inch wide and
en cut the strips into bite-sized cubes
at will heat through quickly.

2 **Saucing the meat.** While the white
sauce simmers, parboil and drain diced
vegetables—in this case, carrot,
green pepper and celery. Stir the meat
into the finished sauce. Add the
vegetables and heat, stirring to prevent
burning *(above)*. Season to taste.

3 **Adding the topping.** Spread the
mixture evenly in a flat baking dish. Mix
equal proportions of dry bread
crumbs and freshly grated cheese, such
as Parmesan, and sprinkle the
mixture over the surface of the sauce.

4 **Gratinéing the mixture.** Slide
the dish under a preheated broiler about
5 inches [13 cm.] from the heat. Broil
for 3 to 5 minutes or until the top browns.
Or place the dish in the upper third of
a 375° F. [190° C.] oven for 15 to 20
minutes until the crust forms.

Presenting Leftovers with Flair

A cooked chicken or turkey—skinned, boned, cut into bite-sized chunks and covered in sauce—may be presented not only as the gratin demonstrated on page 81 but also as a filling for the attractive, edible containers pictured here: bread cases or the thin pancakes called crepes. Both the filling and the containers lend themselves to any number of variations. Incorporating sautéed fresh mushrooms or parsley into the filling is traditional. But you might prefer to add pieces of roasted pepper or parboiled asparagus tips for a new flavor, or you could color the sauce with puréed tomato or spinach.

You can change the taste of the bread cases by using a whole wheat or rye loaf instead of a white one. The batter for the crepes may be enhanced by adding brandy or substituting beer for the milk or water called for in the recipe *(page 169)*. Or you can give the batter color as well as flavor by adding a pinch of saffron—for a delightful yellow tint—or a teaspoon [5 ml.] of finely chopped herbs for flecks of green. Whatever you do, remember that the batter for the crepes must never be thicker than light cream or the crepes will be too heavy.

Plan on serving two or three crepes to each person as a main course; if you decide to serve your chicken filling in bread cases, allow one case for each person. Make the case from a large, stale, unsliced loaf. Firm-crumbed bread can be shaped easily; if you use light-textured bread, freeze it for a few hours before cutting it into hollow cubes.

Wafer-thin Crepes for Stuffing

1 **Mixing the batter.** In a mixing bowl, whisk together the ingredients for the batter. Melt 1 or 2 tablespoons [15 or 30 ml.] of butter in the crepe pan and add the butter to the batter. Whisk the mixture until all the butter is blended into it. Then let the batter rest at room temperature for at least 30 minutes.

2 **Pouring the batter.** With a paper towel, lightly wipe the pan to remove excess warmed butter in it. Heat the butter almost to the smoking point, th pour in the batter and quickly spread by tilting the pan until the base is cove with a very thin layer. Cook the crepe a minute or so until it slides easily ba and forth when you shake the pan.

Making Bread Cases to Fill

1 **Cutting the bread case.** Trim the crust from a firm loaf. From it cut out a 3-inch [8-cm.] cube and, with a knife, carve the four inside edges of the cube; make these walls about ½ inch [1 cm.] thick and cut down to within ½ inch of the base. Insert the knife horizontally ½ inch above the base *(above)* and swivel it to free the center section.

2 **Completing the bread case.** Lift out the center section. If it cannot ea: be lifted, slice along the original inside cuts again until the center sectio completely detached. Shake out any loose crumbs remaining in the case.

3 **Turning the crepe.** Slide a round-tipped knife under the crepe and turn it. Cook the other side for half a minute until it is pale gold. (It will be spotted, unlike the first side.) Slide the crepe onto a warmed dish. Cook the rest of the crepes, but do not add butter unless the crepes stick; usually the butter in the batter will keep the pan greased.

4 **Filling the crepe.** As each crepe is cooked, stack it on top of the others. When the batch is done, turn the stack over. Take each crepe in turn and, holding it across the palm of one hand, spoon the filling onto the spotted side. Cup your hand to prevent the filling from running. Then roll up the crepe around the filling.

5 **Serving the crepes.** Arrange the filled crepes in a buttered, ovenproof dish, flap side underneath. Sprinkle them with grated cheese, dot the crepes with butter and heat them in a hot oven until the cheese is lightly browned. To serve, slip a spoon under each crepe and, lightly pressing down on the top with a fork, lift up the crepe.

3 **Buttering the case.** With a pastry brush, spread melted butter on all the surfaces of the case, inside and out. Put all of the cases on a rack, place the rack in a shallow tray to catch any butter that drips, and set the tray in an oven preheated to 325° F. [160° C.].

4 **Flavoring with garlic.** Bake the cases for 25 to 30 minutes, turning them until all the outside surfaces are crisp and golden. Remove the cases from the oven and lightly rub all the surfaces with a peeled clove of garlic.

5 **Serving the bread cases.** Spoon the prepared filling into each case. To finish, sprinkle a pinch of chopped parsley over the filling, or garnish with equal quantities of chopped parsley, chervil and chives, together with a few leaves of finely chopped tarragon.

A Time-honored Method for Preserving Goose

Goose will keep for months if it is simply salted, cooked and sealed under an airproof cover of its own rendered fat (recipe, page 164). Although freezing makes this method of preservation unnecessary today, the unique flavor of goose stored in this old-fashioned way is ample reason to try it. Traditional as an ingredient in a cassoulet—a French dish made by baking white beans and meats in an herb-flavored sauce—preserved goose also is delicious when heated and served with lentils or sautéed potatoes.

The art of salting and sealing poultry was developed by the farmers of southwest France, who needed to save the meat of large numbers of geese bred, force fed and then slaughtered only for their livers—the famed foie gras. Only a force-fed foie-gras goose yields enough fat for the whole process; but smaller geese, as well as ducks, can be preserved by the same technique if their fat is supplemented with lard.

1 **Collecting the fat.** Pull out the thick cluster of fat from the bird's cavity and add to it the fat trimmed from the gizzard. Cut up the goose by the method shown on pages 14-15, divide the breast into quarters, and trim off the excess skin — another bountiful source of fat. Refrigerate the fat and skin until you are ready to render them.

2 **Salting the goose.** The goose pieces must be salted for at least 24 hours. Sprinkle a thick layer of coarse salt over the bottom of a glazed pot larg enough to hold the pieces. In the pot, alternate layers of the goose and the s· seasoned with mixed spices. Top with a layer of salt. Cover and leave in a cc place or in the refrigerator.

Rendering the Fat of a Bird

The body cavity and skin of goose, duck, turkey and chicken contain large quantities of fat that can be used for sautéing or for preserving poultry. But the fatty globules first have to be refined—or rendered—by melting out the pure fat from the tissues that contain the globules. The melting must be done in water; if fat is cooked over direct heat, the tissues around the globules will burn and impart an acrid taste to the fat. After all the water evaporates, the fat is strained to remove the skin and the tissues—called cracklings—which can make a delicious snack or soup garnish.

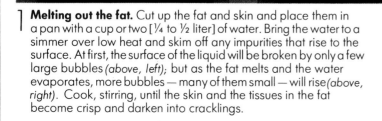

1 **Melting out the fat.** Cut up the fat and skin and place them in a pan with a cup or two [¼ to ½ liter] of water. Bring the water to a simmer over low heat and skim off any impurities that rise to the surface. At first, the surface of the liquid will be broken by only a few large bubbles (above, left); but as the fat melts and the water evaporates, more bubbles — many of them small — will rise (above, right). Cook, stirring, until the skin and the tissues in the fat become crisp and darken into cracklings.

2 **Straining the fat.** Soak cheesecloth or muslin in cold water, wring it dry and drape it in a double layer over a sieve. Strain the fat through the sieve into a heatproof container. Remember to save the cracklings.

3 Removing salt and herbs. When you remove the pieces of goose a day later, brush off all loose particles of salt and herbs clinging to them and wipe each piece clean with a cloth or paper towel. The salt will have drawn off moisture from the goose and will have begun to penetrate the flesh and preserve it.

4 Cooking the goose. Pour or spoon the rendered goose fat *(box, opposite)* into a heavy saucepan and set the pan over low heat. If the fat does not cover all the pieces, supplement it with lard. Add the goose. Simmer slowly, turning the pieces occasionally, until the meat is so tender it can be cut with a spoon — from 1 to 2½ hours, depending on the age of the bird. Remove the meat and set it aside to cool, but continue to simmer the fat until spitting stops, indicating that all moisture has evaporated. Strain the fat through a cheesecloth-lined sieve.

5 Preparing the preserving pot. Wash out the salting pot and sterilize it by filling it with boiling water. Turn the pot upside down to drain and let it air-dry. When the pot is dry and cool, pour in a little strained fat. Swirl and tilt the pot so that the fat will coat the sides and bottom as it cools and congeals. This coating will form a seal between the pot and its contents. Put in a layer of goose, skin side down to avoid trapping air beneath the concave inner surfaces. Cover with melted fat. Repeat until all of the pieces are used, covering each layer with fat.

6 Sealing the pot. Pour a 1-inch [2½-cm.] layer of fat over the contents. Let the pot cool. Refrigerate any unused fat. Next day, the layer of fat will have shrunk to expose some meat. Melt the refrigerated fat and pour in enough to cover the goose again. Cover the pot and store it: a cellar or cool pantry is traditional, but a refrigerator is better if there is room for the pot. The goose will be ready in three to four weeks. To serve, let the pot warm to room temperature and remove the desired pieces. When the pot is returned to storage, the fat will congeal and seal over again.

A Gleaming Centerpiece for the Table

Set in the place of honor at a cold buffet, a whole cooked bird glazed with aspic excites the eye as well as the palate. In addition to making poultry look appetizing, the aspic keeps the bird moist and contributes its own subtle flavor to the finished dish; aspic is to cold food what sauce or gravy is to hot food.

In the 19th Century heyday of haute cuisine, chefs took great pains to make aspic of crystal clarity. To achieve this effect, they simmered a meat stock with a paste made of egg whites and finely ground lean beef. After the egg-and-beef mixture had absorbed any particles that clouded the stock, the mixture was removed by straining the hot stock through muslin.

For an informal meal, there is no need to go to such lengths. The aspic used here to glaze a duck requires nothing more elaborate than basic veal stock *(recipe, page 168)* enriched by the addition of a glass of Madeira or sherry. The gelatin in veal bones is a natural setting agent and the stock should readily jell in a refrigerator, producing a translucent, amber-colored aspic.

Any bird, whether roasted, poached or braised, can be coated with aspic after it has been well chilled. Whether you make a fresh batch or reheat refrigerated or frozen stock to incorporate the wine, cool the stock until it is just on the point of setting. Spooned over a cold bird, the stock will form a thin glaze almost on contact. Then continue applying cool stock to build up the aspic to the desired thickness. Return the bird to the refrigerator for a short time before the application of each new layer in order to set the aspic. When the glazing has been completed, refrigerate the bird until you are ready to serve it.

1 **Cooling stock.** Fill a bowl with crushed ice and set a smaller, thin-walled glass or metal bowl in the ice. Pour a ladleful of veal stock into the small bowl and stir it with a spoon. As soon as the stock begins to congeal, it is ready for use. When it solidifies, warm it for a moment over low heat until it liquefies again.

2 **Coating the bird.** Put the chilled bird on a rack above a platter or pan. Spoon slightly thickened stock over the bird until the skin is covered with a thin glaze. Warm the stock that drips into the platter and rechill it for subsequent layers. Chill the bird for 10 minutes after every coat and before decorating.

3 **Decorating the bird.** To make an eye-catching presentation, dip thinly sliced olives and blanched tarragon leaves in chilled stock and arrange them in a pattern on the glaze. Refrigerate, and continue applying layers of stock over the decorations until the aspic reaches the desired thickness.

Anthology
of Recipes

rawing upon the cooking traditions and literature of more
an 20 countries, the Editors of Time-Life Books and the consul-
nts for this volume have selected 200 published poultry rec-
es for the Anthology that follows. The selections range from
e simple to the unusual—from poached chicken delicately
avored with tarragon to a mouth-watering dish of stuffed guin-
hen with raspberries. The Anthology also spans nearly 2,000
ars and includes recipes by 123 writers—from the Roman
astronome Apicius to such distinguished exponents of the clas-
c culinary art as Escoffier and Curnonsky, as well as such
odern authorities as Elizabeth David and James Beard. But
ere are also recipes by little-known authors of now rare and
t-of-print books held in private collections, many of them nev-
before published in English. Whatever the sources, the em-
asis of the recipes is on authentic dishes meticulously pre-
red with fresh, natural ingredients that blend harmoniously.

Since many early recipe writers did not specify amounts of
gredients, the missing information has been judiciously in-
rted and, where appropriate, clarifying introductory notes—
inted in italics—have been added. Modern terms have been
bstituted for archaic language, but to preserve the character
the original recipes and to create a true anthology, the au-
ors' texts have otherwise been changed as little as possible.
me instructions have necessarily been expanded, but in any
rcumstance where cooking directions still seem somewhat
rupt, the reader need only refer to the appropriate demonstra-
ons in the front of the book to find the technique explained.

For ease of use, the Anthology is organized by poultry type.
ecipes for standard preparations—stocks, pastry, batter and
asic sauces—appear at the end of the Anthology. The serving
iggestions in some recipes are, of course, optional.

All recipe ingredients are listed in order of use, with both the
istomary U.S. and the new metric measurements provided in
parate columns. The metric quantities supplied here reflect
e American practice of measuring solid ingredients, such as
our or sugar, by volume rather than by weight, as Europeans
. And to make the quantities simpler to measure the figures
ave been rounded off to correspond to the gradations on metric
oons and cups. (One cup, for example, equals 237 milliliters;
these recipes, however, a cup appears as a more readily mea-
rable 250 milliliters.) Similarly, weight, temperature and lin-
ir metric equivalents are rounded slightly. The U.S. and met-
c figures, therefore, are not exactly equivalent; necessary
ljustments have been made within recipes. Working with ei-
ier set of figures will produce equally good results, but the two
easuring systems should not be mixed.

Chicken

Chicken with Cucumbers

Poularde à la Charles Monselet

To serve 6 to 8

two 2 to 3 lb.	chickens, cut into serving pieces	two 1 to 1½ kg.
	salt and pepper	
10 tbsp.	butter	150 ml.
	oil	
1 lb.	fresh mushrooms with the stems removed and the caps quartered	½ kg.
16	boiling onions, finely chopped	16
6	large, ripe tomatoes, peeled, seeded and chopped	6
1 cup	heavy cream	¼ liter
2	small cucumbers, peeled, halved lengthwise, seeded and trimmed into chunks that resemble olives	2
	ground thyme	
½ tsp.	finely chopped fresh tarragon	2 ml.

Season the chicken pieces with salt and pepper. Heat the butter in a sauté pan, add the chicken pieces and cook rapidly until they are golden. Add a little oil if necessary. Remove the pieces and cover with foil to keep them warm.

Toss the mushrooms briefly in the butter remaining in the pan; remove them also and keep them warm.

Place the onions in the pan, put the chicken pieces on top of them and cover with the mushrooms. Cover the pan with a piece of buttered paper before putting on the lid, so that the cooking will take place in a sealed, moist atmosphere and the onions will not color. Place over low heat.

After 15 minutes, add the tomatoes and adjust the seasoning if necessary. After a further 10 to 12 minutes, add the cream, tilting the pan from side to side to mix in the cream thoroughly. Discard the buttered paper but replace the lid and leave the pan at a slow simmer.

While the dish is cooking, blanch the cucumber pieces in boiling water until they are tender. Drain them and add them to the chicken pieces in the pan.

Now comes the final delicate touch: add a pinch of thyme and the tarragon to the pan and simmer for a few minutes. To serve, arrange the chicken pieces on a warmed platter and pour the contents of the sauté pan over them.

CURNONSKY
CUISINE ET VINS DE FRANCE

Sautéed Chicken Breasts with Almonds

Suprêmes de Volaille Amandine

To serve 6

3	whole chicken breasts, cut into halves	3
	flour	
	salt and freshly ground white pepper	
8 tbsp.	butter	120 ml.
2 tbsp.	fresh lemon juice	30 ml.
½ cup	blanched almonds, split into halves	125 ml.
1 tsp.	finely chopped garlic	5 ml.
1 tbsp.	finely chopped onion	15 ml.
¼ cup	dry white wine	50 ml.
2 tsp.	finely chopped fresh parsley	10 ml.

Bring a pan of salted water to a boil and put in the chicken breasts. Boil them for 2 minutes and drain. Remove all the skin and breastbone, but leave attached the tiny tip of wing bone, if there is one, on each breast half. Dry the breast halves thoroughly on paper towels.

Mix some flour with a little salt and pepper, and dust the chicken breasts with it. Heat half the butter in a heavy pan. Put in the chicken breasts and brown the halves very slowly on each side. Add the lemon juice, and season with salt and pepper. Cover the pan and sauté gently, over low heat, until the chicken is tender. Remove the chicken halves, set them aside, and add to the pan the almonds, garlic, onion and another 2 tablespoons [30 ml.] of butter. Shake the pan over medium heat until the almonds are nicely browned. Then stir in the rest of the butter alternately with the wine.

Return the chicken to the pan and reheat. Arrange the chicken breast halves in a warmed, shallow serving dish. Spoon the almonds and sauce over the chicken and sprinkle with chopped parsley.

DIONE LUCAS AND MARION GORMAN
THE DIONE LUCAS BOOK OF FRENCH COOKING

Chicken Sauté with Vinegar

Volaille de Bresse Sautée au Vinaigre

To serve 4

3 lb.	chicken, cut into serving pieces	1½ kg.
10 tbsp.	butter	150 ml.
	salt and pepper	
4	shallots, chopped	4
1 cup	wine vinegar	¼ liter

Heat 7 tablespoons [105 ml.] of the butter in an ovenproof skillet big enough to hold the pieces of chicken. Season the pieces with salt and pepper, and brown them lightly. The butter should remain light in color. Cover the skillet and continue cooking the chicken in a hot oven, preheated to 425° F. [220° C.], for about 20 minutes.

When tender, place the pieces of chicken on a platter, cover and keep warm.

Sauté the shallots, without letting them brown, in the butter left in the skillet. Deglaze the skillet with the wine vinegar. Boil to reduce the vinegar by half and beat the remaining butter into the sauce. Pour the sauce over the pieces of chicken, carefully coating them.

PAUL BOCUSE
PAUL BOCUSE'S FRENCH COOKING

Sautéed Chicken with Garlic

Sauté Dauphinois

To serve 6 to 8

two 2 lb.	chickens, cut into small serving pieces	two 1 kg.
	salt and pepper	
⅓ cup	olive oil (or half olive oil and half butter)	100 ml.
24	garlic cloves, unpeeled	24
1	bouquet garni	1
¼ cup	finely chopped fresh parsley	50 ml.

Season the chicken pieces with salt and pepper, and place them in a large sauté pan containing the hot oil (or butter mixed with oil). Cook over high heat for 5 to 6 minutes, turning the pieces from time to time. Reduce the heat to low, cover the pan and leave the chicken to cook for another 15 minutes. Remove the lid occasionally to turn the pieces.

Add the garlic cloves and bouquet garni. Cook for another 20 minutes or so. Remove the bouquet garni, then transfer the chicken and garlic to a warmed platter and sprinkle with chopped parsley.

The guests should squeeze the garlic cloves (which become as soft as butter) out of the skins onto their plates and eat the cloves along with the chicken.

Another excellent *sauté dauphinois* can be prepared by replacing the garlic with 1 pound [½ kg.] of quartered green peppers. In this case the peppers should be added after the chicken has cooked, covered, for only 5 minutes so that the quarters can cook for about 30 minutes.

CURNONSKY
CUISINE ET VINS DE FRANCE

Chicken Sauté, Hunter-Style

Pollo alla Cacciatora

To serve 6

3 lb.	chicken, cut into 8 serving pieces	1½ kg.
3 tbsp.	oil	45 ml.
4 tbsp.	butter	60 ml.
	salt and freshly ground pepper	
½ lb.	fresh mushrooms, sliced (about 2½ cups [625 ml.])	¼ kg.
¼ cup	chopped onion	50 ml.
½ cup	dry white wine	125 ml.
1 tbsp.	flour	15 ml.
1 cup	boiling chicken stock	¼ liter
2 tbsp.	brandy	30 ml.
4	ripe tomatoes, peeled, seeded and chopped	4
1 tbsp.	chopped fresh parsley	15 ml.
1 tbsp.	chopped fresh tarragon (or substitute 1 tsp. [5 ml.] dried tarragon)	15 ml.

Dry the chicken pieces thoroughly on paper towels. Heat the oil and half of the butter in a very large skillet over fairly high heat and brown the chicken, a few pieces at a time, for about 2 minutes on each side. As the chicken pieces brown, remove them from the pan and put in fresh pieces.

When all the chicken pieces are browned, return only the thighs and drumsticks to the pan, cover tightly, reduce the heat to low and simmer for 10 minutes. Add the breast and wings, and simmer for 15 minutes longer, or until all of the pieces are tender. Remove them from the pan and put them on a warmed platter, season them with salt and pepper, and cover with foil to keep them warm.

Sauté the mushrooms in the remaining butter in a separate skillet for about 8 minutes, remove the pan from the heat and set it aside.

Drain off most of the fat from the skillet in which the chicken cooked, add the onion and cook over medium heat until the onion is golden. Add the wine, raise the heat and cook until the wine has evaporated. Stir in the flour, cook for 1 minute, add the boiling stock and cook until the sauce is thickened. Heat the brandy in a ladle over medium heat, ignite it and add it to the sauce. When the flame dies, add the tomatoes and herbs to the sauce, season with salt and pepper, and simmer all ingredients for 10 minutes.

Return the pieces of chicken to the pan, add the mushrooms, simmer for 3 minutes and turn the chicken and sauce onto a warmed serving platter.

LUIGI CARNACINA
GREAT ITALIAN COOKING

Chicken and Mushrooms with Cream

Poulet à la Crème

To serve 4

3 to 4 lb.	chicken	1½ to 2 kg.
6 tbsp.	butter	90 ml.
	salt and pepper	
½ cup	sliced fresh mushrooms	125 ml.
2 tbsp.	flour	30 ml.
2 cups	heavy cream	½ liter

Put half the butter into a fireproof casserole, sauté the chicken until golden and season with salt. Cover and cook gently for barely an hour. Add the mushrooms and cook uncovered for 10 minutes longer.

Separately, prepare a roux with the remaining butter and the flour. Let it cook for 10 minutes and whisk it with the cream to make a sauce. Season with salt and pepper. Cut the chicken into pieces. Combine the chicken pieces and sauce with the cooking juices and mushrooms in the casserole. Serve at once.

CURNONSKY
A L'INFORTUNE DU POT

Sautéed Chicken Breasts with Cheese from the Jura

Suprêmes de Volaille Jurassienne

To serve 4

2	whole chicken breasts	2
½ cup	flour	125 ml.
¼ tsp.	grated nutmeg	1 ml.
	salt and freshly ground black pepper	
2	eggs, lightly beaten	2
¾ cup	bread crumbs	175 ml.
¼ cup	grated Swiss cheese	50 ml.
⅓ cup	butter, melted	75 ml.
1	lemon, cut lengthwise into 4 wedges	1

Split the chicken breasts in half and bone them. Remove and discard the skin. Season the flour with nutmeg, salt and pepper. Dredge the breasts lightly in the flour mixture, then in the eggs, then in a mixture of bread crumbs and Swiss cheese. In a large skillet, brown the chicken breasts on all sides in the melted butter. Cook for about 5 minutes, or until done. Serve hot with lemon wedges.

NIKA STANDEN HAZELTON
THE SWISS COOKBOOK

Chicken Sauté with Cream

Poulet Sauté à la Crème

To serve 4

3 to 4 lb.	chicken, cut into serving pieces	1½ to 2 kg.
7 tbsp.	butter	105 ml.
1 cup	heavy cream	¼ liter

In a sauté pan or skillet, sauté the chicken, without browning it, in 4 tablespoons [60 ml.] of the butter. When done, transfer the chicken to a warmed serving platter and keep it warm. Deglaze the pan juices with the cream. Boil down to half. At the last moment add 3 tablespoons [45 ml.] of butter cut into small pieces and swirl the butter into the pan juices away from the heat.

Coat the chicken with the sauce.

PROSPER MONTAGNÉ
LAROUSSE GASTRONOMIQUE

Breasts of Chicken with Brandy

To serve 6

3	chicken breasts, boned	3
	salt	
1½ tsp.	finely chopped fresh thyme (or substitute ½ tsp. [2 ml.] dried thyme)	7 ml.
4 tbsp.	butter	60 ml.
¼ cup	brandy	50 ml.
1 cup	heavy cream	¼ liter
1 tsp.	paprika	5 ml.
	toast points, made from 3 slices firm-textured white bread with crusts removed, halved diagonally into triangles, and sautéed in butter	
	fresh asparagus tips, boiled in salted water for 3 minutes or until tender, and drained	
1	truffle, chopped (optional)	1

Skin and halve the chicken breasts and remove the wing tips but not the main wing bones. Sprinkle the chicken with salt, pepper and thyme, and dredge the halves in flour to coat them lightly. Sauté the breasts in butter in a heavy skillet, adding butter as needed. Be sure the breasts are only lightly browned (not cooked through to the center). Heat the brandy, pour it over the chicken breasts, and ignite it. Add the cream, cover the skillet and simmer for 10 minutes, turning the breasts once. Add the paprika and season to taste.

Arrange the breasts on a warmed platter and surround them with toast points. Garnish with asparagus tips. Strain the sauce remaining in the skillet over the chicken and asparagus. Sprinkle the top with chopped truffle, if desired.

HENRY PAUL PELLAPRAT
THE GREAT BOOK OF FRENCH CUISINE

Sautéed Chicken with Provençal Herbs

Poulet Sauté aux Aromates de Provence

To serve 4

3 lb.	chicken, cut into serving pieces	1½ kg.
¼ cup	olive oil	50 ml.
	salt and pepper	
½ cup	dry white wine	125 ml.
3	medium-sized ripe tomatoes, peeled, seeded and chopped	3
1	garlic clove, chopped	1
1	anchovy fillet, rinsed with water and drained	1
	savory and marjoram	
1	bay leaf, crushed	1
3	sprigs basil	3
½ cup	pitted black olives	125 ml.

Sauté the chicken in the olive oil. Season with salt and pepper. Remove the chicken pieces. Deglaze the pan with the white wine. Add the tomatoes, garlic, anchovy, a pinch each of savory and marjoram, the bay leaf and the basil sprigs. Allow this scented mixture to simmer for 10 minutes. Then add the olives. Return the chicken to the pan to warm in the sauce, and serve.

JEAN-NOËL ESCUDIER AND PETA J. FULLER
THE WONDERFUL FOOD OF PROVENCE

Chicken Sauté, Normandy-Style

Poulet Sauté d'Yvetot

To serve 4

3 lb.	chicken, cut into serving pieces	1½ kg.
4 tbsp.	butter	60 ml.
3	apples, peeled, cored and finely chopped	3
¼ cup	Calvados	50 ml.
	salt and pepper	

Sauté the chicken pieces in butter in a sauté pan or skillet. Meanwhile, spread the chopped apples in a smooth layer in a casserole. After 20 minutes, or when the chicken is half-cooked, remove it from the pan and lay the pieces on top of the apples. Deglaze the skillet with Calvados. Taste the pan juices for seasoning and add them to the casserole.

Cover the casserole and put it in a moderate oven preheated to 350° F. [180° C.] for 20 to 30 minutes.

MICHEL BARBEROUSSE
CUISINE NORMANDE

Creamed Chicken with Jerusalem Artichokes

Poulet aux Topinambours

To serve 4

3½ lb.	chicken, cut into 8 serving pieces	1½ kg.
1¼ lb.	Jerusalem artichokes	⅔ kg.
	salt and freshly ground pepper	
1 tbsp.	unsalted butter	15 ml.
¼ tsp.	crushed dried thyme	1 ml.
¼ tsp.	crushed dried oregano	1 ml.
¾ cup	dry white wine	175 ml.
¾ cup	heavy cream	175 ml.

Break the artichokes into segments so that they may be peeled more easily. Cut each segment into two or three pieces, depending on size, and trim each piece with a knife or vegetable peeler. The peeled pieces should be about the same size and shape—1½ to 2 inches [4 to 5 cm.] in diameter. Put the artichoke pieces in a casserole and cover with cold water, add ½ teaspoon [2 ml.] of salt and bring to a boil over high heat. Simmer for 8 minutes. By this time the pieces should be half-cooked and floating on the surface of the water. Drain them in a colander.

Salt and pepper the pieces of chicken. Melt the butter in a large, heavy saucepan equipped with a cover. Sauté the chicken on all sides, starting skin side down, until all the pieces are nice and brown (about 6 to 8 minutes on medium heat). Add the thyme, oregano, wine and artichokes. Bring to a boil and simmer, covered, for 15 minutes. Add the cream, ½ teaspoon [2 ml.] of salt and ½ teaspoon of ground pepper, and boil on high heat for 5 to 6 minutes, uncovered, to reduce and thicken the sauce. Place the pieces of chicken on a warmed serving platter, taste the sauce for seasoning as it might need more salt and pepper. Pour the sauce and artichokes over the chicken and serve immediately.

JACQUES PÉPIN
A FRENCH CHEF COOKS AT HOME

Chicken with Sweet Red Peppers

Poussins aux Piments Doux

To peel peppers easily, follow the instructions on page 11.

	To serve 2 to 4	
two 1½ lb.	chickens, halved	two ¾ kg.
4 tbsp.	butter	60 ml.
	salt	
	ground allspice	
	dried marjoram	
6	large sweet red peppers, roasted or broiled, peeled, seeded, deribbed and cut lengthwise into thin strips	6
¾ cup	dry white wine	175 ml.

In a large sauté pan, sauté the chickens in butter until colored. Season with salt, allspice and marjoram.

Add the peppers to the chickens, pour in the wine and bring to a boil. Reduce the heat to a simmer and cook, with the pan covered, for about 25 to 30 minutes or until the juices run clear when you prick the chicken with a skewer.

Place the chickens on a serving dish and arrange the garnish of peppers on top of them.

LÉON ISNARD
LA CUISINE FRANÇAISE ET AFRICAINE

Chicken Sauté with Tomato Sauce

Le Poulet Sauté aux Tomates

	To serve 4	
3 lb.	chicken, cut into 10 serving pieces	1½ kg.
	salt and pepper	
½ cup	olive oil	125 ml.
6	medium-sized onions, quartered	6
1	shallot, chopped	1
10	sprigs parsley	10
	dried thyme	
2	garlic cloves, crushed	2
6	tomatoes, peeled, seeded and coarsely chopped	6
¾ cup	dry white wine	175 ml.
10 to 12	black olives	10 to 12
	fresh lemon juice	

Season the chicken pieces with salt and pepper. In a large skillet, heat 5 tablespoons [75 ml.] of olive oil. Stir in the onions, the shallot, the parsley and a pinch of thyme. Allow the onions to cook until golden and then remove all of these ingredients and put them aside.

In the same skillet, heat the remaining olive oil and fry the chicken pieces until golden brown. Then add the garlic, the tomatoes, the reserved onion mixture and the white wine. Reduce the liquid to half by vigorous boiling for 10 to 15 minutes, stirring frequently.

About 3 minutes before serving, throw in the black olives and add a dash of lemon juice.

A quicker variation calls for reducing the tomatoes in a separate pan, moistening the pan in which the chicken has just cooked with a glass of white wine or stock, and adding the tomatoes, olives and a slice of lemon just before serving.

Another variation is to add, 10 minutes before serving, a few fresh button mushrooms cooked in their own juices or dried cepes that have been soaked and drained.

JACQUES MÉDECIN
LA CUISINE DU COMTÉ DE NICE

Chicken Sautéed with Cucumbers

Poulet Sauté à la Doria

	To serve 4	
2½ to 3 lb.	chicken, cut into serving pieces	1 kg.
	salt and pepper	
1 tbsp.	oil	15 ml.
4 tbsp.	butter	60 ml.
2 or 3	cucumbers, peeled, halved lengthwise, seeded and trimmed into olive-shaped pieces	2 or 3
½ cup	veal stock	125 ml.
1 tsp.	fresh lemon juice	5 ml.
3 tbsp.	brown butter, made by cooking 4 tbsp. [60 ml.] of butter over low heat until browned	45 ml.

Season the chicken pieces with salt and pepper. In a sauté pan or skillet with a heatproof handle, brown the pieces in oil and butter. Add the cucumbers, cover the pan and complete the cooking in a moderate oven preheated to 350° F. [180° C.]. The chicken will be done after 10 to 15 minutes.

Arrange the chicken and the cucumbers on a warmed platter. Deglaze the sauté pan with the veal gravy and lemon juice, and pour the mixture over the chicken. Sprinkle the chicken with the brown butter.

AUGUSTE ESCOFFIER
A GUIDE TO MODERN COOKERY

Brittany Chicken Sauté

Poulet Sauté Bretonne

To serve 4 or 5

4 lb.	chicken, cut into serving pieces	2 kg.
4 tbsp.	butter	60 ml.
3	medium-sized leeks, white part only, sliced and stewed in butter	3
1	small onion, sliced and stewed in butter	1
3 oz.	fresh mushrooms, finely sliced and sautéed in butter (about 1 cup [¼ liter])	100 g.
½ cup	cream	125 ml.
½ cup	velouté sauce, made with chicken stock (recipe, page 168)	125 ml.

Lightly cook the chicken pieces in the butter for approximately 15 minutes without coloring them. Add the leeks and onion. Cover the pan and set it in a moderate oven, preheated to 350° F. [180° C.], for 20 minutes. About 5 minutes before the chicken is quite cooked, add the mushrooms.

Arrange the chicken on a warmed serving platter. Add the cream and velouté sauce to the vegetables. Reduce the liquid to half its volume, then pour the sauce and the vegetables over the chicken.

AUGUSTE ESCOFFIER
A GUIDE TO MODERN COOKERY

Sautéed Chicken with Parmesan

Poulet Sauté au Parmesan

To serve 3

3 lb.	chicken, cut into serving pieces	1½ kg.
8 tbsp.	butter	120 ml.
½ tsp.	salt	2 ml.
2 tbsp.	flour	30 ml.
⅔ cup	light cream	150 ml.
6 tbsp.	freshly grated Parmesan cheese	90 ml.
3	egg yolks	3
4 tbsp.	fresh bread crumbs	60 ml.

In a sauté pan or skillet, brown the chicken pieces over moderate heat for 20 minutes in 2 tablespoons [30 ml.] of butter. Sprinkle on the salt.

In another pan cook the flour in the rest of the butter, without browning. Stir in the cream, 1 tablespoon [15 ml.] of Parmesan and salt to taste. Stir these over low heat. Remove the pan from the heat and finish thickening the sauce by stirring a spoonful into the egg yolks to warm them, then mixing the heated yolks with the remaining sauce.

Sprinkle 2 tablespoons of the Parmesan on the bottom of a heatproof dish, arrange the chicken pieces in the dish, coat with the sauce and put in the oven, preheated to 400° F. [200° C.], for 5 minutes. Sprinkle on the remaining Parmesan, mixed with the bread crumbs, and brown for another minute or two in the oven, then serve.

ALI-BAB
ENCYCLOPEDIA OF PRACTICAL GASTRONOMY

Chicken with Vegetables

Poulets à la Medina-Coeli

This recipe originally appeared in "L'Art de la Cuisine Française au 19ème Siècle" by Antonin Carême, who was called "the chef of kings and the king of chefs." The Malaga called for here is a sweet, fortified wine.

To serve 8

two 2 to 3 lb.	chickens, cut into serving pieces	two 1 to 1½ kg.
4 tbsp.	butter	60 ml.
	salt and pepper	
4 oz.	lean salt pork, diced, blanched in boiling water for 10 minutes and drained	125 g.
20	small boiling onions, parboiled for 5 minutes	20
2 or 3	carrots, shaped into small olives and parboiled for 5 minutes	2 or 3
1	bouquet garni	1
1	whole garlic bulb, unpeeled	1
½ lb.	fresh button mushrooms	¼ kg.
1 tsp.	Hungarian paprika	5 ml.
1 cup	Malaga	¼ liter

Sauté the chickens in the butter in a large sauté pan. Add the salt pork, onions, carrots, bouquet garni, garlic, mushrooms, salt, pepper and paprika. Moisten with two thirds of the Malaga wine and bring the contents of the pan to a boil. Reduce the heat to low and cook, covered, for approximately 40 minutes; the wine should be reduced to a light syrupy consistency. Move the chicken to a heated platter, discard the bouquet garni and the garlic, and garnish the chicken pieces with the salt pork, carrots and mushrooms. Add the remaining Malaga wine to the pan. Simmer for a few minutes, then pour the sauce over the chicken and serve.

BERTRAND GUÉGAN
LA FLEUR DE LA CUISINE FRANÇAISE

Chicken Sauté with Tomatoes

Poulet Sauté aux Tomates

The preparation of tomatoes called for in this recipe is designed to eliminate excess liquid and acidity, and is rarely described in cookbooks. Peel the tomatoes, halve them horizontally and remove the seeds. Salt generously and leave them to drain upside down in a sieve for about 2 hours. Rinse off the salt before using the tomato halves. Draining gives a result that no squeezing by hand can produce and is essential to the quality of the finished dish.

To serve 8 to 10

three 3 lb.	chickens, cut into serving pieces	three 1½ kg.
¼ cup	olive oil	50 ml.
4 tbsp.	butter	60 ml.
	salt and pepper	
	chicken or veal stock	
6	large ripe tomatoes, peeled, halved, seeded, salted, drained and rinsed	6
1	garlic clove	1
	cayenne pepper	
1 tbsp.	finely chopped fresh parsley	15 ml.

Place the chicken legs in a skillet with equal quantities of butter and oil; cover and cook approximately 25 minutes or until they are three quarters done. Add the breasts, season them with salt and pepper, and finish cooking them together with the legs. Drain the chicken pieces, leaving the fat in the skillet. Arrange the pieces in a casserole and moisten with a little stock; keep them warm.

Take the tomato halves from the sieve and cut each in two. Place the resulting quarters in a skillet with some of the fat in which the chicken was cooked; season and add the garlic clove; sauté over a high heat without breaking up the tomato pieces. As soon as the excess moisture has evaporated, remove the garlic clove, dust the tomatoes with a pinch of cayenne pepper and add the chopped parsley.

Arrange the chicken pieces in a pyramid on a warmed platter, surround them with the tomatoes and moisten with their own juice.

URBAIN DUBOIS AND ÉMILE BERNARD
LA CUISINE CLASSIQUE

Chicken Sauté with Lime Flowers

Poularde au Tilleul

This recipe was created by M. René Lasserre, the proprietor of the Chez Lasserre restaurant in Paris, in honor of Les Floralies, an annual flower show. Dried lime flowers, which are obtainable from pharmacies, health food stores or herbal specialists, lend a delicate flavor to poultry and game.

To serve 4

4 lb.	chicken, cut into serving pieces	2 kg.
	salt and pepper	
4 tbsp.	butter	60 ml.
2 tbsp.	dried lime flowers	30 ml.
½ cup	dry white wine	125 ml.
¼ cup	chicken stock	50 ml.
3 tbsp.	heavy cream	45 ml.

Season the chicken pieces with salt and pepper, and sauté them in butter in a casserole. Cover and continue cooking over low heat for 20 minutes. Sprinkle with 1 tablespoon [15 ml.] of lime flowers 5 minutes before the end of the cooking time. With a mortar and pestle, grind enough of the remaining lime flowers to make about ½ teaspoon [2 ml.]. Steep the rest of the flowers in ½ cup [125 ml.] of boiling water to make a strong tea.

Remove the chicken pieces and keep them warm. Deglaze the pan with the white wine and reduce. Add the chicken stock and ground lime flowers. Bind the sauce with the cream and simmer the sauce, without letting it reach a boil, for 10 minutes. Finally, add the lime-flower tea.

Arrange the chicken pieces on a platter and cover with the sauce. Serve with rice.

ROBERT COURTINE
MON BOUQUET DE RECETTES

Chicken Sauté Archduke

Poulet Sauté Archiduc

To serve 4 to 6

4 to 5 lb.	chicken, cut into serving pieces	2 to 2½ kg.
8 tbsp.	butter	120 ml.
2 tbsp.	chopped onion	30 ml.
	Hungarian paprika	
½ cup	dry white wine	125 ml.
¾ cup	heavy cream	175 ml.
1 tsp.	fresh lemon juice	5 ml.
2	cucumbers, peeled, halved lengthwise, seeded, cut into chunks and simmered in butter	2

Sauté the chicken in 4 tablespoons [60 ml.] of the butter without coloring it. When it is half-cooked, after about 30 minutes, add the onion that has been lightly cooked in 1 tablespoon [15 ml.] of the butter with a good pinch of paprika. Cook for another 20 to 30 minutes until the chicken is done. Remove the chicken from the pan and keep hot.

Dilute the cooking juices remaining in the pan with the white wine. Boil down by half, pour in the cream and cook at the boiling point for a few moments. Incorporate the rest of the butter, add the lemon juice and strain the sauce.

Arrange the chicken on a hot dish, garnish with the cucumber chunks and coat with the sauce.

PROSPER MONTAGNÉ
THE NEW LAROUSSE GASTRONOMIQUE

Marinated Fried Chicken

Chicharrones de Pollo

A recipe from the Dominican Republic.

To serve 4

3½ to 4 lb.	chicken, chopped into 16 small pieces by dividing the wings, thighs, drumsticks and breasts into halves	1½ to 2 kg.
¼ cup	dark rum	50 ml.
¼ cup	soy sauce, preferably the Japanese type	50 ml.
¼ cup	strained fresh lime juice	50 ml.
½ tsp.	salt	2 ml.
	freshly ground black pepper	
1 cup	flour	¼ liter
2 cups	vegetable oil	½ liter

Warm the rum in a small pan over low heat. Off the heat, ignite the rum with a match and gently shake the pan back and forth until the flame dies. Add the soy sauce and lime juice to the rum. Place the chicken in a deep bowl and pour in the rum mixture, turning the pieces with a spoon to coat them evenly. Marinate at room temperature for about 2 hours, or in the refrigerator for at least 4 hours, turning the chicken pieces occasionally.

Preheat the oven to the lowest setting and line a large shallow baking dish with a double thickness of paper towels. Pat the pieces of chicken completely dry with paper towels and season them with the salt and a few grindings of pepper. Dip them in the flour and shake vigorously to remove the excess. In a heavy 10- to 12-inch [25- to 30-cm.] skillet, heat the oil over a high heat until it is very hot but not smoking.

Fry five or six pieces of chicken at a time for about 6 minutes on each side, turning them with tongs or a slotted spoon and regulating the heat so they color richly and evenly without burning. As they brown, transfer the pieces to the lined baking dish and keep them warm in the oven.

Serve the chicken as soon as all the pieces are cooked, accompanied if you like with hot boiled rice.

FOODS OF THE WORLD/THE COOKING OF THE CARIBBEAN ISLANDS

Tangerine Peel Quick-fried Chicken in Hot Sauce

Instructions for chopping a chicken into 16 to 20 pieces are given in the recipe on page 100.

To serve 4

2 lb.	chicken	1 kg.
3	slices fresh ginger root	3
1	onion, sliced	1
	salt	
3 tbsp.	soy sauce	45 ml.
3 tbsp.	dry sherry	45 ml.
6 tbsp.	vegetable oil	90 ml.
2	fresh hot chilies, stemmed, seeded and chopped	2
1 tbsp.	dried tangerine peel, crumbled (or substitute peel from 1 large fresh tangerine, broken into small pieces)	15 ml.
2 tsp.	wine vinegar	10 ml.
2 tsp.	sugar	10 ml.
	black pepper	
1 tsp.	sesame-seed oil	5 ml.

Chop the chicken through the bones into 16 to 20 pieces. Place them in a deep bowl. Add the ginger and onion, sprinkle with salt and 1 tablespoon [15 ml.] each of the soy sauce and sherry. With your fingers, work this marinade into the chicken and leave the chicken to marinate for half an hour; then remove the ginger and onion.

Heat the vegetable oil in a large wok or skillet. When hot, add the marinated chicken. Turn and fry for 3½ minutes, then remove and drain the chicken and pour away any excess oil from the pan.

Add the chilies and tangerine peel to the oil remaining in the pan. Stir fry over high heat for 15 seconds; return the chicken to the pan. Turn the chicken over just once. In a bowl, mix the rest of the sherry and soy sauce, the vinegar, sugar and pepper. Pour the mixture evenly over the chicken. Stir fry for another ½ minute, sprinkle with sesame-seed oil and serve.

KENNETH LO
CHINESE FOOD

Stir-fried Chicken with Fresh Mushrooms

Ma Ku Chi Pien

To serve 4

6 oz.	boneless chicken breast	180 g.
2	medium-sized zucchini	2
⅓ lb.	fresh mushrooms	150 g.
¼ cup	thinly sliced carrots, parboiled	50 ml.
¼ cup	peanut or corn oil	50 ml.
1 tbsp.	dry sherry	15 ml.
1 tsp.	salt	5 ml.
½ tsp.	cornstarch combined with 3 tbsp. [45 ml.] water	7 ml.

Marinade

2 tsp.	cornstarch	10 ml.
2 tbsp.	cold water	30 ml.
½ tsp.	salt	2 ml.

Slice the chicken breast with the grain into 2-by-1-by-⅛-inch [5-cm.-by-2½-cm.-by-3-mm.] pieces; there should be about 1 cup [¼ liter]. Combine the sliced chicken with the marinade ingredients and, using your hand, mix well. The chicken can be either cooked right away or covered and kept in the refrigerator for up to 24 hours.

Cut the zucchini lengthwise into halves, then slice diagonally into ½-inch [1-cm.] pieces—about 4 cups [1 liter]. Slice the mushrooms, about 2 cups [½ liter], and set both vegetables on a large plate with the sliced parboiled carrots.

Heat a pan or wok over medium heat until it becomes very hot. Add 2 tablespoons [30 ml.] of the oil, then add the chicken and stir fry to separate the slices. If the chicken seems to stick to the pan, add a little more oil. As soon as the chicken separates into slices, sprinkle it with the sherry, mix well and transfer to a plate.

Reheat the pan, add the remaining 2 tablespoons [30 ml.] oil and stir fry the zucchini, mushrooms and carrots over moderately high heat for about 2 minutes. Add the salt and mix well. Add the cooked chicken. Stir to combine with the vegetables and to heat through.

Mix the cornstarch-and-water combination very well and pour slowly into the pan, continuing to stir until the sauce thickens and clear glaze coats the chicken and vegetables. Serve hot, accompanied by boiled rice.

FLORENCE LIN
FLORENCE LIN'S CHINESE ONE-DISH MEALS

Chicken Pieces with Vinegar Sauce

Spezzatino di Pollo all'Aceto

To serve 6

3 lb.	chicken, cut into serving pieces	1½ kg.
4	anchovy fillets, soaked in water for 10 minutes and patted dry	4
2	garlic cloves	2
½ cup	white wine vinegar	125 ml.
	salt and freshly ground pepper	
	flour	
½ cup	oil	125 ml.
3	sprigs rosemary (or substitute 1 tsp. [5 ml.] dried rosemary)	3

In a mortar, pound the anchovy fillets and the garlic to a paste. Add the vinegar and blend until smooth. Season the chicken with salt and pepper, and dust with flour.

Heat the oil, seasoned with the rosemary, in a skillet until the oil almost smokes. Then brown the chicken, a few pieces at a time, on both sides. As the pieces become brown, remove them from the pan and add fresh ones. When all are browned, return only the legs and thighs to the pan, cover tightly, reduce the heat and simmer for 10 minutes. Add the breasts and wings, and simmer for another 15 minutes. When all the chicken pieces are fully cooked, transfer them to a warmed platter and cover with foil to keep them warm.

Drain off all but 2 tablespoons [30 ml.] of the fat from the pan. Add the anchovy and vinegar mixture and reduce it over a high heat to half its original quantity. Return the pieces of chicken to the pan, cover tightly and simmer over very low heat for 5 minutes. Transfer the chicken to a warmed serving platter and spoon the sauce over it.

LUIGI CARNACINA
GREAT ITALIAN COOKING

Fried Chicken

To serve 4 to 6

3 lb.	chicken, cut into serving pieces	1½ kg.
½ cup	flour	125 ml.
1 tsp.	salt	5 ml.
¼ tsp.	pepper	1 ml.
½ tsp.	curry powder, preferably Madras-style (optional)	2 ml.
½ cup	milk, or as needed	125 ml.
	butter	

Preheat the oven to 350° F. [180° C.].

Pat the chicken dry. Mix the flour, salt, pepper and curry powder in a bag. Dip the chicken pieces in the milk, then shake them in the bag, a few pieces at a time, until coated.

Melt enough butter to lightly coat the bottom of a heavy skillet and quickly brown the chicken in it. Melt additional butter—about 4 tablespoons [60 ml.]—in a small pan.

Use a flat baking pan large enough to hold all the chicken without piling it up. Place the chicken pieces skin side down in the pan, pour over the melted butter and bake them on the lower rack of the oven for about 25 minutes. Baste and turn the pieces. Bake them for another 35 minutes, or until browned and done.

To cook on top of the stove, flour the chicken following the same preparation methods as above. Then place the chicken pieces in a heavy, greased skillet and brown them over low heat. Cover the pan and steam until the pieces are almost done—about 1 hour and 10 minutes. Remove the cover, raise the heat and let the chicken pieces crisp for 10 minutes.

JANE MOSS SNOW
A FAMILY HARVEST

Chicken Breasts Suprême

To serve 6

3	whole chicken breasts, boned to make 6 pieces	3
	salt	
7 tbsp.	butter	105 ml.
2 tbsp.	flour	30 ml.
	white pepper	
½ cup	chicken stock	125 ml.
¼ cup	dry white wine	50 ml.
¼ cup	heavy cream	50 ml.

Sprinkle the boned breasts lightly with salt. Heat 5 tablespoons [75 ml.] of the butter in a 12-inch [30-cm.] skillet. Add the chicken breasts and cook for 4 minutes over medium heat. Turn the breasts and cook for another 4 minutes or so, until done. Test with your finger to see that they feel springy. Remove the chicken breasts from the skillet, and keep them warm.

In a saucepan, melt the 2 remaining tablespoons [30 ml.] of butter. Blend in the flour, ¼ teaspoon [1 ml.] of salt and white pepper. Stir in the chicken stock and cook over medium heat, stirring until thickened. Add the wine and simmer for 2 minutes. Just before serving, stir in the heavy cream and heat. Pour the sauce over the chicken. Serve with rice sprinkled with fresh parsley, and green beans.

ELEANOR GRAVES
GREAT DINNERS FROM LIFE

Deep-fried Marinated Chicken

Toriniku No Tatsuta-age

To serve 4

12 oz.	chicken breast, skinned and boned	⅓ kg.
1 tbsp.	finely chopped fresh ginger root	15 ml.
½ cup	soy sauce	125 ml.
3 tbsp.	*sake* (strong rice wine)	45 ml.
	cornstarch	
	vegetable oil for deep frying	
2	scallions	2

Cut the chicken into bite-sized pieces and place them in a bowl. Mix the ginger with the chicken. Pour on the soy sauce and *sake,* and mix. Marinate for 30 minutes. Lift out the chicken pieces and roll them in the cornstarch, shaking to remove the excess.

Heat 2 to 3 inches [5 to 8 cm.] of oil in a tempura pan or a saucepan to about 340° F. [175° C.] on a frying thermometer, or until bubbles form on wooden chopsticks stirred in the oil. The heat should be a little lower than moderate.

Fry the chicken pieces, a few at a time, until golden brown. Drain them on the rack of the tempura pan or on paper towels. Arrange the pieces on a warmed platter.

Cut the scallions crosswise into 1-inch [2½-cm.] pieces, then cut them lengthwise into fine strips. Crisp them for a few minutes in cold water, then squeeze them dry in a kitchen cloth. Add to the platter with the chicken and serve.

ELISABETH LAMBERT ORTIZ WITH MITSUKO ENDO
THE COMPLETE BOOK OF JAPANESE COOKING

Deep-fried Eight-Piece Chicken

To serve 8

3 to 4 lb.	chicken, cut into 8 serving pieces	1½ to 2 kg.
2	slices fresh ginger root, finely chopped	2
1	scallion, finely chopped	1
1	egg, lightly beaten	1
¼ cup	flour	50 ml.
2 tbsp.	dry sherry	30 ml.
	oil for deep frying	

Add the ginger and scallion to the beaten egg, along with the flour and sherry. Blend to a smooth batter.

Dip the chicken pieces in the batter to coat them. Meanwhile, heat the oil. Add the chicken, a few pieces at a time, and deep fry until golden. The breast and wings need less cooking than the drumsticks and should be removed from the hot oil first. Drain on paper towels and serve.

GLORIA BLEY MILLER
THE THOUSAND RECIPE CHINESE COOKBOOK

Southern Fried Chicken with Cream Gravy

To serve 4

2½ lb.	chicken, cut into serving pieces	1¼ kg.
	salt	
1 cup	flour	¼ liter
1 cup	lard	¼ liter
	Cream gravy	
2 tbsp.	flour	30 ml.
¾ cup	chicken stock	175 ml.
½ to ¾ cup	light cream	125 to 175 ml.
	salt and white pepper	

Sprinkle the chicken pieces with salt on all sides. Put the flour in a sturdy paper bag. Drop the chicken into the bag a few pieces at a time and shake the bag until each piece is thoroughly coated with flour. Remove the chicken pieces from the bag and vigorously shake them free of all excess flour. Lay them side by side on a sheet of wax paper.

Preheat the oven to 200° F. [100° C.].

Over high heat, melt the lard in a heavy 10- to 12-inch [25- to 30-cm.] skillet. The fat should be ¼ inch [5 mm.] deep. If it is not, add a little more. When a light haze forms above the fat, add the chicken pieces, starting them skin side down. Since the legs and thighs will take longer to cook than the breasts and wings, put them into the pan first.

Cover the pan and fry the chicken over moderate heat for about 6 to 8 minutes, checking every now and then to make sure the chicken does not burn. When the pieces are deep brown on one side, turn them over and cover the pan again. Continue frying until all the pieces are cooked. Transfer the finished chicken to a baking dish and place the dish in the oven to keep the chicken warm while you make the gravy.

Pour off all but 2 tablespoons [30 ml.] of fat from the skillet. Add the flour, and stir until the fat and flour are well combined. Pour in the chicken stock and ½ cup [125 ml.] of the light cream. Cook over moderate heat, beating with a whisk until the gravy is smooth. If the gravy is too thick for your taste, stir in the remaining cream to thin it. Strain the gravy through a fine sieve if you wish. Taste for seasoning, then pour into a heated gravy boat and serve with the fried chicken arranged attractively on a heated serving platter.

FOODS OF THE WORLD/AMERICAN COOKING

Deep-fried Chickens

Petits Poulets Frits

	To serve 8	
two 2 to 2½ lb.	chickens, quartered and the wing tips removed	two 1 kg.
	salt and pepper	
1 to 2 tbsp.	chopped fresh parsley	15 to 30 ml.
⅓ cup	fresh lemon juice	75 ml.
	flour	
3	eggs, beaten	3
	bread crumbs	
	oil for deep frying	
2	large bunches fresh parsley (optional)	2

Season the chicken quarters with salt and pepper, and sprinkle them with chopped parsley and then with the lemon juice. Marinate the pieces in a bowl for at least 1 hour, turning them occasionally. Dry and flour each piece separately, roll it in the beaten eggs and cover it with bread crumbs.

Twelve to 15 minutes before serving, immerse the legs, which take longest to cook, in 2 to 3 inches [5 to 8 cm.] hot oil preheated to 375° F. [190° C.]; 5 minutes later, add the breasts. When the pieces are done and nicely colored, drain them, salt them lightly and arrange them on a folded napkin or a bed of parsley that has been deep fried for a few seconds.

URBAIN DUBOIS
ÉCOLE DES CUISINIÈRES

Pan-fried Chicken with Mustard

To serve 4

3½ lb.	chicken, cut into 8 serving pieces	1½ kg.
2 tbsp.	Dusseldorf-style prepared mustard	30 ml.
1 tbsp.	Dijon-style prepared mustard	15 ml.
2	egg yolks	2
2 tbsp.	heavy cream	30 ml.
2 cups	dry white bread crumbs	½ liter
	flour	
	salt and freshly ground black pepper	
	corn oil	

Skin the chicken pieces, using absorbent paper to give you a better grip on them and to pat each piece dry.

In a medium-sized bowl, blend the mustards smoothly with the egg yolks and cream. Spread out the bread crumbs on one sheet of wax paper and a little flour on another.

Season each chicken piece with salt and freshly ground black pepper. Dust it on all sides with flour. Dip it in the mustard mixture, turning it over to make sure it is entirely coated, and roll it in bread crumbs, patting them on firmly. Place all the pieces on a plate and chill for 3 to 4 hours to firm up the coating and allow the mustard flavor to penetrate.

When ready to fry the chicken, select one large, deep skillet (or two small ones) that will hold all the pieces in one layer. Pour in corn oil to a depth of about 1 inch [2½ cm.] and place the pan(s) over moderate heat.

When the oil is hot enough to make a bread cube froth on contact, add the chicken pieces; the oil should not quite cover them. Fry them over moderate heat for 15 to 20 minutes, turning the pieces occasionally with tongs or two spoons to avoid piercing the chicken. When the chicken is cooked through, crusty and golden brown, drain the pieces on absorbent paper and serve immediately.

Note: if you have to fry the chicken in two batches — or if it is not to be served immediately — you can keep it hot in an oven, preheated to the lowest setting, for 15 to 20 minutes.

ROBERT CARRIER
THE ROBERT CARRIER COOKERY COURSE

Fried Chicken with Cream Gravy and Mush

To serve 6 to 8

two 2 to 3 lb.	chickens, cut into serving pieces	two 1 to 1½ kg.
	salt and pepper	
	flour	
5 tbsp.	lard	75 ml.
Mush		
1 cup	white cornmeal	¼ liter
1 quart	boiling water	1 liter
1 tsp.	salt	5 ml.
1	egg yolk	1
Cream gravy		
1 tbsp.	butter	15 ml.
½ tbsp.	flour	7 ml.
1 cup	light cream	¼ liter
	salt and black pepper	

To make the mush, dribble the cornmeal into rapidly boiling salted water, stirring constantly, then let boil over direct

heat for 2 or 3 minutes and continue cooking for 1 hour in a double boiler. Let it cool slightly, add the egg yolk, beat well and set it aside to get cold.

Meanwhile, sprinkle the chicken pieces with salt and pepper, cover them with a towel and let them stand for 30 minutes. Dry each piece carefully and roll it in flour. Heat the lard in a heavy iron skillet; when the fat is very hot, but not smoking, put in the chicken (frying only a few pieces at a time). Turn them to brown on both sides, keeping the heat at an even temperature so that the chicken will not brown before it cooks through. As the pieces are cooked, drain them on absorbent paper, place them on a hot platter and keep them in a warm part of the stove until ready to serve.

Drop the mush, a tablespoonful [15 ml.] at a time, into the remainder of the hot fat in which the chicken was fried, turning to fry on both sides. The cakes should be about ½ inch [1 cm.] thick and the circumference of a water glass. Fry each cake a golden brown on each side and arrange in a border around the chicken pieces.

Use the same skillet to make the gravy. Melt the butter and sift in the flour; when well mixed with the butter and remaining grease and the bits left from frying the mush, add the cream, a little salt and a little black pepper. Let the gravy thicken, then pour it into a sauceboat and serve.

SHEILA HIBBEN
AMERICAN REGIONAL COOKERY

Erskine Caldwell's Genuine Southern Fried Chicken

To serve 6

two 3 to 4 lb.	chickens, cut into serving pieces	two 1½ to 2 kg.
5 cups	milk	1¼ liters
3 or 4	eggs, beaten	3 or 4
	salt	
	Tabasco sauce	
	flour	
	bread crumbs	
	oil or fat for deep frying	

Soak the chicken pieces overnight in the milk, to which the eggs, some salt and a dollop of Tabasco have been added. Drain and dry the chicken pieces, roll them in a mixture of half flour and half bread crumbs, and fry them in deep fat until they are brown. Finish the cooking in a moderate oven, preheated to 350° F. [180° C.], for 10 to 15 minutes; but do not allow the chicken to dry out.

Serve the chicken with baked yams, broiled tomatoes and a tossed green salad.

BERYL BARR AND BARBARA TURNER SACHS
THE ARTISTS' & WRITERS' COOKBOOK

Garlic-fried Chicken

Spezzatino di Pollo Fritto

To serve 4

3½ lb.	chicken	1½ kg.
1	egg, lightly beaten	1
¾ cup	flour	175 ml.
2 tsp.	salt	10 ml.
½ tsp.	black pepper	2 ml.
5	garlic cloves, 3 pressed or mashed to a paste and 2 left whole	5
½ cup	vegetable oil	125 ml.
½ cup	olive oil	125 ml.
1 or 2	lemons, cut into wedges	1 or 2

Have the butcher chop the chicken, bones and all, into 1-inch [2½-cm.] pieces. Wash and dry the pieces. Dip them in the egg, then in a mixture of the flour, salt, pepper and mashed garlic. Let the pieces stand a few minutes to dry.

Heat the oils in a large skillet and add the whole cloves of garlic. When the cloves are browned, remove them. Add the chicken pieces. Fry them for 20 to 30 minutes or until browned and tender. Serve garnished with lemon wedges.

ROMEO SALTA
THE PLEASURES OF ITALIAN COOKING

Crackling Fried Chicken

The malt sugar called for in this recipe has the consistency of honey and is obtainable, in jars, from Oriental food stores.

To serve 4

2½ to 3 lb.	chicken	1 to 1½ kg.
2 tsp.	salt	10 ml.
4	slices fresh ginger root, finely chopped	4
½ tbsp.	malt sugar (or substitute ordinary sugar)	7 ml.
1½ tbsp.	white wine vinegar	22 ml.
1½ tbsp.	light soy sauce	22 ml.
2 tbsp.	water	30 ml.
1½ tbsp.	dry sherry	22 ml.
3 tbsp.	cornstarch	45 ml.
	vegetable oil for deep frying	

Mix the salt and ginger together and rub the chicken with them, inside and out. Marinate for 3 hours in an airy place.

Chop the chicken into 16 to 20 pieces the Chinese way. To do so, you will need a very sharp, heavy cleaver. Divide the chicken into four pieces by splitting it in half lengthwise and cutting off each leg. Chop each of the legs crosswise into three pieces and each wing into two pieces, giving 10 pieces. Then chop each of the two body pieces into three across and right through the breastbone, producing six pieces. You can split the larger pieces in two, to end up with 16 to 20 pieces.

Mix the sugar, vinegar, soy sauce, water, sherry and cornstarch into a paste. Rub the pieces of chicken with half of this paste and leave them to dry in an airy place for 2 hours. Rub in the rest of the paste and leave to dry for 1 more hour.

Heat the oil in a deep fryer until very hot. Deep fry the chicken in two lots for 3 to 3½ minutes each, when the pieces should be very crisp. Serve hot.

KENNETH LO
CHINESE FOOD

Marinated Fried Whole Chicken

Marinade de Poulet

If bitter, Seville orange juice is not available, the juice of sweet oranges can be mixed with a little lemon juice to use as a substitute. The chickens should be split and flattened by the method shown on page 45, Steps 1 and 2, and page 47, Step 5.

To serve 4

two 2 lb.	chickens, split down the back and flattened	two 1 kg.
½ lb.	lard	¼ kg.
2 cups	flour, or thin crepe batter (recipe, page 169)	½ liter
1 cup	heated Seville orange juice (optional)	¼ liter
	Marinade	
⅓ cup	dry white wine	100 ml.
⅓ cup	wine vinegar	100 ml.
⅓ cup	Seville orange juice	100 ml.
	ground allspice	
	cayenne pepper	
	salt	
1	large onion, thinly sliced	1
1 tbsp.	fines herbes	15 ml.

Place the flattened chickens in a dish with the marinade liquid, and season with the spices and salt. Add the onion and fines herbes, and marinate for 2 to 3 hours. Turn the chickens in the marinade several times so that they are thoroughly flavored, then drain them. Flour the chickens, or coat them with very thin batter, and fry them in the lard until they turn an attractive golden brown. The authentic sauce to serve with this is heated orange juice; or you can boil up the marinade, strain it and serve that as the sauce.

NICOLAS DE BONNEFONS
LES DÉLICES DE LA CAMPAGNE

Fried Chicken Florentine

To serve 4

3½ lb.	chicken, cut into serving pieces	1½ kg.
2 cups	flour	½ liter
1	egg, lightly beaten	1
1½ cups	olive oil	375 ml.
	Marinade	
3 tbsp.	olive oil	45 ml.
¼ cup	fresh lemon juice	50 ml.
¼ tsp.	salt	1 ml.
	pepper	
2 tsp.	chopped fresh parsley	10 ml.

Make a marinade of oil, lemon juice, salt, a pinch of pepper and the parsley. Pour it over the chicken pieces in a casserole and let stand for about 2 hours, turning the pieces occasionally. Take the chicken out of the marinade, dry the pieces well, flour them thoroughly, dip them into the beaten egg and fry them in deep olive oil for about 15 minutes.

ADA BONI
THE TALISMAN ITALIAN COOK BOOK

Chicken Kiev

An easy way to bone chicken breasts is shown on page 32.

To serve 6

3	chicken breasts, skinned, boned and halved	3
	salt	
¼ tsp.	pepper	1 ml.
2 tbsp.	finely cut fresh chives	30 ml.
6 tbsp.	unsalted butter, cut into 6 finger-sized pieces and frozen hard	90 ml.
½ cup	flour	125 ml.
2	eggs, lightly beaten	2
1½ cups	fresh bread crumbs	375 ml.
	vegetable oil for deep frying	

Flatten the boned breasts to a thickness of about ¼ inch [½ cm.] by placing them between two pieces of wax paper and pounding them lightly with a kitchen mallet or rolling pin. Discard the paper and lay out the flattened breasts, boned side uppermost. Salt to taste, and sprinkle the breasts with the pepper and chives. Place a finger of frozen butter on each breast half. Roll up the butter in the breast meat as you would wrap a package, tucking in the ends at the beginning of the roll. Dip the rolled breasts in flour, then in the beaten

eggs, and finally roll them in the bread crumbs. Chill in the refrigerator for 3 hours or more. Heat the oil to 365° F. [185° C.] in a saucepan or deep skillet; the oil should be deep enough to cover the rolled breasts. Deep fry the breasts for 4 to 5 minutes or until golden brown. Drain them on paper towels and serve immediately.

CARL LYREN
365 WAYS TO COOK CHICKEN

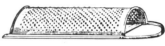

Chicken with Walnuts, Peking-Style

The bean paste in this recipe may be either the whole or ground soybean type. Both are sold in Oriental food stores.

To serve 6

1	whole chicken breast, skinned, boned and diced	1
1 tsp.	salt	5 ml.
1 tbsp.	cornstarch	15 ml.
1	egg white	1
1 cup	walnuts, blanched in boiling water for 3 minutes, drained and skinned	¼ liter
2 tbsp.	vegetable oil plus enough additional for deep frying	30 ml.
1	green pepper, halved, seeded, deribbed and diced	1
1	sweet red pepper, halved, seeded, deribbed and diced	1
2 tbsp.	bean paste	30 ml.
2 tbsp.	sugar	30 ml.
1 tbsp.	dry white wine	15 ml.
	chicken stock (optional)	

Mix the chicken with the salt, cornstarch and egg white, tossing well. Put the walnuts into a strainer and deep fry them in enough oil heated to 300° F. [150° C.] to cover them by 1 inch [2½ cm.]. Dip them up and down in the oil to get them as brown as you like; but they burn easily, so be careful. Drain them well and set aside. Reserve the oil.

Sauté the peppers in 1 tablespoon [15 ml.] of fresh oil for 1 minute. Drain them. Add another tablespoon of oil to the pan and sauté the bean paste for 3 minutes, stirring constantly. Add the sugar.

Deep fry the chicken pieces in the reserved oil heated to 375° F. [190° C.] for 1 minute. Drain the pieces and put them into the bean paste. Add the wine. If the sauce is too thick for your taste, thin it with up to ¼ cup [50 ml.] of chicken stock. Toss furiously. Add the peppers and walnuts, and allow to heat through, stirring constantly.

YU WEN MEI AND CHARLOTTE ADAMS
100 MOST HONORABLE CHINESE RECIPES

Marinated Fried Chicken, Greek-Style

Kotopoulo Tiganito Marinato

To serve 4 or 5

2½ lb.	chicken, cut into serving pieces	1 kg.
	salt and freshly ground pepper	
¾ cup	flour	175 ml.
	olive, corn or peanut oil	
	small tomatoes or tomato wedges	
	watercress and parsley sprigs	

Marinade

¼ cup	olive oil	50 ml.
¼ cup	white wine vinegar	50 ml.
¼ cup	fresh lemon juice	50 ml.
½ cup	dry white wine	125 ml.
2	garlic cloves, chopped	2
1	small onion, sliced	1
1	bay leaf, crushed	1
1 tsp.	dried thyme, marjoram or oregano	5 ml.
2	peppercorns, crushed	2
2 or 3	juniper berries	2 or 3
4	coriander seeds, cracked	4

Combine all the marinade ingredients in a bowl. Place the chicken in the marinade, coating the pieces on all sides. Cover and refrigerate for at least 2 hours or overnight if desired. Drain the chicken, then season lightly with salt and pepper. Put the flour in a paper bag, add the chicken pieces and shake lightly until they are coated with flour.

Pour oil into a heavy skillet to a depth of ½ inch [1 cm.] and heat almost to the smoking point. Slip the chicken into the hot oil and fry to a light chestnut color on all sides. Using tongs, remove the chicken to a roasting pan, discarding the oil remaining in the skillet.

Bake in a moderate oven, preheated to 350° F. [180° C.], for 30 minutes or until tender, pouring off the oil as it collects in the pan. (The chicken will now be crisp and a rich chestnut color.) Arrange the chicken on a platter, alternating tomatoes, watercress and parsley around the edge.

VILMA LIACOURAS CHANTILES
THE FOOD OF GREECE

Broiled Herbed Chicken

To serve 4

2 to 2½ lb.	chicken, quartered	1 kg.
6 tbsp.	butter	90 ml.
	parsley sprigs	
1½ tsp.	dried thyme	7 ml.
	salt and pepper	
1 to 2 tbsp.	vegetable oil	15 to 30 ml.

Lift the skin of each of the chicken quarters carefully with your fingers, being careful not to tear the skin or detach it except from the main part of the flesh. In so doing you will be forming pockets. Soften the butter. Chop several large parsley sprigs and blend them into the butter until you have a slightly greenish paste. Add the thyme.

Smear the paste all over the flesh of the chicken under the skin until you have a good, thick coating. Fold back the skin into its normal position and press down firmly. Sprinkle the chicken with salt and pepper.

Place the chicken on a rack in the broiling pan, skin side down, and broil 4 inches [10 cm.] from the heat source for 20 minutes, basting the pieces once with oil. Turn them, baste again and continue to cook for another 20 minutes, basting them with their juices and additional oil if necessary. The chicken will be crisp and brown when done.

JANE MOSS SNOW
A FAMILY HARVEST

Chicken Stuffed with Figs

Le Poulet Farci aux Figues

To serve 4

2½ to 3 lb.	chicken with the gizzard, heart and liver reserved	1 to 1½ kg.
6 tbsp.	butter	90 ml.
2	medium-sized onions, finely chopped	2
10	firm ripe black figs, each peeled and cut lengthwise into 8 pieces	10
1 cup	raw unprocessed rice	¼ liter
2 cups	water	½ liter
	salt and black pepper	
	olive oil	
	cayenne pepper	

In a large fireproof casserole, heat 4 tablespoons [60 ml.] of the butter over medium heat and cook the onions gently in this until they are transparent. Do not allow them to brown.

Chop the chicken giblets coarsely. Add the figs and the giblets to the onions and leave them to cook until the giblets lose their pink color. Then add the rice and stir until the grains are well coated with butter.

Add the water, salt to taste and a little pepper, and bring to a boil. Reduce the heat and simmer gently for 25 to 30 minutes, or until all the liquid has been absorbed. Remove the casserole from the heat and add the remaining butter.

Preheat the oven to 400° F. [200° C.]. Dry the inside of the chicken well and stuff it with about two thirds of the fig mixture, reserving the rest. Sew up the chicken.

Place the chicken, back uppermost, in a fairly deep roasting pan. Smear the bird with oil, sprinkle with salt and cayenne pepper, and place the pan on the middle shelf of the oven. Leave the bird to cook for about 45 minutes. To test whether the chicken is cooked, pierce one of the thighs with a skewer. The juice released should be pale yellow. If it is pink, cook for a further 5 to 10 minutes.

Transfer the chicken to a platter. Remove the sewing thread. Leave the bird to cool for 5 minutes, as this will make it easier to carve. Stir the reserved fig and rice mixture with a fork, reheat it over a low heat and serve it separately.

JACQUES MÉDECIN
LA CUISINE DU COMTÉ DE NICE

Stuffed Chicken, Cyprus-Style

Kotopoulo Yemisto Kypriotiko

To serve 5 or 6

2½ to 3 lb.	chicken with the liver reserved	1 to 1½ kg.
	vegetable oil or butter	
½ cup	slivered blanched almonds	125 ml.
¾ cup	raw unprocessed long-grain rice	175 ml.
½ cup	dry white wine	125 ml.
1¼ cups	water	300 ml.
	salt	
1 tsp.	ground cinnamon	5 ml.
	sugar	
½ cup	dried currants	125 ml.

Wash and dry the chicken, and set it aside. To prepare the stuffing, heat 3 tablespoons [45 ml.] of oil or butter in a medium-sized saucepan and sauté the almonds and liver. When the almonds and liver are lightly browned, remove them from the pan with a slotted spoon. Chop the liver and set it aside with the nuts. Add the rice to the fat in the pan and sauté over medium heat, stirring constantly. Then pour in the wine and water, and add the salt, cinnamon and a pinch of sugar. Cover and cook for 12 minutes, or until the rice is almost tender. Stir in the almonds, liver and currants and remove the pan from the heat.

Spoon the stuffing into the cavity of the chicken and close tightly with skewers. Truss the chicken and brush the sur-

face lightly with melted butter or oil. Set the bird on a rack in a roasting pan, breast side up, and roast it in a preheated moderate oven at 350° F. [180° C.] for 1¼ hours or until tender. Turn the bird with two wooden spoons every 20 minutes and baste it frequently with the pan drippings. When the bird is roasted, remove the stuffing from the cavity and transfer it to the center of a warmed platter. Carve the chicken and arrange the pieces around the stuffing. Serve warm. Note: for a popular mainland variation, substitute pine nuts, nutmeg, a little chopped celery and parsley, and bread—that has been soaked in water and then squeezed—for the almonds, cinnamon and rice.

VILMA LIACOURAS CHANTILES
THE FOOD OF GREECE

Chicken with Anchovies

Poulet aux Anchois

This 19th Century recipe, originally for a spit-roasted chicken, has been adapted for oven roasting. The salted anchovies called for in the recipe must be filleted, washed and patted dry before use. If you substitute already filleted, canned anchovies, soak them in water for 10 minutes and dry them with paper towels before you chop them. The technique for stuffing a chicken under the skin is demonstrated on page 46.

To serve 4

3 to 3½ lb.	chicken	1½ kg.
8	salted anchovy fillets, washed, dried and chopped	8
3 oz.	lean salt pork with the rind removed, blanched in boiling water for 10 minutes, drained and chopped	100 g.
2 tbsp.	finely chopped fresh parsley	30 ml.
4 or 5	scallions, chopped	4 or 5
	freshly ground black pepper	
	grated nutmeg	
4 or 5	thin slices fresh pork fat	4 or 5
½ cup	veal or ham stock	125 ml.

Mix together three quarters of the anchovies with the other chopped ingredients. Season with pepper and nutmeg, and spread the stuffing mixture under the skin of the chicken. Bard, or cover, the breast of the chicken with the pork fat. Truss the bird and roast it in a moderate oven preheated to 350° F. [180° C.] for about 1 hour, removing the pork fat after 45 minutes. Transfer the chicken to a warmed platter. Degrease the roasting juices before deglazing the pan with the stock to which the remaining anchovies have been added.

OFFRAY AINÉ
LE CUISINIER MÉRIDIONAL

Chicken with Olives

Entrée de Poulardes aux Olives

The original 1691 recipe calls for Champagne, which at that period could have been either a sparkling white wine or a non-sparkling red wine. The latter makes more sense in the context of this recipe. The orange called for is a bitter-flavored Seville; you can substitute any orange by squeezing it ahead of time and stirring in 2 tablespoons [30 ml.] lemon juice.

To serve 4

3½ to 4 lb.	roasting chicken	1½ to 2 kg.
1	slice fresh pork fat	1
1 tbsp.	chopped fresh parsley	15 ml.
3 tbsp.	chopped scallions	45 ml.
1 oz.	lean salt pork, chopped, blanched for 10 minutes in boiling water and drained	50 g.
1 tbsp.	flour	15 ml.
¼ cup	chicken or veal stock	50 ml.
¾ cup	dry red wine	175 ml.
1 tbsp.	capers, rinsed, drained well and chopped	15 ml.
2	anchovy fillets, soaked in water for 10 minutes, patted dry and chopped	2
½ cup	olives (ripe, green or both), pitted and crushed	125 ml.
1 tbsp.	olive oil	15 ml.
1	bouquet garni made of parsley, chervil, tarragon, chives, thyme and a bay leaf	1
1 cup	velouté sauce *(recipe, page 168)*	¼ liter
	Seville orange	

Choose a very tender, plump chicken; bard its breast by covering it with a generous slice of pork fat and place the chicken in the oven. While the chicken is roasting, make the sauce by first sautéing the chopped parsley and scallions for a few minutes with the chopped salt pork. Stir in the flour. Add the stock, wine, capers, anchovies, olives, olive oil and bouquet

garni and simmer 30 to 40 minutes. Bind the sauce with the thickened stock, season well and degrease.

Remove the roasted chicken from its pan, cut off the legs at the joints and make slits in the thighs, wings and breast. Crush all sections slightly with the flat of a knife blade, then put them in a fireproof casserole with the sauce and all their juices. Cover the casserole and simmer gently over the lowest possible heat for 15 to 20 minutes, basting regularly.

Before serving, arrange the chicken sections on a platter, cover them with the sauce and squeeze the juice of an orange over the top. Serve hot.

MASSIOLOT
LE CUISINIER ROIAL ET BOURGEOIS

Chicken Tandoor-Style

Tandoori Murg

At the Moti Mahal restaurant, Delhi, the tandoor oven in which this dish is cooked is fired with layers of wood and then with charcoal that is heated white. Western cooks may use an ordinary oven, an oven broiler or an outdoor grill.

To serve 4

two 2½ lb.	chickens, skinned and halved	two 1 kg.
1 tsp.	salt	5 ml.
¼ to ⅓ cup	fresh lime or lemon juice	50 to 75 ml.
8 tbsp.	butter, melted	120 ml.
	black pepper	
2	limes or lemons, cut into wedges	2
1	tomato, sliced	1
1	onion, sliced	1
	Marinade	
1½ cups	unflavored yogurt	375 ml.
4	garlic cloves, crushed	4
1 to 2 tsp.	cayenne pepper	5 to 10 ml.
2 tsp.	ground cumin seed	10 ml.
1 tsp.	ground coriander	5 ml.
1 tsp.	ground ginger	5 ml.
½ to 1 tsp.	red vegetable food coloring (optional)	2 to 5 ml.
	black pepper	

You can use the skinned chicken halves as they are, but it is better to discard the wings, the rib bones and the backbones.

With a sharp knife make shallow gashes all over the skinned halves. Rub the chicken with the salt and then some of the lime or lemon juice.

In a large bowl combine the yogurt, garlic, cayenne, cumin, coriander, ginger, food coloring and black pepper. Brush the chicken thoroughly with this mixture, getting deep into the gashes. Marinate the chicken, refrigerated, in the mixture for 4 to 5 hours, or overnight.

Preheat the oven or oven broiler to 450° F. [230° C.], or start a charcoal fire and get the coals white-hot.

Thread each chicken half along its length on a long metal skewer and cook for 5 minutes on one side, then turn and cook for 5 minutes on the other side. Brush with melted butter and cook for 10 minutes more on each side, or until the chicken is done and the surface is golden brown.

Sprinkle with the remaining lime or lemon juice and with black pepper. Garnish with lime or lemon wedges and tomato and onion slices. Serve hot.

LEE FOSTER (EDITOR)
THE NEW YORK TIMES CORRESPONDENTS' CHOICE

Roast Chicken Oregano, Peloponnesos-Style

Kota Fournou Ladorigani

To serve 4 or 5

2½ to 3 lb.	roasting chicken	1 to 1½ kg.
	salt and freshly ground pepper	
¼ cup	olive oil	50 ml.
3 tbsp.	fresh lemon juice	45 ml.
1½ tsp.	dried oregano	7 ml.
	sliced tomatoes and cucumbers	

Season the chicken, inside and out, with salt and pepper, then truss it. Place the chicken in a roasting pan. Whisk the olive oil, lemon juice and 1 teaspoon [5 ml.] of the oregano together in a small bowl and brush the mixture over the chicken. Roast the chicken in a preheated moderate oven at 350° F. [180° C.] for 1¼ hours, turning every 20 minutes and basting with the remaining marinade. When the juices run clear after you prick a thigh with a skewer, transfer the chicken to a heated platter. Sprinkle the remaining oregano on the chicken and serve it warm, garnished with the tomatoes and cucumbers.

VILMA LIACOURAS CHANTILES
THE FOOD OF GREECE

Roast Chicken with Parsley

Volaille "Truffée" au Persil

The fromage blanc called for in this recipe is a fresh cheese made from skimmed milk and containing no fat solids. To prepare a homemade version, blend 1½ cups [375 ml.] of low-fat ricotta cheese and 4 tablespoons [60 ml.] of low-fat unflavored yogurt with a pinch of salt until the mixture is smooth and there is no trace of graininess. Refrigerate the mixture, covered, for 12 hours before using.

To serve 4

2½ lb.	chicken	1¼ kg.
	salt and pepper	
1 tsp.	salad oil	5 ml.
	Parsley garniture	
5 tbsp.	finely chopped fresh parsley	75 ml.
1 tbsp.	finely chopped fresh chives	15 ml.
2 tsp.	finely chopped fresh tarragon	10 ml.
2	shallots, finely chopped	2
2	mushrooms, finely chopped	2
1 tbsp.	*fromage blanc* (or substitute farmer cheese)	15 ml.
	salt and pepper	
	Sauce	
¾ cup	chicken stock	175 ml.
1	garlic clove, crushed but not peeled	1
1 tbsp.	finely chopped fresh parsley	15 ml.

In a mortar, mix together to a paste all the ingredients of the parsley garniture. Salt and pepper to taste.

Remove any excess fat from inside the tail opening of the bird. Working from the neck opening, with your fingers—do not cut anything—gently separate the skin from the breast meat, all the way to the tops of the drumsticks. Spread the parsley garniture as evenly as possible between the skin and the flesh, then pat the skin back into place. Salt and pepper the inside of the bird, truss the bird and paint the skin lightly with the oil.

Preheat the oven to 425° F. [220° C.]. Roast the bird for 20 minutes, then turn the heat down to 350° F. [180° C.], and roast it for about another 40 minutes, or until the juices inside the bird run clear with no trace of pink. *(Do not baste it with fat that accumulates in the pan. If you wish, baste occasionally with a spoonful of hot chicken stock.)*

Remove the bird to a carving board and let it rest in a warm place. Discard as much fat as possible from the roasting pan. On top of the stove, over low heat, add to the pan the stock, garlic and 1 tablespoon [15 ml.] of parsley. Stir and scrape all the brown glaze into the sauce. Let it reduce by about one third, then strain it through a fine-mesh strainer into a small saucepan. Taste for seasoning and keep it warm.

To serve, quarter the bird and present it on a warmed oval platter, with the juices from the carving board and the sauce poured over it.

MICHEL GUÉRARD
MICHEL GUÉRARD'S CUISINE MINCEUR

Split, Stuffed Baked Chicken

Poulet Fendu Farci au Four

Carving presents no problem when this chicken is split and stuffed as shown on pages 45-47.

	To serve 4	
3 to 3½ lb.	chicken	1½ kg.
1 tsp.	crumbled mixed dried thyme, oregano and savory	5 ml.
3 tbsp.	olive oil	45 ml.
	Stuffing	
3 oz.	fresh white cheese (ricotta or cream cheese)	100 g.
¾ cup	fresh white bread crumbs	175 ml.
4 tbsp.	butter	60 ml.
	salt and pepper	
1 tbsp.	finely chopped fresh marjoram leaves and flowers (if unavailable, substitute fines herbes)	15 ml.
1	large egg	1
1	medium-sized onion, finely chopped, stewed gently in 1 tbsp. [15 ml.] butter for 15 minutes and cooled	1
1 lb.	small firm zucchini, cut into julienne strips, salted, squeezed, sautéed in 2 tbsp. [30 ml.] butter and cooled	½ kg.
	freshly grated Parmesan cheese	

Split the chicken along the back, flatten it out and loosen the skin. Sprinkle the chicken on both sides (but not beneath the skin) with the dried herbs. Pat and rub generously with olive oil, then leave to marinate for an hour or two.

Mash the white cheese, bread crumbs and butter together with the salt, pepper and fresh herbs, using a fork; mash in the egg also. Then mix in the onion and the zucchini, and finally the Parmesan, adding enough to bring the stuffing to a firm, stiff consistency.

Stuff the chicken, taking a handful of stuffing at a time and forcing it into place, pushing it beneath the skin with the fingers of one hand while molding the outside of the skin with the other hand. Cover the drumsticks and thighs well before worrying about the breasts. When all of the stuffing is in place, fold the neck-skin flap (if there is any) over the throat opening and tuck the flap beneath the bird.

With a small, sharply pointed knife, pierce the web of skin and thin flesh between the inside of one thigh and the tip of the breast, making a slit just large enough to receive the drumstick tip. Gently force the drumstick up and push its tip through the slit. Repeat with the other drumstick.

Place the bird in a roasting pan and mold the surface with your hands to force the skin and stuffing into a plump version of the bird's natural form. Salt and pepper the bird, and roast it in a preheated oven, starting at 450° F. [230° C.] and turning the oven down to about 375° F. [190° C.] some 10 minutes later. Start basting regularly after 30 minutes. Count 50 minutes to 1 hour of roasting time, depending on the size of the chicken. If, after about 40 minutes, it seems to be coloring too rapidly, turn the oven down further, placing a sheet of aluminum foil loosely over the bird.

Transfer the bird to a heated platter. But do not attempt to serve the roasting juices—they are too fat and the dish needs no sauce; instead, chill the scrapings and juices, discarding the fat, and use them for flavoring leftovers.

RICHARD OLNEY
SIMPLE FRENCH FOOD

Roast Chicken with Onion

Poulet à l'Oignon

This recipe has been adapted from a 19th Century original version by the French chef Louis Eustache Ude. An easy way to flavor a chicken under the skin, as called for here, is demonstrated on page 46.

	To serve 4	
2½ to 3 lb.	chicken	1 to 1½ kg.
	salt and pepper	
1	medium-sized onion, thinly sliced	1
½ cup	butter, softened	125 ml.
	chicken stock (optional)	

Season the inside of the chicken with salt and pepper. With your fingers, carefully loosen the skin over the breast meat, poking down toward the legs as far as you can go without tearing the skin. Insert the onion slices under the loosened skin so that they form a layer between it and the flesh. With wooden picks, fasten down any loose ends of skin to keep the onion snugly lodged as the chicken roasts.

Before placing the chicken in a preheated oven, 375° F. [190° C.], spread the softened butter over the skin that covers the onions. Salt and pepper the entire bird to taste. Place it in a shallow earthenware dish or open roasting pan, and do not give the chicken another thought for 45 minutes. Then baste it with the fat and juices that have collected in the pan. Repeat the basting process twice, and roast the bird for a total of 1½ hours.

Serve the chicken hot out of the oven, as soon as possible, to savor the crackling golden skin with the tender slices of onion oozing juice underneath. (Add a small quantity of boiling chicken stock to the pan juices if more sauce is wanted.)

For an accompaniment, parboil potato balls for 2 minutes. Drain well, then sprinkle them with paprika and roast them along with the chicken, basting the potato balls at the same time you attend to the chicken.

ESTHER B. ARESTY
THE DELECTABLE PAST

Elizabeth Frink's Roast Lemon Chicken

To serve 4

3 lb.	chicken	1 ½ kg.
2	lemons	2
1	small garlic bulb	1
	salt and pepper	
2 tbsp.	olive oil	30 ml.
2 tbsp.	butter	30 ml.
	chopped fresh parsley	

Cut up 1 lemon into 8 pieces; rub the outside of the chicken with the peel side of the pieces and then put the lemon pieces inside the chicken with the garlic. Season with salt and pepper, and pour a mixture half of olive oil and half of butter on top and inside of the chicken.

Roast for 1 ½ hours in a preheated 325° F. [160° C.] oven. Half an hour before taking the chicken out of the oven, pour freshly squeezed juice from the second lemon over the top and sprinkle the chicken with chopped parsley.

BERYL BARR AND BARBARA TURNER SACHS (EDITORS)
THE ARTISTS' AND WRITERS' COOKBOOK

Stuffed Roast Chicken, Toulouse-Style

Poulet à la Toulousaine

To serve 6

3 lb.	chicken	1 ½ kg.
½ lb.	lean ham, thinly sliced and cut into 1-inch [2½-cm.] squares	¼ kg.
1 tbsp.	chopped mixed fresh herbs	15 ml.
	salt and pepper	
2	garlic cloves, peeled	2
7 oz.	garlic sausage, left whole	200 g.
¼ cup	brandy	50 ml.
½ cup	oil	125 ml.

To make the stuffing, mix the ham with the herbs and season with salt and pepper. Stuff the chicken with half of the mixture and then, successively, a garlic clove, the sausage, the other garlic clove and, finally, the remainder of the stuffing. Sew up the chicken and moisten it, first with the brandy, then with the oil. Put the bird on a rack and roast it for 30 minutes in an oven preheated to 425° F. [220° C.], then for 15 minutes at 325° F. [160° C.]. Serve with puréed navy beans.

ODETTE KAHN
LA PETITE ET LA GRANDE CUISINE

Basic Roast Chicken with Stuffing

To serve 4

3 to 3½ lb.	roasting chicken	1 ½ kg.
	salt and freshly ground black pepper	
2 tbsp.	butter, softened	30 ml.
	Bread stuffing	
2 tbsp.	butter	30 ml.
2 or 3	slices bacon	2 or 3
1	onion, finely chopped	1
2 cups	small cubes of trimmed firm-textured white bread	½ liter
3 tbsp.	finely chopped fresh parsley	45 ml.
	crumbled dried thyme and rosemary	
1	egg	1
¼ cup	milk or chicken stock	50 ml.
	salt and freshly ground black pepper	

Preheat the oven to 350° F. [180° C.].

First make the stuffing. In a large skillet, fry the bacon in half of the butter until the bacon is crisp. Remove the bacon, add the chopped onion to the pan and sauté over moderate heat until the onion pieces turn soft and golden. Remove them from the pan with a slotted spoon.

Add the remaining butter to the skillet. When it melts, add the bread cubes and toss over moderate heat until they have taken up all the fat and turned a light golden color.

Crumble the bacon into a mixing bowl. Add the sautéed onion, bread cubes, parsley and a generous pinch each of thyme and rosemary, and toss with a fork until well mixed.

In another, smaller bowl, beat the egg with the milk or stock. Pour this over the bread mixture, tossing with the fork to distribute the liquid evenly. Season with salt and pepper.

Wipe the chicken clean both inside and out. Fill the cavity of the chicken with the bread stuffing. Skewer the vent or sew it up with a few stitches of strong cotton thread. Lay the chicken in a roasting pan. Rub the bird with salt and pepper, and spread with the softened butter.

Roast the chicken for about 1¼ hours, basting it frequently with its own juices (supplemented if necessary with a tablespoon or two [15 or 30 ml.] of boiling water).

To serve, transfer the chicken to a heated serving dish. Discard the skewers or thread and keep the bird hot. Pour 2 or 3 tablespoons [30 or 45 ml.] of water into the roasting pan and bring to a boil over moderate heat, stirring and scraping the base and sides with a wooden spoon to dislodge any crusty bits. Simmer for a minute, stirring. Taste for seasoning; pour into a heated sauceboat and serve with the chicken.

ROBERT CARRIER
THE ROBERT CARRIER COOKERY COURSE

Broiled Chicken Oregano

Kotopoulo Riganato tis Skaras

To serve 4

2½ to 3 lb.	chicken, cut into serving pieces	1 to 1½ kg.
1	garlic clove, halved	1
	salt and pepper	
	fresh or dried oregano leaves	
¼ cup	fresh lemon juice	50 ml.
5 tbsp.	butter, melted	75 ml.

Several hours before serving—or the day before, if time allows—rub the chicken pieces with garlic and place them in a deep china or earthenware bowl. Sprinkle the chicken with salt and pepper, oregano and lemon juice. Cover the bowl and refrigerate the chicken.

When ready to cook, preheat the broiler to its highest setting. Arrange the chicken pieces on the broiler rack and baste with a little of the melted butter. Add the remaining marinade to the rest of the butter. Broil the chicken 3 to 4 inches [7½ to 10 cm.] from the heat for 15 to 20 minutes on each side, basting often.

This chicken is also delicious broiled over charcoal.

THE WOMEN OF ST. PAUL'S GREEK ORTHODOX CHURCH
THE ART OF GREEK COOKERY

Teriyaki Broiled Chicken

To serve 6

three 2 lb.	chickens, halved	three 1 kg.
Teriyaki marinade		
½ cup	olive or peanut oil	125 ml.
⅔ cup	Japanese soy sauce	150 ml.
2 tbsp.	grated fresh ginger root	30 ml.
2	garlic cloves, finely chopped	2
1 tbsp.	grated fresh orange peel or, preferably, tangerine peel	15 ml.
¼ cup	dry sherry	50 ml.
	salt and pepper	

Blend all the marinade ingredients well and pour the mixture over the chicken pieces in a shallow dish or enameled pan. Press the chicken pieces into the marinade and turn them several times while they marinate, which should be a minimum of an hour and as much as 24 hours for maximum flavor. Preheat the broiler. Place the chicken pieces on the rack of a broiler pan and set the pan a little farther from the heating unit than usual (about 6 inches [15 cm.] if you can)

to prevent the soy sauce from caramelizing. Brush the pieces with a little oil and broil them for about 15 minutes on each side, brushing several times with the marinade. To serve spoon the pan juices over the chicken.

JAMES BEARD
JAMES BEARD'S AMERICAN COOKERY

Barbecued Chickens with Rice

This piquant barbecue sauce can be made in large quantities and stored for several weeks in the refrigerator.

To serve 4

two 3 lb.	roasting chickens, halved	two 1½ kg
1 cup	raw unprocessed rice	¼ liter
Barbecue sauce		
3 to 4 tbsp.	sugar	45 to 60 ml.
3 to 4	medium-sized onions, chopped and sautéed	3 to 4
1 to 2 tbsp.	salt	15 to 30 ml.
1 tsp.	ground ginger	5 ml
1 tsp.	celery seed	5 ml.
½ tsp.	cayenne pepper	2 ml.
2 tbsp.	Worcestershire sauce	30 ml.
6	garlic cloves, finely chopped	6
2 cups	herb vinegar	½ liter
1 tsp.	ground nutmeg	5 ml.
1 tsp.	ground allspice	5 ml.
2 cups	canned tomatoes	½ liter
2½ cups	stale beer	625 ml.

To make the barbecue sauce, first caramelize 1 to 2 tablespoons [15 to 30 ml.] of sugar by heating it in a heavy saucepan over medium heat until it is nut brown. Add the other ingredients and bring to a boil. When the sauce cools, add 1 tablespoon [15 ml.] of sugar—or more, to taste.

Marinate the halved chickens in the barbecue sauce for 2 to 3 hours. Remove the chickens and broil them over hot coals, basting frequently with the sauce; do not be afraid to scorch the flesh a little. Use a celery rib for a barbecue brush.

Serve with boiled rice to absorb the rich juices.

PHYLLIS JERVEY
RICE & SPICE

Broiled Chicken Breasts Sesame

To serve 3 to 6

	chicken breasts, boned	6
	sesame seeds	

Marinade

1/4 cup	butter, melted	50 ml.
1/4 cup	soy sauce	50 ml.
1/4 cup	dry white wine	50 ml.
1 tsp.	dried tarragon	5 ml.
1 tsp.	dry mustard	5 ml.

Mix together the butter, soy sauce, white wine, tarragon and mustard, and marinate the chicken breasts in the mixture for 2 or 3 hours.

Broil the breasts over a medium charcoal fire for 4 or 5 minutes on each side, starting with the skin side up and basting with the marinade two or three times. Remove the chicken breasts from the fire, again brush with the marinade, then roll them in sesame seeds until they are well coated. Return the chicken breasts to the fire for a minute or two to brown the seeds. Serve with plain buttered rice.

JOSÉ WILSON (EDITOR)
HOUSE AND GARDEN'S PARTY MENU COOKBOOK

Chicken Kabob, Calcutta-Style

Chicken Reshmi Kebab

To serve 2

1 lb.	chicken breasts, skinned, boned and cut into 1/2-inch [1-cm.] cubes	1/2 kg.

Marinade

3 tbsp.	butter, melted	45 ml.
2 tsp.	ground coriander	10 ml.
1	medium-sized onion, finely chopped	1
1	garlic clove, finely chopped	1
2 tbsp.	soy sauce	30 ml.
1 tbsp.	fresh lemon juice	15 ml.
1 tsp.	brown sugar	5 ml.
	salt and black pepper	

Combine all the marinade ingredients in a bowl. Add the chicken cubes and mix thoroughly. Cover and marinate in the refrigerator for 6 or 7 hours or overnight.

Thread the chicken cubes on skewers and place them on a rack 4 or 5 inches [10 or 13 cm.] from the heat under a preheated broiler or over a charcoal fire. Broil until the cubes are cooked and a golden color, turning the skewers once. This takes about 5 to 6 minutes on each side. Serve hot.

LEE FOSTER (EDITOR)
THE NEW YORK TIMES CORRESPONDENTS' CHOICE

Chicken Devil's-Style

Pollo alla Diavola

Anything cooked *alla diavola* in Italy usually has been grilled over abundant hot coals, of which the devil himself should have enough, and the seasonings are also hot but not so hot as to ruin taste buds. In the case of this dish, the flavor is heightened with red pepper, black pepper and lemon.

To serve 4

two 2 to 2 1/2 lb.	chickens	two 1 to 1 1/4 kg.
1/2 cup	olive oil	125 ml.
3	dried red chilies, stemmed and seeded (or substitute 3 or 4 dashes of Tabasco sauce)	3
2	lemons	2
	freshly ground pepper	
	salt	

Start your charcoal grill.

On a stove burner, heat the olive oil in a small pan over medium heat. Add the chili pods and sauté them until they are deep, dark brown. Turn off the heat, cool the olive oil and throw away the browned chilies. (The alternative is to add Tabasco to the olive oil to make it hot without cooking it.)

Cut the chickens in half, crack the legs and wing joints loose, and spread them out, skin side up, on a board or clean counter. Pound the chicken halves well with a meat mallet to flatten them out.

Add the juice of 1 of the lemons to the seasoned olive oil along with 3 or 4 twists of pepper. Put the chicken halves in a big bowl, pour the seasoned olive oil over them, and turn the pieces over and over to coat them well. Let the chicken stand for 1 to 2 hours, turning the halves from time to time.

When your grill is heaped with hot coals, put the marinated chicken halves on to cook, skin side down. Sprinkle the chicken with salt and a bit more pepper, and grill thoroughly, turning and basting from time to time with the remaining marinade. The chicken is done when it is tender and has a dark brown crust all over (some spots may well be charred).

You can use the broiler in your oven, but an oven broiler never seems to get hot enough. If you want to try, preheat the broiler, put the chicken as close to the flame or coil as possible and broil it, turning it frequently and basting it often.

Serve the chicken hot with lemon wedges.

MARGARET AND G. FRANCO ROMAGNOLI
THE ROMAGNOLIS' TABLE

Broiled Skewered Chicken
Kababe Morgh

To serve 4

two 2 lb.	chickens, each cut into 8 serving pieces	two 1 kg.
1 cup	finely grated onion	¼ liter
½ cup	fresh lemon juice	125 ml.
2 tsp.	salt	10 ml.
4 tbsp.	butter, melted	60 ml.
⅛ tsp.	ground saffron (or saffron threads, pulverized with a mortar and pestle) dissolved in 1 tbsp. [15 ml.] warm water	½ ml.

In a stainless-steel, enameled or glass bowl combine the onion, lemon juice and salt, stirring until they are thoroughly blended. Add the chicken and turn the pieces to coat them well. Marinate at room temperature for at least 2 hours or in a refrigerator for 4 hours, turning the pieces occasionally.

Light a layer of coal in a charcoal broiler and let it burn until a white ash covers the surface, or preheat the stove broiler at its highest setting.

Remove the chicken from the marinade and string the pieces tightly on four long skewers, pressing the pieces together firmly. If you are broiling the chicken under a stove broiler, suspend the skewers side by side across the length of a large roasting pan that is deep enough to allow about 1 inch [2½ cm.] of space under the meat.

Stir the melted butter and dissolved saffron into the marinade and brush the chicken on all sides with 2 to 3 tablespoons [30 to 45 ml.] of the mixture. Broil about 3 inches [8 cm.] from the heat source for 10 to 15 minutes, turning the skewers occasionally and basting the chicken frequently with the remaining marinade. The chicken is done if colorless juices trickle out when a thigh is pierced with the point of a small sharp knife. Serve at once.

FOODS OF THE WORLD/MIDDLE EASTERN COOKING

Lemon Chicken

To serve 6

4 lb.	chicken pieces	2 kg.
	salt and pepper	
½ cup	oil	125 ml.
1 cup	fresh lemon juice	¼ liter
½ cup	dry white wine	125 ml.

Dry the chicken with paper towels, sprinkle salt and pepper on both sides of each chicken piece, then arrange the pieces in a nonmetal dish that holds them snugly in one layer. Add ¼ cup [50 ml.] of the oil to the lemon juice and beat together with a fork. Pour this marinade mixture over the chicken.

Turn the pieces until all surfaces are coated with the marinade. Cover tightly and marinate the chicken in a cool place for at least 6 hours. (Marinating it overnight in the refrigerator is better yet.) Remove and turn the chicken pieces once or twice.

Preheat the broiler to its highest setting. Lift the chicken pieces out of the marinade and dry them on paper towels. Place the pieces on a baking sheet, brush them with oil, and sprinkle with salt and pepper. Broil the chicken to a golden brown (about 4 to 5 minutes). Turn the pieces over and repeat. Transfer the chicken pieces to a large skillet or casserole and pour over them the marinade and white wine. Bring to a boil over high heat, then cover and simmer over low heat for 20 to 25 minutes, or until the chicken pieces are tender.

To serve hot, place the chicken pieces on a warmed platter and spoon some cooking sauce over them. Pass the rest of the sauce separately.

To serve cold, chill the chicken in the refrigerator in its cooking liquid, which will turn into a jelly. Scrape the lemon jelly into a small bowl and place spoonfuls of it around the chicken pieces. Decorate with a few black olives.

CAROL CUTLER
THE SIX-MINUTE SOUFFLÉ AND OTHER CULINARY DELIGHTS

Broiled Skewered Chicken, Japanese-Style
Yakitori

The mirin called for in this recipe is a sweet rice wine obtainable at Oriental food stores.

To serve 2

1 lb.	chicken, skinned, boned and cut into 1-inch [2½-mm.] cubes	½ kg.
½ lb.	fresh mushrooms	¼ kg.
6 to 8	scallions, trimmed and cut into 1-inch [2½-cm.] lengths	6 to 8
½ lb.	chicken livers, halved	¼ kg.
⅓ cup	soy sauce	75 ml.
¼ cup	*mirin*	50 ml.
2 tbsp.	sugar	30 ml.

Halve the mushrooms, if they are large. Soak bamboo skewers approximately 6 to 8 inches [15 to 20 cm.] long in water for 15 minutes or so. Then thread alternate pieces of chicken, mushroom, scallion and liver on the skewers. Mix together the soy sauce, *mirin* and sugar, and baste the skewered ingredients with the mixture. Place the skewers over a charcoal fire prepared in a hibachi or barbecue grill, or under a preheated oven broiler and cook about 3 inches [8 cm.] from

heat for 8 to 10 minutes. Baste frequently with the sauce
d turn the skewers several times until the chicken and
ers are cooked.

Chicken livers are often omitted from *yakitori*. Other
getables such as tiny boiling onions or green peppers may
substituted or added.

SANDRA TAKAKO SANDLER
THE AMERICAN BOOK OF JAPANESE COOKING

Broiled Chicken with a Deviled Topping

*structions for flattening the bird without cutting it in half
pear on page 45, Steps 1 and 2, and page 47, Step 5. Instruc-
ns for halving the bird and then flattening it appear on
ges 48-49.*

To serve 4		
/2 lb.	chicken, flattened, or halved and flattened	1 ¼ kg.
	salt and freshly ground black pepper	
tbsp.	butter, melted	90 ml.
Deviled topping		
tbsp.	butter, softened	60 ml.
tsp.	strained fresh lemon juice	5 ml.
tsp.	Worcestershire sauce	10 ml.
tsp.	finely chopped garlic	2 ml.
tsp.	dry mustard	2 ml.
tsp.	salt	1 ml.
	freshly ground black pepper	
cup	fresh bread crumbs	175 ml.

emove the grid from your broiling pan and preheat the
oiler at its highest setting.

Prepare the topping by first creaming the softened but-
r. Beat in the lemon juice, Worcestershire sauce, chopped
arlic, dry mustard and a few grindings of black pepper.
hen the ingredients are thoroughly combined, stir in (do
ot beat in) the fresh bread crumbs. Set the bowl aside.

Pat the chicken dry with paper towels, brush both sides
venly with 2 tablespoons [30 ml.] of the melted butter and
ay the chicken, skin side down, on the cold grid. Sprinkle it
venly with salt and pepper.

Place the grid with the chicken in the preheated broiling
an. The surface of the chicken should be about 4 inches
0 cm.] from the source of the heat. Baste the chicken every
minutes with the remaining melted butter.

After 20 minutes turn the chicken over with tongs. Brush
e skin side, now uppermost, with melted butter, sprinkle it
venly with salt and pepper, and return the chicken to the
broiler. Baste with the remaining butter (or with pan juices)
after 5 minutes.

Five minutes or so before the chicken is done, spread the
topping quickly and evenly over the chicken pieces, using a
spatula. Broil for the remaining 5 minutes, or until the topping is a deep golden brown.

Transfer the chicken, crumbed side up, to a warmed serving platter. Serve at once.

MICHAEL FIELD
COOKING WITH MICHAEL FIELD

Chicken Braised in a Casserole, Farmer's-Style

Poulet en Cocotte à la Fermière

To serve 4		
3 to 4 lb.	chicken, seasoned inside with salt and pepper, and trussed	1 ½ to 2 kg.
6 tbsp.	butter	90 ml.
1	medium-sized onion, finely sliced	1
4	young carrots, thinly sliced	4
1	small celery heart, finely sliced	1
3 or 4	thin slices prosciutto	3 or 4
⅓ cup	shelled fresh peas	75 ml.
½ cup	sliced fresh green beans	125 ml.
½ cup	chicken or veal stock	125 ml.

Melt 4 tablespoons [60 ml.] of the butter in a small sauté
pan. Add the onion and cook gently for 4 to 5 minutes; it
should be no more than straw colored. Add the carrots and
celery. Sweat them gently over very low heat for 15 minutes.
Shake the pan to toss the vegetables, rather than risk breaking them up by turning them with a spoon; they should be
softened but not at all brown. The onion should be a golden
color and the butter should remain clear. Set the pan aside.

Melt the remaining butter in a heatproof casserole over
low heat. Add the chicken and brown it lightly. Remove the
chicken and line the casserole with the prosciutto. Replace
the chicken, breast up, and surround it with all the cooked
and raw vegetables mixed together. Add the stock and cover.

Place the casserole in the oven and cook for 45 to 50
minutes. Make sure that the heat does not go above moderate, since the vegetables will burn if the liquid reduces,
while the cooking of the chicken will not be speeded up.

Test for doneness, and serve.

MADAME SAINT-ANGE
LA CUISINE DE MADAME SAINT-ANGE

Braised Capon, Country-Style

Cappone in Casseruola alla Paesana

To peel peppers easily, follow the instructions on page 11.

	To serve 6	
5 lb.	capon	2½ kg.
	salt and freshly ground pepper	
6 tbsp.	butter	90 ml.
2	onions, sliced	2
2	garlic cloves, crushed	2
3	yellow peppers, peeled, halved, seeded, deribbed and cut into strips	3
1	bouquet garni made up of 3 parsley sprigs, 2 thyme sprigs (or ½ tsp. [2 ml.] dried thyme) and a bay leaf	1
½ cup	dry Marsala	125 ml.
6	ripe tomatoes, peeled, seeded and chopped	6
½ cup	chopped prosciutto	125 ml.
2	medium-sized zucchini, sliced	2
¼ cup	chopped fresh parsley	50 ml.

Season the cavity of the capon with salt and pepper, and truss the bird. Heat the butter in a large, heavy enameled casserole over fairly high heat, then brown the capon on all sides. Adjust the heat during the browning so that the butter does not burn.

Remove the capon from the casserole, add the onions and garlic, and cook until the onions begin to color. Add the pepper strips, cook for 3 minutes longer and then add the bouquet garni, Marsala, tomatoes and prosciutto. Season with salt and pepper, bring to a simmer and return the capon to the casserole.

Cover the casserole and place it in a moderate oven, preheated to 350° F. [180° C.], for 2 hours. About 15 minutes before the capon is fully cooked, add the zucchini slices and the chopped parsley.

Transfer the capon to a warmed serving platter. If the sauce is too thin, reduce it slightly over high heat before spooning it around the capon.

LUIGI CARNACINA
GREAT ITALIAN COOKING

Chicken in Red Wine

Coq au Vin

	To serve 6 to 8	
6 lb.	chicken, preferably a cock 10 to 12 months old, cut into serving pieces	3
	salt and pepper	
2	strips lean salt pork with the rind removed, sliced ⅔ inch [150 mm.] thick and cut into cubes	
2 to 3 tbsp.	oil or butter	30 to 45
3	medium-sized carrots, cut into sections 1 to 2 inches [2½ to 5 cm.] long	
3	medium-sized onions, coarsely chopped	
2 tbsp.	flour	30
¼ cup	brandy	50
3 cups	dry red wine	¾ li
1	bouquet garni made up of a pinch of thyme, a bay leaf and a few sprigs parsley	
½ lb.	mushrooms	¼ k
	salt and freshly ground pepper	
10 to 11 tbsp.	butter	150 165 r
25 or 30	small boiling onions, peeled	25 or
6	slices firm-textured white bread with the crusts removed, halved diagonally	
1	garlic clove	
	chopped fresh parsley	

Parboil the pieces of salt pork for 2 minutes, drain and d them in a towel. Put them to fry over low heat in a larg heavy *sauteuse* or skillet with a bit of oil or butter. When t pieces are golden brown, remove them and put them asid

In the same cooking fat, place the carrots and choppe onions. Keep the heat between medium and low, and allo them to cook, stirring regularly to avoid overbrowning, f 20 to 30 minutes. Remove the vegetables, put them asi and replace them with the chicken pieces, previously salte Cook the chicken over a somewhat higher heat until gent browned on all sides, sprinkle with flour and continue cook, turning the pieces as necessary. Return the sauté onions and carrots to the pan. When the flour has cooked f a few minutes, pour in the brandy, carefully set it alight a stir. When the flames have died, add the wine and raise t heat. Stir the chicken pieces and move them around until t liquid comes to a boil.

At this point, if the skillet is already overfull of the chic en, or if perhaps you have had to use two skillets and bot seem too full to permit adding the vegetables, keep the carrots and onions aside and add them later when the chicken goes into the oven dish.

Transfer the chicken pieces and vegetables to an earthenware, copper or enameled cast-iron casserole with a lid. Stir and scrape the first pan with a wooden spoon to loosen and dissolve the frying adherents, then pour the liquid over the chicken pieces. If they are not completely covered, add enough wine, water or good stock (water is better than indifferent stock) to barely, but entirely, cover them. Add the bouquet garni (or simply sprinkle with thyme, and add the bay leaf and parsley sprigs untied). Put to cook, covered, in the oven, regulating the heat so that the sauce hardly simmers. The length of cooking time depends on the bird's age and "past"—from 30 to 45 minutes for a fryer that has never exercised to 1½ hours for a 10-month-old rooster, and an hour longer still for one that may be too old to have a fine flesh but will produce a marvelous sauce.

Meanwhile cook the boiling onions, seasoned, in butter over very low heat, shaking the pan from time to time, for 20 to 30 minutes. Keep them covered and avoid browning them; if the saucepan is not heavy enough, you may have to use a fireproof pad over the heat source. Remove the onions when they are done and use the same pan to fry the mushrooms. Trim the mushroom stems and cut the caps into two or four pieces (if they are small, leave them whole). Toss them in butter over high heat for 2 or 3 minutes; season with salt and freshly ground pepper.

Transfer the chicken pieces and the carrots to a platter. Pass the cooking liquid through a fine sieve into a saucepan, using a pestle to work the residue. Discard the remains of the bouquet garni. In the saucepan, skim as much fat from the surface of the liquid as possible and bring it to a boil, then position the saucepan over the heat so as to permit its contents to simmer only on one side. Carefully skim off all fat and impurities as they surface over the next 30 minutes or so. If, at this point, the sauce is still too thin, turn up the heat to create a fast boil, stirring constantly until you achieve the right consistency.

Put the chicken pieces and the carrots back in the oven dish, distribute the garnish (sautéed mushrooms, glazed boiling onions and fried pork sections) on top and pour over the sauce. Cover and return to the oven to simmer gently for 15 to 20 minutes.

Brown the triangles of bread in butter over low heat until golden and crisp. (They may be prepared ahead of time and rewarmed in the oven.)

To serve, place the chicken pieces more or less symmetrically on a large, warmed platter. Rub the crouton triangles with the clove of garlic, dip a corner of each triangle in the sauce, then in the chopped parsley, and arrange them around the edge of the platter, parslied tips pointing out. Pour sauce and garnish over the chicken and sprinkle with a bit of chopped parsley. Serve with steamed potatoes.

RICHARD OLNEY
THE FRENCH MENU COOKBOOK

Grandmother's Chicken Casserole

Chicken en Casserole Grand'mère

To serve 4

2½ to 3 lb.	chicken	1 to 1½ kg.
1	garlic clove, peeled	1
2 tbsp.	lard or rendered bacon fat	30 ml.
	salt and pepper	
¼ cup	water	50 ml.
¼ lb.	fat salt pork, diced, blanched in boiling water for 5 minutes and drained	125 g.
¼ lb.	fresh mushrooms	125 g.
12	small boiling onions, peeled	12
	sugar	
2 tbsp.	butter	30 ml.
2 or 3	medium-sized potatoes, diced	2 or 3
	chopped fresh parsley	

Put the garlic inside the chicken cavity. Truss the bird as for roasting, and place it in a casserole with the lard (or bacon fat) and a little salt. Put it in an oven, preheated to 400 to 425° F. [200 to 220° C.], and cook, uncovered, for about 30 minutes or until it is a good brown all over, turning the chicken occasionally and basting it with the fat. Pour off the fat and reserve. Add 2 or 3 tablespoons [30 or 45 ml.] of water and stir in all the brown crust from the sides of the casserole. Set the chicken aside in the casserole.

In a skillet, sauté the salt pork in the fat reserved from the casserole. When golden brown, remove the pork and set it aside. Cook the mushrooms in the fat left in the skillet, season with salt and pepper, and set aside. Put the onions in another skillet with 2 tablespoons [30 ml.] of water, a sprinkling of sugar and ½ tablespoon [7 ml.] of butter, then cook slowly until the water cooks away and the onions take on a good brown color.

Add the salt pork, mushrooms and onions to the chicken and, if the gravy has reduced too much, add a little more water. Cover the casserole, reduce the oven heat to 350 to 375° F. [180 to 190° C.] and cook 30 minutes longer or until the chicken is done, basting often.

Cook the potatoes in the remaining butter until brown and tender, and put them on top of the other vegetables in the casserole. Sprinkle with chopped parsley and serve all from the casserole. Other vegetables like peas and asparagus can be added if desired.

LOUIS DIAT
FRENCH COOKING FOR AMERICANS

Chicken Breasts Baked with Onion

Oignonnade à la Bretonne

To serve 6

6	chicken breasts, skinned, boned and halved	6
2 cups	finely chopped fresh mushrooms	½ liter
4 tbsp.	butter	60 ml.
2 cups	finely chopped onions	½ liter
½ cup	reduced veal stock, made from 1 cup [¼ liter] veal stock	125 ml.
2 cups	heavy cream	½ liter
	salt and pepper	

Sauté the mushrooms in 2 tablespoons [30 ml.] of the butter. In another pan, gently cook the onions in the remaining butter until they are transparent.

Spread half of the onions over the bottom of a shallow heatproof casserole or pudding dish. Lay the chicken breasts on top, and cover with the rest of the onions and all the mushrooms. Pour in the veal stock and the cream. Add salt and pepper, and cook uncovered in an oven, which has been preheated to 325° F. [170° C.], for about 20 minutes. When the chicken is tender and the cream has reduced to a coating consistency, serve immediately with freshly cooked peas.

ÉDOUARD NIGNON
ÉLOGES DE LA CUISINE FRANÇAISE

Chicken in Beer

Coq à la Bière

To serve 4

2½ to 3 lb.	chicken	1 to 1½ kg.
4 tbsp.	butter	60 ml.
	salt and pepper	
1 tbsp.	chopped shallots	15 ml.
½ cup	gin	125 ml.
1 cup	heavy cream	¼ liter
½ lb.	fresh mushrooms, diced (2½ cups [625 ml.])	¼ kg.
2 cups	dark beer	½ liter
	cayenne pepper	
2 tbsp.	chopped fresh parsley	30 ml.

Truss the chicken. Melt 2 tablespoons [30 ml.] of the butter in a fireproof casserole over moderate heat and turn the chicken in it until golden. Add salt and pepper, cover and cook for half an hour over low heat. Remove the chicken to a heated dish and keep it covered in a warm place.

In the same casserole, cook the shallots. When they are golden, put back the chicken, pour on the gin and flame it. Add 1 tablespoon [15 ml.] of butter, 2 tablespoons [30 ml.] of the cream and the mushrooms. Pour in the beer, season with salt, pepper and a little cayenne, cover and simmer for 15 minutes. When the chicken is well cooked, put it on a chopping board and cut it into four pieces, then put it on the serving dish and keep it covered in a warm place.

Pour the rest of the cream into the casserole and boil vigorously for several minutes to thicken the liquid. Adjust the seasoning if necessary. Take the casserole off the heat and add the rest of the butter. Let it melt in the sauce, off the heat, and pour the sauce over the chicken.

Sprinkle with chopped parsley and serve hot.

RAYMOND OLIVER
LA CUISINE

Kubab Chicken

The technique for drawing back the skin of a chicken, called for in this recipe, is demonstrated on page 37.

If any readers interested in the intricacies of spice cookery should ever come across an old book called *Indian Domestic Economy and Receipt Book,* published in Madras in 1850, and acknowledged simply to the author of *Manual of Gardening for Western India* without further clue to his identity, they should snap it up. This is the pot-roasted chicken recipe that evolved from a recipe in that book.

To serve 4

2 to 2½ lb.	chicken	1 kg.
2 tsp.	coriander seeds	10 ml.
12	black peppercorns	12
6	cardamom pods, opened and the seeds reserved	6
½ tsp.	ground cloves	2 ml.
1 tsp.	salt	5 ml.
½ inch	fresh ginger root, peeled and sliced	1 cm.
5 tbsp.	butter, preferably clarified	75 ml.
1 or 2	lemons	1 or 2

Pound together all the spices and seasonings until they are reduced to a paste, then work them with 1 tablespoon [15 ml.] of butter.

Draw back the skin of the chicken and, with a small knife, make incisions in the legs and breast. Spread the spice mixture into the incisions and smooth the skin back into place. Leave for a couple of hours before cooking.

Put 4 tablespoons [60 ml.] of butter into a deep, heavy oven pot and heat it. Put in the chicken, lying on its side.

Cover the pot closely. Bake in a moderate oven, preheated to 350° F. [180° C.], for 50 minutes to an hour, turning the chicken over onto its other side at half time. Then remove the lid and turn the chicken breast upward and roast for another 10 minutes.

Serve the chicken with the cooking liquid poured over it and lemon quarters around the dish. Boiled rice or saffron rice makes a good accompaniment, although I prefer a salad.

On occasion I have varied the spice mixture, omitting the ginger root and cloves, using cinnamon, saffron, whole cardamom and a little ground ginger. The salt is important.

ELIZABETH DAVID
SPICES, SALT AND AROMATICS IN THE ENGLISH KITCHEN

Chicken Stew, Jewish-Style

Tafina de Poule

According to religious law, Orthodox Jews are forbidden to cook on their Sabbath (Saturday). Traditionally, a hearty stew, or cholent, was prepared on Friday evening, and was then left to cook overnight in the cooling embers of a baker's wood-fired oven. The casserole was collected the following day and eaten at lunchtime while it was still warm. This recipe for tafina—a type of cholent—has been adapted for cooking in a contemporary gas or electric home oven.

To serve 4

3 to 4 lb.	chicken, cut into serving pieces	1½ to 2 kg.
2 tbsp.	olive oil	30 ml.
10	medium-sized onions, quartered	10
4	large tomatoes, peeled, seeded and coarsely chopped	4
2 lb.	fresh broad beans, shelled and peeled (or substitute fresh lima beans, shelled)	1 kg.
	salt and pepper	
2 cups	water	½ liter
20	small dried, pitted prunes	20

In a heavy casserole sauté the chicken pieces over high heat in the olive oil. When the pieces are golden brown, add the onions and sauté them until they begin to color. Add the tomatoes and broad beans. Season with salt and pepper, pour in the water and reduce the heat. Simmer, covered, for about 30 minutes. Add the prunes. Cook at the barest simmer over low heat, using a fireproof pad under the casserole, or bake in a cool oven, preheated to 300° F. [150° C.], for 5 to 6 hours. Check from time to time to be sure that there is enough water, and if necessary add some.

EDOUARD DE POMIANE
CUISINE JUIVE GHETTOS MODERNES

Chicken with Tomatoes and Honey

Poulet aux Tomates et au Miel

To serve 4

3 lb.	chicken, whole or cut into serving pieces, with the gizzard, heart and liver reserved	1½ kg.
15	medium-sized tomatoes, peeled, seeded and chopped	15
⅔ cup	butter	150 ml.
⅛ tsp.	ground saffron	½ ml.
1	onion, grated	1
	salt and pepper	
3 tbsp.	thick honey	45 ml.
2 tsp.	ground cinnamon	10 ml.
½ cup	blanched almonds	125 ml.
	oil	
2 tsp.	sesame seeds, toasted	10 ml.

Place the chicken or chicken pieces in a fireproof casserole together with the giblets. Cover with the tomatoes and add the butter, saffron, grated onion, salt and pepper. Cover and cook over moderate heat, stirring and shaking frequently.

After about 50 minutes (or longer for a whole chicken), when the chicken is cooked so that the flesh comes away easily from the bones, remove the chicken and giblets. Raise the heat and continue cooking the tomatoes until all their liquid has evaporated and they have the consistency of a thick stew. Stir, scraping the bottom of the casserole to keep the tomato mixture from sticking, while adding the honey and cinnamon. Return the chicken to the casserole, turning it gently so that it warms through and becomes impregnated with the sauce. Remove the casserole from the stove.

A few minutes before serving, fry the almonds in a little oil. Arrange the chicken on a warmed platter, pour the tomato sauce over the chicken, and garnish with the almonds and sesame seeds. Serve at once.

LATIFA BENNANI SMIRES
LA CUISINE MAROCAINE

Chicken with Eggplant

Braniya

To serve 4 to 6

4 to 5 lb.	chicken, cut into serving pieces	2 to 2½ kg.
¼ cup	olive oil	50 ml.
5	garlic cloves, peeled	5
	salt and pepper	
½ tsp.	ground saffron	2 ml.
3	medium-sized eggplants, peeled and cubed	3
½ cup	water	125 ml.

Sauté the chicken with the garlic cloves in olive oil in a skillet set over moderate heat. As soon as the chicken pieces have browned, season them with salt, pepper and saffron, and add the eggplant. Moisten with the water, cover the pan and cook gently over low heat for 20 minutes or until the chicken is done and the eggplant is tender.

LÉON ISNARD
LA CUISINE FRANÇAISE ET AFRICAINE

Spiced Chicken Cooked in Milk

To serve 3 or 4

4 to 4½ lb.	stewing chicken	2 kg.
1 tsp.	coriander seeds	5 ml.
1 inch	slice fresh ginger root	2½ cm.
2 or 3	cardamom pods	2 or 3
¼ tsp.	ground cloves	1 ml.
	salt and ground black pepper	
2	lemons	2
2 quarts	milk	2 liters
2	eggs, beaten	2
	pistachio nuts or roasted almonds for garnish	

Roast the coriander seeds for 2 or 3 minutes in a moderate oven; peel the ginger root and chop it coarsely; pound both in a mortar with the cardamoms and the ground cloves, after removing the husks of the cardamoms. Add salt and ground black pepper. Prick the chicken all over with a fork, rub it with lemon; then press some of the spices onto the chicken and put some more inside. Place the chicken in a heatproof casserole and leave for an hour or two.

Bring the milk to a boil with the remainder of the spices. Pour it over the chicken and cook very slowly for about 2½ hours—for the first hour on top of the stove, with the casse-role covered; for the remainder of the time in the oven, without the lid. When the chicken is quite tender, take the casse-role out of the oven and leave it to cool.

When cold, cut all the flesh from the chicken in nice pieces; measure about 2 cups [½ liter] of the sauce, heat it up. Add the sauce gradually, through a sieve, to the 2 whole beaten eggs and heat the mixture in a double boiler till thick. Pour this sauce over the chicken.

Serve cold, garnished with a few halves of pistachio nuts or roasted almonds and quarters of lemon.

ELIZABETH DAVID
SUMMER COOKING

Chicken and Sweetbread Fricassee

Fricassée de Poulets

This recipe has been adapted from the original version, published in 1674 and held in the Bibliothèque Nationale in Paris. The author is known only by his initials: L.S.R. Fresh lemon juice may be substituted for the unripe-grape juice called for in the original version. To prepare artichoke bottoms, break off the stems of fresh artichokes, pull or cut off all the leaves, scoop out the chokes, and trim the meaty bottoms into smooth saucer shapes.

To serve 6

3 lb.	chicken, cut into serving pieces	1½ kg.
2 oz.	lean salt pork, blanched in boiling water for 5 minutes, drained and diced	75 g.
4 tbsp.	butter	60 ml.
	salt and pepper	
1	bouquet garni	1
1 or 2	whole cloves	1 or 2
2 tbsp.	finely cut fresh chives	30 ml.
1½ cups	fresh mushroom caps, raw or briefly sautéed in butter	375 ml.
2	sweetbreads, parboiled in salted water for 15 minutes, drained, peeled and sliced	2
2 or 3	fresh artichoke bottoms, quartered and parboiled for 10 minutes	2 or 3
12	fresh asparagus tips	12
1 cup	veal or chicken stock	¼ liter
2	egg yolks, mixed with 1 tbsp. [15 ml.] juice from unripe grapes	2

In a large sauté pan, fry the salt pork in the butter. Add the chicken pieces, salt, pepper, bouquet garni, cloves, chives and mushroom caps. Sauté, stirring and turning regularly over moderate heat for 8 to 10 minutes. Pour in the stock, scrape the bottom of the pan, add the sweetbreads and simmer, covered, for another 15 minutes or so.

Skim off the fat. Stir in the artichoke bottoms and asparagus tips, and simmer gently for 5 minutes. Then mix the egg yolks and unripe-grape juice with a ladleful of the cooking liquid. Away from the heat, stir the mixture back into the stew and continue stirring over low heat until the sauce is lightly thickened.

Decorate as you see fit with lemon slices, fried parsley, nasturtium flowers or pot-marigold petals, pomegranate slices or foie gras.

L.S.R.
L'ART DE BIEN TRAITER

Chicken in Saffron and Garlic Sauce

Gallina en Pepitoria

To toast saffron, as called for in this recipe, fold it in a piece of paper, and place the paper on a fireproof pad over low heat until it begins to brown. Crush the toasted saffron with a pestle in a mortar or bowl.

To serve 6

4 to 5 lb.	stewing chicken, cut in small serving pieces, with the liver reserved	2 to 2½ kg.
1/4 to 1/3 cup	olive oil	50 to 75 ml.
1	medium-sized onion, finely chopped	1
2	garlic cloves, finely chopped	2
2 tbsp.	pine nuts	30 ml.
1	slice French or Italian bread, crusts removed	1
2	sprigs parsley, chopped	2
2	hard-boiled egg yolks	2
1/4 tsp.	pulverized, toasted saffron threads (or substitute ground saffron)	1 ml.
	boiling water	
	salt and pepper to taste	

Heat 2 to 3 tablespoons [30 to 45 ml.] of the olive oil in a fireproof casserole. Dry the chicken carefully with a paper tow-

el. When the oil almost begins to smoke, fry the chicken with the onion and garlic.

In a skillet, fry the pine nuts in 2 tablespoons [30 ml.] of olive oil. Remove the nuts to a large mortar. Fry the bread and the chicken liver (cover the skillet until the liquid has cooked out of the liver in order to avoid spattering grease). Remove the bread and chicken liver to the mortar with the pine nuts and use a pestle to mash them to a fine paste along with the parsley, egg yolks and saffron. Dilute the mixture with a little boiling water.

When the chicken is golden but not brown, sprinkle it with salt and pepper, pour the mixture from the mortar over it and add boiling water to cover. Stir. Cook slowly, covered, until the chicken is almost tender, then remove the lid to allow the sauce to thicken. To serve, remove the chicken to a warmed serving dish and strain the sauce over it.
Note: a stewing chicken will take 1½ to 2½ hours to cook. The recipe can be made with young chickens, which may be tender in just 30 minutes. If the sauce is too thin when the chicken is done, remove the chicken, boil the sauce until it is reduced to the desired consistency, then reheat the chicken in the sauce.

BARBARA NORMAN
THE SPANISH COOKBOOK

Chicken with Fresh Herbs and Cream

Jeune Poulet à l'Américaine

To serve 4

3 lb.	chicken, cut into serving pieces	1½ kg.
4 tbsp.	butter	60 ml.
5	shallots, chopped	5
1/3 cup	Madeira	75 ml.
1/2 cup	brandy	125 ml.
2 tbsp.	puréed tomato	30 ml.
1/2 cup	heavy cream	125 ml.
	salt and pepper	
	ground ginger	
	finely chopped fresh tarragon, basil and savory	

Melt the butter in a casserole over moderate heat. Add the chicken pieces and brown them quickly on all sides. Add the shallots and make a sauce by stirring in the Madeira, brandy, puréed tomato and heavy cream. Season with salt, white pepper, ginger and a large pinch of each of the fresh herbs.

Put the lid on the casserole, bring everything to a boil and complete the cooking by placing the casserole in a preheated moderate oven at 350° F. [180° C.] for 20 minutes or until the chicken is tender. Serve from the casserole.

LÉON ISNARD
LA CUISINE FRANÇAISE ET AFRICAINE

Chicken Fricassee with Sage

Chicken Fricassée alla Salvia

To serve 4

4 lb.	chicken, cut into serving pieces	2 kg.
1 tbsp.	butter	15 ml.
1 tbsp.	olive oil	15 ml.
	salt and pepper	
1 cup	dry white wine	¼ liter
2 oz.	prosciutto, thinly sliced and cut into fine julienne strips	75 g.
1 tbsp.	chopped fresh sage	15 ml.

Melt the butter in a large skillet and add the oil and the chicken. Sprinkle the chicken with salt and pepper, and brown it slowly and thoroughly on all sides. When it is well browned, pour the wine over the chicken and add the prosciutto and sage. Lower the heat, cover the skillet and cook slowly until the chicken is done, about 40 minutes. Serve immediately with the pan gravy.

ADA BONI
THE TALISMAN ITALIAN COOK BOOK

Chicken Fricassee

La Fricassée de Poulet

To serve 8

two 3 lb.	chickens, cut into serving pieces	two 1½ kg.
4 tbsp.	butter	60 ml.
2	medium-sized onions	2
1	sprig thyme	1
	salt	
2 tbsp.	flour	30 ml.
¼ cup	water	50 ml.
3 cups	heavy cream	¾ liter
¼ cup	dry white wine	50 ml.
	freshly ground pepper	
2	egg yolks	2

Place the chicken in a sauté pan with the butter, onions and thyme. Season with salt, cover the pan and place it over moderate heat. Check frequently and adjust the heat if necessary so that the meat gives up its moisture but does not brown. When the chicken pieces are firm, remove the thyme and the onions; sprinkle the chicken with flour and stir frequently. After 10 minutes, stir in the water, scraping any residues from the bottom and sides of the pan.

Pour about 6 tablespoons [90 ml.] of the cream, and all of the wine, over the chicken. Simmer gently and add a further 2 cups [½ liter] of cream, a little at a time. The sauce should be rich, smooth and of a consistency that will coat a spoon.

Simmer for 25 to 30 minutes and, if the sauce becomes too thick, add more cream. Taste to see if the sauce is sufficiently salted; season it with a little pepper.

Remove the pan from the heat and let it stand for 1 minute. Beat the egg yolks into the remaining cream and stir them into the fricassee.

LUCIEN TENDRET
LA TABLE AU PAYS DE BRILLAT-SAVARIN

Chicken in the Style of Nice

Poulet Niçoise

To serve 4 or 5

3½ lb.	chicken, cut into serving pieces	1½ kg.
4 to 6 tbsp.	olive oil	60 to 90 ml.
2	large onions, sliced	2
3 to 4	green peppers, halved, seeded, deribbed and cut into thin strips 2½ inches [6 cm.] long	3 to 4
3	medium-sized tomatoes, peeled, seeded and coarsely chopped	3
3	garlic cloves	3
	salt and pepper	
2 or 3	small zucchini, peeled and cut into large dice	2 or 3
1	small eggplant, peeled and cut into large dice	1
	flour	
	chopped fresh parsley or basil	

Heat 2 tablespoons [30 ml.] of oil in a sauté pan or skillet and sauté the chicken pieces until they are golden brown. Meanwhile, in a casserole, gently sauté the onions and peppers in 2 tablespoons of oil. When they are soft, add the tomatoes and 2 garlic cloves. Continue to cook until the vegetables are almost tender. Add the chicken pieces, season and simmer, covered, for 45 minutes.

Meanwhile, lightly flour the diced zucchini and eggplant, and sauté them in the oil remaining in the sauté pan until golden brown; add more oil if necessary. Arrange the contents of the casserole on a serving dish and garnish with the zucchini and eggplant. Finely chop the remaining garlic clove and sprinkle it over the dish with the parsley or basil.

RAYMOND ARMISEN AND ANDRÉ MARTIN
LES RECETTES DE LA TABLE NIÇOISE

Chicken Stovies

The word "stovies" comes from the French étouffer—to stew in an enclosed vessel. This dish is a legacy of the 17th Century "Auld Alliance" between Scotland and France, and was once popular at Highland rural weddings.

To serve 4

3 to 4 lb.	stewing chicken, cut into serving pieces	1½ to 2 kg.
6	medium-sized potatoes, cut into chunks	6
1	onion, sliced (or substitute 2 shallots)	1
	salt and pepper	
8 tbsp.	butter, cut into bits	120 ml.
2 cups	water	½ liter

In a buttered fireproof casserole, arrange alternate layers of potatoes, onion and chicken, sprinkling each layer with salt and pepper, and dotting liberally with butter. Add the water and cover tightly. Simmer very gently on top of the stove for 2 to 3 hours, or until the chicken is tender. If necessary, add a little hot water occasionally to prevent burning.

F. MARIAN MC NEILL
THE SCOTS KITCHEN

Chicken Célestine
Le Poulet Célestine

To serve 4

3½ to 4 lb.	chicken, cut into serving pieces	1½ to 2 kg.
4 tbsp.	butter	60 ml.
½ lb.	fresh button mushrooms	¼ kg.
1	medium-sized tomato, peeled, seeded and diced	1
¾ cup	dry white wine	175 ml.
½ cup	veal or chicken stock	125 ml.
1 tbsp.	Cognac	15 ml.
	salt and pepper	
	cayenne pepper	
1 tbsp.	finely chopped fresh parsley	15 ml.
1	garlic clove, finely chopped	1

In a heavy enameled iron casserole, heat the butter until it turns a nut-brown color. Add the chicken pieces and sauté them over high heat to seal in the juices, turning the pieces frequently until they are golden on all sides. Add the mushrooms and tomato, and sauté for 5 minutes. Pour in the wine, the stock and the Cognac. Season with salt and pepper, and a pinch of cayenne. Cover and cook over low heat for 15 minutes, or until done.

Remove the chicken pieces to a warmed platter. Skim off any fat from the sauce and, if the sauce is plentiful and thin, reduce it over high heat. Sprinkle the sauce with chopped parsley and garlic before pouring it over the chicken.

LUCIEN TENDRET
LA TABLE AU PAYS DE BRILLAT-SAVARIN

Jambalaya of Chicken
Le Jambalaia

In the United States, jambalaya is a highly seasoned stew prized by Louisianians who choose among several basic ingredients—poultry, meat (usually ham) or seafood—adding vegetables and rice. New Orleans cooks believe the dish has Spanish origins, and suspect the name comes from "jamón" or ham. But in France this mild version of jambalaya was well known in 19th Century Provence, where the name was said to be of Arabic origin.

To serve 4 to 6

4 to 5 lb.	stewing chicken	2 to 2½ kg.
3	medium-sized onions	3
2 or 3	carrots, whole or halved lengthwise	2 or 3
1	bouquet garni	1
1	rib celery	1
4	garlic cloves	4
2 cups	dry white wine	½ liter
	salt and pepper	
1 cup	raw unprocessed long-grain rice	¼ liter
1 tbsp.	olive oil	15 ml.
¼ tsp.	ground saffron	1 ml.

Truss the chicken and place it in a pot just large enough to contain the bird with the vegetables placed around it. Pour in the wine and add enough water to cover the bird. Bring slowly to a boil over moderate heat, skimming frequently. Cover and cook at a simmer until done (2 to 3 hours depending on the age of the chicken).

When the bird is almost tender, ladle 2 cups [½ liter] of the cooking liquid into a bowl and degrease it. Then, in a separate pot, fry the rice and saffron gently in the oil. When the rice turns opaque, moisten it with the degreased liquid. Bring the liquid to a boil over high heat, reduce the heat to very low and cook the rice, covered, for 18 minutes. Remove the pot from the stove and leave the rice to rest, covered, for a further 5 minutes. Carve the chicken and serve with the rice.

RENÉ JOUVEAU
LA CUISINE PROVENÇALE

Chicken with Port
Poulet au Porto

To serve 4 to 6

4 lb.	roasting chicken, trussed	2 kg.
2	onions, finely chopped	2
3	carrots, finely chopped	3
	bouquet garni	
4 tbsp.	butter	60 ml.
	salt and pepper	
⅔ cup	port	150 ml.
⅓ cup	heavy cream	75 ml.

Cook the chopped onions and carrots along with the bouquet garni in 1 tablespoon [15 ml.] of the butter for about 10 minutes in a covered pan.

Put the rest of the butter into a heavy, fireproof casserole. Sauté the chicken until golden all over. Add the onions and carrots. Season with salt and pepper, cover the casserole and cook gently for about 1 hour. Turn the chicken from time to time so that it cooks evenly.

Add the port 5 minutes before the end of the cooking time. When the chicken is cooked, transfer it to a warmed platter. Pour the cream into the casserole. Let it bubble for a few minutes to reduce, then pour the sauce over the chicken.

Serve with tomatoes, green beans and chanterelle mushrooms sautéed in butter.

ROBERT COURTINE
MON BOUQUET DE RECETTES

Pickled Chicken
Pollo en Escabeche

To serve 6

3½ lb.	chicken, cut into serving pieces	1½ kg.
	salt and freshly ground pepper	
3	medium-sized onions, thinly sliced	3
6	large garlic cloves	6
1	fresh green chili	1
1	bay leaf	1
1 tsp.	dried oregano	5 ml.
1 cup	olive oil	¼ liter
½ cup	white wine vinegar	125 ml.

Season the chicken pieces with salt and pepper, and place them in a heavy, enameled casserole with the onions and garlic. Tie the chili pepper, bay leaf and oregano in a small

square of cheesecloth and add to the casserole. Pour the oil and vinegar over the chicken, bring to a boil, reduce the heat, cover and simmer gently for 30 minutes. If the onions are very watery, continue cooking, with the casserole only partially covered to reduce the sauce, for 15 minutes longer—or until the chicken is tender. Otherwise, continue cooking with the casserole covered as before. Discard the cheesecloth package. Serve the chicken from the casserole with white rice or any plainly cooked starchy vegetable.

Pickled chicken is equally good served cold. Refrigerate and serve with the jellied sauce, lettuce, sliced tomato, radishes, avocado and olives.

ELISABETH LAMBERT ORTIZ
THE COMPLETE BOOK OF CARIBBEAN COOKING

Indonesian Simmered Chicken
Ajam Smoor

The sweet Indonesian or tart, dark soy sauce and the cellophane mung-bean noodles called for in this recipe are obtainable from Oriental food stores.

To serve 5 or 6

3 lb.	chicken, trussed	1½ kg.
1 cup	water	¼ liter
¼ cup	Indonesian soy sauce (or substitute 2 tbsp. [30 ml.] dark molasses mixed with 1 tbsp. [15 ml.] dark soy sauce)	50 ml.
1	onion, thinly sliced	1
6	black peppercorns, crushed	6
¼ cup	vegetable oil	50 ml.
6	slices fresh ginger root	6
3 tbsp.	chopped onion, sautéed in oil	45 ml.
4	whole cloves	4
¼ tsp.	grated nutmeg	1 ml.
1	slice lemon	1
4 oz.	cellophane noodles, soaked in cold water for 2 or 3 minutes and drained	125 g.
	salt	
¼ cup	rusk crumbs (or substitute dry bread crumbs)	50 ml.

Place the trussed chicken in a saucepan with the water, soy sauce, onion slices and peppercorns. Bring to a boil, reduce the heat and simmer, covered, for 15 to 20 minutes. Remove the chicken and pat it dry. Leave the chicken whole or cut it into serving pieces before browning it rapidly in the oil in a large, heavy skillet.

Place the browned chicken in a heavy fireproof casserole with the ginger, sautéed onion, cloves, nutmeg and lemon slice. Pour in the cooking liquid from the saucepan. Bring to a boil again, reduce the heat, cover and simmer slowly until well done. Add the noodles for the last 10 minutes of cooking. Transfer the chicken and noodles to a warmed platter. Taste the liquid for seasoning, add salt if necessary, and thicken the liquid slightly with the rusk crumbs.

Serve with boiled rice.

HUGH JANS
VRIJ NEDERLAND

Chicken California

This remarkable old San Joaquin Valley recipe has some authentic Mexican touches, but is more interesting as an excellent example of California ranch cookery at the beginning of the century.

To serve 4 to 6

4 to 5 lb.	chicken, cut into serving pieces	2 to 2½ kg.
½ cup	olive oil	125 ml.
½ cup	cornmeal, stone-ground if possible, plus extra for thickening sauce	125 ml.
	salt	
1 cup	finely chopped onion	¼ liter
3	garlic cloves, finely chopped	3
½ tsp.	grated nutmeg	2 ml.
1 tsp.	cumin seeds	5 ml.
1 tsp.	ground coriander	5 ml.
1 cup	water	¼ liter
1 cup	dry red wine	¼ liter
4 tbsp.	chili powder	60 ml.
1 cup	blanched almonds	¼ liter
1 cup	green olives	¼ liter
	chopped fresh coriander (*cilantro*) leaves, if available	
1 tsp.	sesame seeds	5 ml.

Heat the olive oil in a deep braising pan or heavy iron or cast-aluminum skillet. Roll the chicken in the cornmeal and brown quickly on both sides. Salt while it is browning. When nicely colored, add the onion, garlic, nutmeg, cumin and ground coriander. Turn the chicken so that the flavors of the seasonings blend. Add the water and wine, and bring to a boil. Reduce the heat, cover and simmer till the chicken is just tender—about 45 minutes to 1 hour. Do not let it overcook. Add the chili powder, turn the chicken pieces and simmer a few minutes more.

Transfer the chicken to a warmed platter. Add the almonds and olives to the sauce. Blend a little cornmeal with

water and stir it into the sauce. Continue to stir until the sauce thickens slightly. Correct the seasoning and pour the sauce over the chicken. Sprinkle with chopped coriander leaves, if available, and the sesame seeds.

Serve with rice or cornmeal, and a good salad of oranges and onions flavored with a little rosemary. Beer goes well with this menu.

JAMES BEARD
JAMES BEARD'S AMERICAN COOKERY

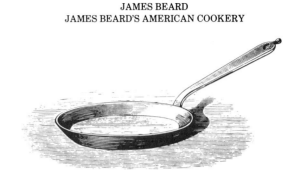

Chicken with Red and Green Peppers

Le Poulet aux Poivrons de Fanny

To serve 4

4 lb.	chicken, cut into serving pieces	2 kg.
2 tbsp.	butter	30 ml.
2 tbsp.	olive oil	30 ml.
	salt and pepper	
	cayenne pepper	
1 tsp.	Hungarian paprika	5 ml.
3	onions, finely chopped	3
3	shallots, finely chopped	3
3	garlic cloves, finely chopped	3
6	medium-sized tomatoes, peeled, seeded and chopped	6
5 or 6	red and green peppers, halved, seeded, deribbed and finely chopped	5 or 6
1	bouquet garni of bay leaf, thyme, sage and savory	1
½ cup	ripe olives	125 ml.
½ cup	green olives	125 ml.

Heat the butter and olive oil in a large fireproof casserole and sauté the chicken pieces until they are golden brown. Season with salt, pepper, cayenne to taste and paprika. Add the onions, shallots, garlic, tomatoes, and red and green peppers along with the bouquet garni. Cover the casserole and cook slowly for about 2 hours. A few minutes before serving, add the olives and check the seasoning. Serve with boiled rice or fresh egg noodles.

MICHEL BARBEROUSSE
CUISINE PROVENÇALE

Brut~10/89

Chicken Casserole, Portuguese-Style

To serve 4

2½ lb.	chicken, cut into serving pieces	1 kg.
3	tomatoes, peeled, seeded and chopped	3
6 oz.	smoked lean ham, thinly sliced and cut into ½-inch [1-cm.] squares	175 g.
8	small boiling onions	8
1 tbsp.	Dijon-style prepared mustard	15 ml.
1	large garlic clove, finely chopped or crushed	1
6 tbsp.	dry white wine	90 ml.
6 tbsp.	tawny or white port	90 ml.
	salt and black pepper	
4 tbsp.	butter	60 ml.
3 tbsp.	brandy	45 ml.

Combine the tomatoes, ham, onions, mustard, garlic, white wine and port in a shallow baking pan or casserole. Season the chicken pieces with salt and pepper, and arrange them in a single layer on top of the tomato mixture. Dot with butter. Bake in a moderate oven at 350° F. [180° C.] for 1 hour or until the chicken is browned and tender. Sprinkle with brandy. Serve the chicken with the sauce spooned over.

SHIRLEY SARVIS
A TASTE OF PORTUGAL

Broiled Chicken with Ginger Sauce

K'ao Chi Kuan

To serve 4

12	chicken thighs (or substitute 6 legs, halved, or a whole chicken, cut into 12 pieces)	12
1 tsp.	salt	5 ml.
2 tbsp.	finely chopped fresh ginger root	30 ml.
2	scallions, finely chopped	2
1	garlic clove, finely chopped	1
2 tbsp.	peanut oil	30 ml.
¼ cup	soy sauce	50 ml.
1 tbsp.	sugar	15 ml.
1 tbsp.	sesame-seed oil	15 ml.

Sprinkle the salt over the chicken pieces and set aside. Then set aside the ginger root, scallions and garlic in separate piles on a plate. Heat a skillet or wok. Add the oil and lightly brown the ginger, then add the scallions and garlic and stir

fry for 1 minute. Add the soy sauce and sugar, and bring to a boil. Turn off the heat and add the sesame-seed oil. Put the chicken pieces in this sauce and marinate for at least 1 hour.

Preheat the broiler to 450° F. [230° C.]. Place the chicken pieces meat side up on the rack of the broiler pan and broil about 4 inches [10 cm.] from the heat for 25 minutes, or until golden brown. Baste once with the leftover marinade. Turn the chicken pieces and broil for 20 minutes more. Do not baste again so that the skin may become crispy. Serve hot.

FLORENCE LIN
FLORENCE LIN'S CHINESE ONE-DISH MEALS

Chicken Stuffed with Parsnips

To serve 4

3½ lb.	chicken	1½ kg.
1 tbsp.	rendered chicken fat or butter	15 ml.
1	small parsnip, diced	1
1	small onion, chopped	1
	salt and pepper	
1 cup	chicken stock	¼ liter
1	bouquet garni	1
2 tbsp.	butter, creamed	30 ml.
1 tbsp.	chopped fresh parsley	15 ml.

Stuffing

2	medium-sized parsnips, peeled, quartered lengthwise and the cores removed	2
1 tbsp.	rendered chicken fat or butter	15 ml.
1	small onion, chopped	1
4	slices lean bacon, chopped	4
2 tsp.	chopped fresh sage	10 ml.
	salt and pepper	

Preheat the oven to 350° F. [180° C.].

To make the stuffing, boil the parsnips in salted water until tender. Drain and mash them to a purée. Melt 1 tablespoon [15 ml.] fat in a small skillet and cook the onion and bacon in this until the onion is soft. Remove from the heat and mix in the mashed parsnips, sage, and salt and pepper. Stuff the chicken with this mixture and truss it.

Melt the other tablespoon of chicken fat in a large, fireproof casserole over moderate heat and brown the chicken all over. Remove the chicken and set aside. Lower the heat, stir in the diced parsnip and onion, cover and sweat them for 5 minutes. Set the chicken on top. Season. Pour the stock over the chicken and tuck in the bouquet garni. Cover and cook in the oven for 1½ hours.

Remove the chicken, carve it and scoop out the stuffing.

Arrange the carved pieces on a warmed serving platter with the stuffing and cover with foil to keep warm. Strain the juices from the casserole and skim them if necessary. Return them to the casserole over moderate heat on top of the stove. Whisk in the creamed butter and parsley, and simmer gently for 2 minutes. Serve the sauce and the chicken separately.

GAIL DUFF
FRESH ALL THE YEAR

Chicken Bouillabaisse

Bouillabaisse de Poulet

To serve 4

2½ to 3 lb.	chicken, cut into serving pieces, with the liver reserved	1 to 1½ kg.
1 tsp.	ground saffron	5 ml.
2 tbsp.	*pastis* or other anise-flavored liqueur	30 ml.
¾ cup	olive oil	175 ml.
	salt and pepper	
2	onions, chopped	2
4	garlic cloves, crushed	4
6	tomatoes, peeled, seeded and chopped	6
10	small sprigs fennel	10
2 tbsp.	finely chopped fresh parsley	30 ml.
4	potatoes, peeled and thickly sliced	4
4	slices dry coarse bread, moistened with a little olive oil	4
	Sauce	
1	garlic clove	1
4	small fresh chilies, stemmed, seeded and coarsely chopped	4
2 tbsp.	olive oil	30 ml.
	reserved chicken liver, sautéed	

In an earthenware bowl, marinate the chicken pieces for 20 minutes with the saffron, liqueur, ¼ cup [50 ml.] of the olive oil, salt and pepper.

Heat the rest of the olive oil in a fireproof casserole, and add the onions and garlic. Cook until they begin to brown. Add the tomatoes and, when everything is well blended, add the fennel, parsley, chicken and marinade. Pour on boiling water until the ingredients are well covered. Season with salt, cover the casserole and simmer for 10 minutes. Add the potatoes and simmer for about 20 minutes more, until both potatoes and chicken are well cooked. Uncover the casserole and boil rapidly for several minutes to thicken the broth.

Pour the broth into a soup tureen over the slices of bread. Arrange the chicken pieces, potato slices and vegetables on a platter and keep them hot until the soup course is finished.

To make the sauce, pound together in a mortar the garlic clove, chilies and olive oil. Add the sautéed chicken liver and two cooked potato slices, and continue to pound. Moisten with 4 to 6 tablespoons [60 to 90 ml.] of the broth and mix well. Serve the resulting smooth sauce in a sauceboat to accompany both courses of the bouillabaisse.

RAYMOND OLIVER
LA CUISINE

Chicken Braised with Forty Cloves of Garlic

Poulet aux Quarante Gousses d'Ail

To serve 4

4 lb.	chicken	2 kg.
	salt and pepper	
1	small bouquet garni of fresh parsley and thyme, and a bay leaf	1
1 cup	olive oil	250 ml.
40	garlic cloves, unpeeled	40
1	large bouquet garni of fresh rosemary, thyme, sage and parsley, and a bay leaf, wrapped in a folded rib of celery	1
	flour-and-water paste, containing a little oil	
8	croutons, made from 4 slices firm white bread with crusts removed, sliced diagonally into triangles and browned in olive oil	8

Season the inside of the chicken with salt and pepper, place the small bouquet garni in the cavity and truss the bird. Put the olive oil into a heatproof casserole with the garlic cloves and the large bouquet garni. Place the chicken in the casserole and turn it several times so that it is well coated with the oil. Seal the lid of the casserole with the flour-and-water paste. Place the casserole in a moderate oven preheated to 325° F. [160° C.] and cook for about 1½ hours.

Transfer the casserole to the table and remove the lid just before serving. A delicious aroma of garlic will be released. The chicken will be tender and fragrant. Serve with croutons and let each person spread his croutons with garlic, squeezed from their skins. (Let me point out that cooked garlic disagrees with no one.)

JEAN-NOËL ESCUDIER AND PETA J. FULLER
THE WONDERFUL FOOD OF PROVENCE

Chicken in Cream, Mountain-Style

Poulet à la Montagnarde

To serve 4

3 to 4 lb.	chicken, cut into serving pieces	1½ to 2 kg.
	salt and pepper	
	flour	
3 tbsp.	butter	45 ml.
1 cup	heavy cream	¼ liter
1 tbsp.	fresh lemon juice or white wine vinegar	15 ml.
	cooked ham, diced	
	asparagus tips, boiled in salted water for 5 minutes, drained and patted dry	

Season the chicken pieces with salt and pepper, and coat them with flour. Cook the pieces gently in the butter without allowing them to brown. When they have become firm, put them in a fireproof earthenware casserole or a deep pan, and pour the cream over them. Simmer gently, covered, for about 20 minutes. Adjust the seasoning, add the lemon juice, and scatter the diced ham and asparagus tips over the dish.

SIMIN PALAY
LA CUISINE DU PAYS

Sautéed Chicken with Sorrel

To serve 6

two 2½ to 3 lb.	chickens, cut into serving pieces	two 1 to 1½ kg.
	salt and freshly ground black pepper	
2 tbsp.	butter	30 ml.
1 tbsp.	olive oil	15 ml.
4 to 5 cups	loosely packed sorrel leaves	½ to ¾ liter
3 tbsp.	finely chopped shallots	45 ml.
1 cup	dry white wine	¼ liter
½ cup plus ⅓ cup	heavy cream	125 ml. plus 75 ml.
1	egg yolk	1

Sprinkle the chicken with salt and pepper. Heat the butter and oil in a heavy skillet equipped with a lid. Add the chicken pieces, skin side down, and cook about 5 minutes or until golden brown. Turn over the pieces and reduce the heat. Cook about 10 minutes, uncovered.

Meanwhile, stack the sorrel leaves and cut them into fine shreds. This is called a chiffonade of sorrel. Set it aside.

Scatter the shallots around the chicken pieces and cook briefly. Sprinkle the chicken with the chiffonade and add the wine. Cover and cook for about 5 minutes. Uncover and add ½ cup [125 ml.] of the cream. Turn the chicken pieces about in the sauce, but leave them skin side up. Cover, and remove the skillet from the heat.

When ready to serve, uncover the skillet. Cook the chicken in the sauce over high heat for about 5 minutes. Blend the remaining ⅓ cup [75 ml.] of cream with the egg yolk and stir it into the sauce. Cook just until the sauce bubbles up. Do not cook longer or the sauce may curdle. Serve the chicken with the sauce spooned over.

CRAIG CLAIBORNE
CRAIG CLAIBORNE'S FAVORITES FROM THE NEW YORK TIMES

Chicken Braised in Red Wine

Poulet en Meurette

This is a recipe of Monsieur Austin de Croze, a distinguished gastronome of the 1920s and 1930s.

To serve 6 to 8

two 2½ lb.	chickens, cut into serving pieces	two 1 kg.
10 oz.	lean salt pork with the rind removed, blanched in boiling water for 10 minutes, drained and diced	300 g.
30	boiling onions	30
1	bouquet garni of fresh parsley and thyme	1
3	garlic cloves, finely chopped	3
½ lb.	fresh mushrooms	¼ kg.
	salt and pepper	
3 cups	dry red wine	¾ liter
8 tbsp.	butter	120 ml.
½ cup	flour	125 ml.
4	slices firm white bread with crusts removed, halved diagonally into triangles, rubbed with garlic and fried in butter	4
1 tbsp.	chopped fresh parsley	15 ml.

Cover the bottom of a fireproof casserole with the salt-pork dice, the onions, the parsley and thyme bouquet, and the garlic. Add the chicken and mushrooms. Season with salt and pepper. Add the wine and braise for 35 to 40 minutes.

Work together the butter and flour to form a smooth paste, or *beurre manié*, and stir this into the simmering braising juices to thicken them into a light sauce. Serve the chicken and its sauce from the casserole, garnishing the top with the bread croutons.

The dish can be prepared in the same way with white wine, in which case it is called *poulet pochouse*.

CURNONSKY
CUISINE ET VINS DE FRANCE

Chicken Vinaigrette

Pollo a la Vinagreta

To serve 4

4 lb.	chicken, cut into serving pieces	2 kg.
	salt	
2 tbsp.	olive oil	30 ml.
4	medium-sized onions, thinly sliced (about 2 cups [¼ kg.])	4
1	small whole garlic bulb	1
1	bay leaf	1
1 tsp.	vinegar	5 ml.

Season the chicken pieces with salt, put them in a saucepan with the olive oil, onions, garlic, bay leaf and vinegar. Bring to a boil over high heat, cover the pan and then cook gently over low heat, shaking the pan from time to time, until the chicken is done (20 to 25 minutes). Drain the chicken pieces and serve them at once—discarding the cooking liquid or pressing it through a sieve to make a sauce.

VICTORIA SERRA, TRANSLATED BY ELIZABETH GILI
TIA VICTORIA'S SPANISH KITCHEN

Chicken in Yogurt

Murghi Dehin

To serve 4

3 lb.	roasting chicken, skinned and cut into serving pieces	1½ kg.
1½ cups	unflavored yogurt	375 ml.
1	large sweet red pepper, quartered, seeded, deribbed and grated or pounded to a paste	1
1 tsp.	Hungarian paprika	5 ml.
1	2-inch [5-cm.] piece fresh ginger root, grated	1
2 or 3	dried green chilies, crushed	2 or 3
16	large garlic cloves, crushed	16
1 tsp.	salt	5 ml.
5 tbsp.	chopped fresh parsley or coriander	75 ml.

Prick the chicken pieces all over with a very sharp fork. Beat the yogurt and make a marinade with the red pepper, paprika, ginger, dried chilies, garlic and salt. (The garlic is not excessive; yogurt takes care of its pungency.) Marinate the chicken for 10 to 12 hours in a cold place or in the refrigerator, turning the pieces from time to time.

Heat a heavy iron saucepan until the metal is very hot.

Throw in the chicken and marinade so that it makes a light splash, producing steam. Stir in the parsley or coriander leaves and cover immediately. Cook on high heat for 5 minutes; then on medium heat until all the yogurt is dry except for a tablespoon or two at the bottom. Do not let this get brown. Stir the chicken to coat it evenly. Serve hot with all the scrapings from the pan.

DHARAMJIT SINGH
INDIAN COOKERY

Sweet and Sour Chicken in Almond Sauce, Catalan-Style

Myraux ou Myrause de Catalogne

Baptiste Platine de Crémone, who published the original version of this recipe in 1474, declared that it was the finest meat he had tasted: ". . . very nourishing and healthy, it warms the liver and kidneys, fattens the body and relaxes the stomach."

To serve 4

3 lb.	roasting chicken	1½ kg.
	salt and pepper	
4 tbsp.	butter, softened	50 ml.
½ cup	blanched almonds, roasted in a slow oven until lightly browned	125 ml.
2	slices French or Italian bread, toasted in a slow oven until lightly browned	2
½ cup	red wine vinegar	125 ml.
1 tsp.	ground cinnamon	5 ml.
½ inch	fresh ginger root (a piece the size of a hazelnut), peeled and sliced	1 cm.
2 tbsp.	sugar	30 ml.

Season the chicken with salt and pepper, smear it with the butter and roast it in an oven preheated to 375° F. [190° C.] for 40 minutes. Remove the chicken, cut it into serving pieces and put them in a casserole, saving the roasting and carving juices.

Pound the almonds (or grind them in a blender), first alone, then with the toasted bread that has been soaked in the vinegar and finally add all the other flavorings—to which have been added the chicken's roasting and carving juices. If necessary to make a smooth sauce, add a little chicken stock or water. Taste for seasoning, pour the mixture over the chicken pieces, cover the casserole and simmer over a low heat or in a moderate oven preheated to 350° F. [180° C.] until the chicken is done—about 15 minutes. Stir occasionally to prevent sticking. Degrease the sauce, if necessary, before serving.

BAPTISTE PLATINE DE CRÉMONE
LE LIVRE DE HONNESTE VOLUPTÉ

125

Suzanne's Chicken Sauté

Poulet Sauté Suzanne

To serve 4

3 to 4 lb.	chicken, cut into serving pieces	1½ to 2 kg.
¼ cup	olive oil	50 ml.
2 tbsp.	butter	30 ml.
	salt and pepper	
⅓ cup	Cognac	75 ml.
⅓ cup	sweet white wine, such as Muscat	75 ml.
⅔ cup	heavy cream	150 ml.
2	egg yolks	2
	fines herbes, finely chopped	

Season the chicken pieces with salt and pepper. Heat a little olive oil in a sauté pan and sauté the chicken pieces rapidly on all sides. When they are golden brown, remove and drain them. Pour off any oil remaining in the pan and replace it with the butter. Melt the butter over low heat, return the chicken pieces to the pan and turn them in the butter.

Pour in the wine and the Cognac, turn up the heat and reduce the liquid until it thickens slightly. Add all but 2 tablespoons [30 ml.] of the cream. Cover the pan and simmer the chicken very gently for about 15 minutes. Remove the pan from the heat; stir in the egg yolks mixed with the remaining cream, and continue stirring briskly over very low heat until the sauce thickens, taking care not to let it boil. Sprinkle with the herbs and serve.

SUZANNE LABOURER AND X.-M. BOULESTIN
PETITS ET GRANDS PLATS

Chicken Sauté with Garlic

Poulet Canaille

To serve 4

3 to 4 lb.	chicken, cut into serving pieces	1½ to 2 kg.
3 tbsp.	butter	45 ml.
¼ cup	olive oil	50 ml.
30	garlic cloves, unpeeled	30
10	shallots, peeled and finely chopped	10
	salt and pepper	
⅔ cup	dry white wine	150 ml.

Heat the butter and oil in a sauté pan or a cast-iron casserole. Place the chicken pieces in the pan and brown them lightly on one side, over medium heat to avoid burning the fat. Turn the pieces and brown them on the other side. Add the unpeeled garlic cloves and the shallots. Sauté for 10

minutes or until the skins of the garlic cloves are lightly colored. Season liberally with salt and pepper. Add the wine cover the pan, reduce the heat to low and cook gently for about 30 minutes. When the meat is done, uncover the pan and turn the heat very high. Boil the wine, stirring constantly, until the liquid completely evaporates.

Bring the sauté pan to the table and serve the chicken pieces with the garlic cloves. Eat the garlic with the chicken first biting into each clove so that you can slide the tough skin off and discard it on your plate. The taste of the garlic is exquisitely subtle.

GINETTE MATHIOT
À TABLE AVEC ÉDOUARD DE POMIANE

Stewed Chicken, Canary Islands-Style

Pepitoria de Pollo à la Canaria

To serve 4 to 6

4 lb.	roasting chicken, cut into serving pieces	2 kg
	flour	
	salt and pepper	
¾ cup	olive oil	175 ml
2	garlic cloves, finely chopped	2
1	medium-sized onion, chopped	1
2 cups	dry white wine	½ liter
	hot chicken stock	
1	bay leaf	1
⅛ tsp.	dried thyme	½ ml.
1 tsp.	ground saffron	5 ml.
15	blanched almonds, chopped	15
½ cup	coarse bread crumbs	125 ml.
2	hard-boiled eggs, chopped	2
¼ cup	finely chopped fresh parsley	50 ml.

Coat the chicken pieces in flour that has been seasoned with salt and pepper. Shake off the excess flour. Heat all but a tablespoon or two [15 or 30 ml.] of the olive oil in a heavy skillet. Sauté the garlic and onion in it for about 5 minutes, or until soft. Add the chicken pieces and sauté over medium heat until just golden: they should not be brown. Add the white wine and enough chicken stock barely to cover the chicken. Taste for seasoning; add salt and pepper if needed. Add the bay leaf and thyme. Cover and simmer over low heat for about 45 minutes, or until the chicken is almost tender.

Dissolve the saffron in a little hot water and add to the chicken with the almonds. Simmer about 15 minutes longer, or until the chicken is tender. If the sauce looks too thin, cook uncovered to allow evaporation.

Fry the bread crumbs in the remaining olive oil until crisp and brown. Before serving, sprinkle the chicken pieces with chopped hard-boiled egg, bread crumbs and parsley.

NIKA STANDEN HAZELTON
THE CONTINENTAL FLAVOUR

———————◆———————

Senator's Braised Hen

La Poule du Sénateur

One of my friends, a French senator, once declared in front of the cook of a mutual acquaintance that an old hen was good for nothing except enriching the stock of a pot-au-feu. To show him how wrong he was, Mlle. Marthe, the cook, created the following preparation and he freely admitted his error.

	To serve 4	
4 lb.	stewing chicken	2 kg.
3 or 4	slices lean salt pork, blanched in boiling water for 5 minutes, drained and rinsed	3 or 4
	salt and pepper	
¾ cup	dry white wine	175 ml.
9	medium-sized potatoes, diced	9
6 tbsp.	butter	90 ml.
20	small boiling onions	20
1 cup	veal or chicken stock	¼ liter
2 tsp.	cornstarch, mixed with a little water	10 ml.
½ tbsp.	fresh lemon juice	7 ml.
	Marinade	
½ cup	olive oil	125 ml.
	salt	
5 or 6	peppercorns	5 or 6
2 tbsp.	finely chopped fresh parsley and chives	30 ml.
4	shallots, finely chopped	4
3	garlic cloves, crushed	3

Prepare the marinade by mixing the olive oil, salt, peppercorns, parsley and chives, shallots and garlic cloves.

Place the chicken in this marinade and leave it in a cool place (or the refrigerator) for a day. Occasionally spoon the marinade over parts of the chicken that are not immersed, and turn the bird over completely after about 6 hours.

Line the bottom of a fireproof casserole with the salt pork; season the chicken inside, put it on top of the salt pork and strain the marinade over it. Add the white wine, cover and cook over very low heat for about 3 hours. (One can also cook the bird in the oven, but in that case the lid should be sealed with a flour-and-water paste or aluminum foil.)

Meanwhile, fry the diced potatoes in two thirds of the butter until they are golden. In another pan, lightly color the onions in the remaining butter. Half an hour before serving, add the potatoes to the juices in the casserole and pour in the stock. Continue cooking over very low heat.

To serve, first put the chicken on a warmed platter and surround it with the onions and potatoes arranged alternately. Then add the cornstarch to the liquid remaining in the casserole. Simmer the liquid for 1 minute to thicken it, add the lemon juice and mix thoroughly. Carve the chicken, pour the sauce over the pieces and serve on hot plates.

RENAUDET
LES SECRETS DE LA BONNE TABLE

Boiled Fowl with Oysters

Despite the name of this 1861 recipe, the fowl or stewing chicken is poached rather than boiled. The "jar" in which the chicken poaches is an earthenware pot. In this recipe the jar should be covered halfway by the boiling water. The "blade" of mace specified is a blade-shaped strip of the whole spice.

	To serve 3 or 4	
4 lb.	stewing chicken	2 kg.
36	oysters, shucked, with their liquor reserved	36
½ cup	heavy cream	125 ml.
2	egg yolks	2
½ tsp.	ground mace (optional)	2 ml.

Truss a chicken as for boiling. Fill the inside with all but a few of the oysters, which have been bearded and washed in their own liquor. Secure the ends of the chicken, put it into a jar, cover and plunge the jar into a saucepan of boiling water. Keep it boiling for 1½ hours, or rather longer. Then take the gravy that has flowed from the oysters and chicken, of which there will be a good quantity; stir in the cream and yolks of eggs, add a few oysters scalded in their liquor. Let the sauce get quite *hot,* but do not allow it to *boil.* Pour some of it over the chicken and the remainder send to table in a tureen. A blade of pounded mace added to the sauce, with the cream and eggs, will be found an improvement.

MRS. ISABELLA BEETON
THE BOOK OF HOUSEHOLD MANAGEMENT

Poached Chicken with Prune Stuffing
Hindle Wakes

The original name of this recipe probably derives from "Hen de la Wake" or "Hen of the Wake" which means the hen to be eaten during a festive holiday or "wake" in Lancashire dialect. This is a late version of a very old recipe, dating from the Middle Ages. It was collected in its present form near Wigan, about 1900. Hindle wakes is traditionally served cold, and it is as good to eat as it is gay to look at with its white meat, black stuffing and yellow and green trimmings.

To serve 8

4 to 5 lb.	stewing chicken	2 to 2½ kg.
½ cup	wine vinegar	125 ml.
2 tbsp.	brown sugar	30 ml.
1	lemon, quartered	1
	parsley sprigs	
	Stuffing	
1 lb.	large dried prunes, pitted and soaked in water for 10 minutes or more	½ kg.
3 cups	fine white bread crumbs	¾ liter
½ cup	blanched almonds, coarsely chopped	125 ml.
	salt and pepper	
1 tbsp.	finely chopped mixed fresh parsley, marjoram, thyme and chives	15 ml.
2 oz.	beef suet, shredded (about ½ cup [125 ml.])	75 g.
½ cup	dry red wine	125 ml.
	Sauce	
¼ cup	cornstarch	50 ml.
1 cup	reserved chicken poaching stock, cooled and skimmed	¼ liter
	grated zest and juice of 2 lemons	
	salt and pepper	
2	eggs, well beaten	2

Reserve six prunes for decoration. Mix together the remaining prunes and all the other stuffing ingredients, and stuff the chicken. Sew up the breast flap and draw together the skin at the vent. Place the chicken in a large saucepan of water with the wine vinegar and brown sugar. Simmer for 4 hours and allow the chicken to get cold in the stock.

While the chicken is cooling, make the lemon sauce. Mix the cornstarch with the stock and bring to a boil, stirring in the juice of 2 lemons as you do so. Season with salt and pepper, add the grated zest of 1 lemon and boil for 2 minutes. Allow to cool slightly and stir in the well-beaten eggs, hold-ing the pan off the heat. Beat till thick and creamy; on no account should the sauce boil again. Leave it to get cold.

Place the cold chicken on a platter. Pour the sauce over it and decorate with the remaining grated lemon zest, quarters of lemon, halves of the reserved prunes and sprigs of parsley.

Carve with a very sharp knife.

ELISABETH AYRTON
THE COOKERY OF ENGLAND

Stuffed Chicken Baked in Parchment
La Pochette Surprise

To serve 2

2 lb.	chicken, halved	1 kg.
	olive oil	
	fine dry bread crumbs, seasoned with salt and freshly ground white pepper	
	Stuffing	
3	chicken livers, chopped	3
1	chicken heart, chopped	1
7 or 8	shallots, finely chopped	7 or 8
2 tbsp.	finely cut fresh chives	30 ml.
3 tbsp.	finely chopped chervil	45 ml.
20	tarragon leaves	20
2	slices French or Italian bread with crusts removed, soaked in milk and squeezed almost dry	2
1 tbsp.	butter	15 ml.
1	egg	1
	salt and freshly ground white pepper	
	grated nutmeg	

To prepare the stuffing, mix together the livers, heart, shallots, chives, chervil and tarragon in a large mortar or heavy mixing bowl. Add the bread, butter and egg. Pound the mixture, then add salt, pepper and a pinch of nutmeg. Fry a spoonful of the mixture to taste it for seasoning.

Brush the skin side of each chicken half generously with olive oil and pat on salted and peppered crumbs by hand to ensure a good coating. Lay each chicken half skin side down on a large piece of well-greased parchment paper. Fill the interior of each half with stuffing, brush the tops with oil and cover lightly with seasoned crumbs. Fold the edges of the paper securely together and tie each packet with string. This should be done carefully, bearing in mind that the packet, or *pochette,* will be served just as it is.

Bake in a moderate oven, preheated to 350° F. [180° C.], for 30 to 40 minutes, adjusting the heat so that the chicken cooks through without the packet becoming charred. This requires care but great artists often seek a challenge.

Each guest should open his or her own packet—first to discover what is inside and, second, to enjoy to the full the ineffable aroma.

GASTON DERYS
L'ART D'ÊTRE GOURMAND

Poule au Pot Henri IV

This classic recipe is named after the French King Henry IV (1553-1610), whose aspiration it was for all his subjects to be able to poach a chicken every Sunday.

To serve 6

4 lb.	roasting chicken with liver reserved	2 kg.
2 to 2½ quarts	boiling water, salted	2 to 2½ liters
4 or 5	carrots	4 or 5
2 or 3	turnips	2 or 3
1	small cabbage, core removed	1
6	slices French or Italian bread, dried in a moderate oven	6
	Stuffing	
3	eggs	3
1½ cups	bread crumbs	375 ml.
2 to 3 tbsp.	chopped fresh parsley	30 to 45 ml.
	reserved chicken liver, chopped	
2 oz.	ham, diced	50 g.
2 oz.	lean salt pork with the rind removed, diced, blanched in boiling water for 10 minutes and drained	50 g.
2 or 3	shallots, chopped	2 or 3
	salt	

Prepare the stuffing first. Beat the eggs in a bowl. Add the bread crumbs, parsley, chicken liver, ham, salt pork and shallots. Season with salt and stir the mixture well.

Loosely stuff the chicken and truss it as for roasting. Place it in a pot with the boiling water. If you are using old carrots and turnips, cut them into pieces and add them to the pot at this stage. Cover the pot and cook over medium heat.

But if the carrots and turnips are young and tender, leave them whole and add them along with the cabbage after 30 to 40 minutes. Continue cooking for a further 25 to 30 minutes or until the chicken is done.

To serve the stock, strain it into a soup tureen over oven-dried bread slices.

To serve the main dish, carve the chicken, arrange it on a warmed platter surrounded by all the vegetables. Moisten the dish with a few spoonfuls of stock.

TANTE MARGUERITE
LA CUISINE DE LA BONNE MÉNAGÈRE

Chicken Stewed with Eel

Poulet de Ferme Etuvé à la Digoinaise

This recipe is from a book dedicated to Alexandre Dumaine, chef-proprietor of the Hotel de la Côte d'Or in Burgundy from 1931 to the mid-1960s. The eel, which your fish dealer can skin for you, has a gelatinous quality that lends body and a surprising smoothness to the sauce.

To serve 4

2 to 2½ lb.	chicken, cut into serving pieces	1 kg.
6 to 8 tbsp.	butter	90 to 120 ml.
½ lb.	eel, skinned and cut into 1-inch [2½-cm.] slices	¼ kg.
	salt and pepper	
1½ tbsp.	flour	22 ml.
¾ cup	dry white wine	175 ml.
1 cup	water	¼ liter
	bouquet garni	
2	garlic cloves	2
	slices of coarse country bread	

Melt 4 tablespoons [60 ml.] of the butter in a sauté pan. Place the chicken pieces and eel in the pan, season with salt and pepper, cover tightly and cook gently for 10 minutes. Turn the pieces, cover and cook for another 10 minutes.

Remove the chicken and the eel, and keep them hot. Add the flour to the juice in the pan and cook over low heat; stir well and do not allow to color. Add the wine and the water, blending the sauce with a whisk. Put the pieces of chicken and eel back into the sauté pan. Add the bouquet garni and garlic. Cover; simmer for about 50 minutes over low heat.

Sauté a few pieces of bread in the remaining butter in another pan. Place the pieces of chicken and eel on top of the bread in a hot serving dish. Pour the sauce over the chicken and eel and serve very hot.

ALEXANDER WATT
THE ART OF SIMPLE FRENCH COOKERY

Chicken Stuffed with Brains

Poulet à la Franc-Comtoisse

If you can find —and afford —a fresh truffle, this dish provides an elegant use for a few slices of it.

	To serve 4	
2½ to 3 lb.	chicken	1 to 1½ kg.
	salt and pepper	
1	calf's brain	1
2 or 3	fresh truffle slices	2 or 3
4 tbsp.	butter	60 ml.

Season the chicken inside with salt and pepper. Wash the calf's brain under running water; then soak it for a few minutes in cold water and remove the surface membrane. Season the brain with salt and pepper. Tuck the truffle slices into the brain, and ease it into the breast cavity of the chicken. Sew up the opening with strong cotton thread, truss the bird, coat the top with butter and place the bird on a rack in a shallow roasting pan. Cook in a moderate oven preheated to 350° F. [180° C.] for about 1¼ hours. Cover the breast with buttered parchment paper after it becomes golden brown. Leave the paper in place for a few minutes to steam the bird briefly, then remove the paper to let the breast continue browning. To serve, carve the chicken, arrange it on a warmed dish, and pour over it the pan juices from which you have skimmed the fat.

ÉDITIONS GUTENBERG
LA CUISINE LYONNAISE

Steamed Chicken

Djej Mafooar

	To serve 4	
3 lb.	roasting chicken	1½ kg.
¼ tsp.	pulverized saffron threads	1 ml.
1 tsp.	salt	5 ml.
¼ cup	unsalted butter, softened	50 ml.
	ground cumin seed	
	coarse salt	
	cayenne pepper (optional)	

Pound the saffron with the salt and blend with the softened butter. Rub into the skin of the chicken.

Fill the bottom of a *couscoussier* or other type of steamer with water. *The perforated top section should not touch the liquid below.* Bring to a boil. Dampen a strip of cheesecloth and dust it with flour. Use this to make a seal between the top and bottom sections of the steamer. Check all sides for effective sealing: the top and bottom should fit snugly, so that steam rises only through the holes.

Place the chicken in the top section and cover with a double layer of cheesecloth. Put the lid on, making sure it fits tightly. Steam for 1 hour without lifting the lid. Serve at once, as is, with accompanying bowls of ground cumin seed and coarse salt or, if desired, mix the cumin and salt with a sprinkle of cayenne pepper.

PAULA WOLFERT
COUSCOUS AND OTHER GOOD FOOD FROM MOROCCO

Chicken Greater than the Sum of its Parts

Murgi ka Kima

	To serve 2 or 3	
1½ to 2 cups	finely chopped, raw boneless chicken	⅓ to ½ liter
⅓ cup	clarified butter	75 ml.
12	whole cloves	12
1	large onion, halved lengthwise and thinly sliced crosswise	1
	salt	
1 tsp.	ground turmeric	5 ml.
3 tbsp.	fresh lime juice	45 ml.
	Spicy paste	
1 tsp.	finely chopped garlic	5 ml.
1 tsp.	finely chopped fresh ginger root	5 ml.
2 tsp.	chopped onion	10 ml.

To make the spicy paste, whirl the garlic, ginger and chopped onion in a blender, using only as much water as is necessary to facilitate grinding. Reserve.

In a heavy, medium-sized saucepan, heat the butter almost to smoking. Keep the lid of the pan close by. Drop in the cloves, close the pan immediately and shake it over the heat for 1 minute. Remove the cloves with a slotted spoon and discard them. Fry the sliced onion in the same butter.

When the onion is just golden, add the chicken. Salt to taste. Stir and keep turning with a spatula for 5 minutes. Add the turmeric. Continue stirring for 10 minutes. Do not add any water. Add the spicy paste and cook uncovered until the mixture is smooth. (Never add water.) Squeeze the lime juice into the pan, stir and serve very hot.

SHIVAJI RAO AND SHALINI DEVI HOLKAR
COOKING OF THE MAHARAJAS

Roast Chicken, Moroccan-Style

Djej Mechoui

To serve 4

two 2 lb.	chickens, halved or quartered	two 1 kg.
3	scallions, white parts only, chopped	3
1	garlic clove (optional)	1
2 tbsp.	coarsely chopped fresh coriander and parsley	30 ml.
1 tsp.	salt	5 ml.
1½ tsp.	sweet paprika	7 ml.
1½ tsp.	ground cumin	7 ml.
¼ tsp.	cayenne pepper	1 ml.
4 tbsp.	butter, softened	60 ml.

Pound the scallions in a mortar with the garlic, herbs, salt and spices. Blend with the butter to make a paste. Rub the paste all over the prepared chicken pieces. Leave the chicken to marinate at room temperature for at least 1 hour. Heat the charcoal in an outdoor grill or preheat the oven broiler.

Arrange the pieces of chicken skin side up over the coals, or skin side down under the broiler. After 5 minutes turn and baste with any extra paste or the juices in the broiling pan. Continue turning and basting every 5 minutes for approximately 25 minutes or until the pieces are done.

PAULA WOLFERT
COUSCOUS AND OTHER GOOD FOOD FROM MOROCCO

Chicken Adobo

To serve 4

2½ to 3 lb.	chicken, cut into serving pieces	1 to 1½ kg.
6	garlic cloves, finely chopped	6
6	black peppercorns	6
2	bay leaves	2
½ cup	white vinegar	125 ml.
2 tbsp.	dark soy sauce	30 ml.
	salt	
	oil	

In a large skillet with a cover, bring to a simmer the garlic, peppercorns, bay leaves, vinegar, soy sauce and a pinch of salt. Add the chicken pieces, stirring to coat them with the sauce. Bring again to a simmer. Cover and simmer for about 30 minutes or until the chicken is cooked, basting once or twice with the liquid in the skillet. Remove the chicken to a plate and pat the pieces dry with paper towels. Skim the fat from the sauce in the skillet and keep the sauce warm.

In another large skillet heat a thin film of oil and then brown the chicken pieces. Arrange the browned pieces on a warmed platter and pour the sauce over them. Serve hot with plain white rice.

LEE FOSTER (EDITOR)
THE NEW YORK TIMES CORRESPONDENTS' CHOICE

Boiled Stuffed Chicken, Hungarian-Style

Fött Töltött Csirke

To serve 8 to 10

4½ lb.	chicken, boned except for the wings and drumsticks	2 to 2½ kg.
2 to 3 tsp.	salt	10 to 15 ml.
1	onion, finely chopped	1
1 tbsp.	butter	15 ml.
1 lb.	ground veal	½ kg.
½ lb.	chicken livers, trimmed of membranes and patted dry	¼ kg.
1	large bread roll, torn into chunks, soaked in milk and squeezed almost dry	1
2	hard-boiled eggs	2
2	tomatoes, peeled and chopped	2
1 tsp.	Hungarian paprika	5 ml.
2	eggs	2
¼ cup	sour cream	50 ml.
2	garlic cloves, peeled	2
1	carrot, sliced	1
1 tbsp.	chopped fresh parsley	15 ml.
6	sprigs parsley	6
	lemon slices	
	radishes	

Rub the chicken inside and out with salt. Wilt the onion in the butter. Add the veal and chicken livers. Rub the soaked bread roll through a strainer, together with the hard-boiled eggs and tomatoes. Combine this with the meat, paprika, eggs, sour cream and salt. Mix thoroughly. Stuff the chicken with this mixture; sew up all openings. Tie up the bird in a double thickness of muslin or cheesecloth; place it in a pan with water to cover. Add the garlic, carrot and chopped parsley. Cook the bird slowly for 1½ hours or until it is tender — do not overcook.

Remove the chicken, carefully unwrap it and place it on a platter. Cover and chill it overnight. Garnish it with the remaining parsley, lemon slices and radishes. To serve, first remove the wings and legs, then slice the chicken crosswise.

INGE KRAMARZ
THE BALKAN COOKBOOK

Poached Stuffed Chicken

La Véritable Poule au Pot Agenoise

This recipe calls for a well-fattened cockerel or a capon. If you use stewing chicken instead, poach it for 3 hours and add the vegetables toward the end of the cooking time. The technique for stuffing a bird under the skin is shown on page 46, Step 3.

To serve 6

5 to 6 lb.	cockerel or capon with the liver reserved	2½ to 3 kg.
1	slice stale French or Italian bread, rubbed with garlic (optional)	1
8	medium-sized carrots	8
4 or 5	medium-sized turnips	4 or 5
2 or 3	leeks	2 or 3
1	head Boston lettuce	1
	salt and pepper	
	Stuffing	
	reserved chicken liver, chopped	
4 or 5	egg yolks	4 or 5
2 cups	coarsely crumbled dry bread crumbs	½ liter
4 oz.	lean salt pork, blanched in boiling water for 5 minutes, drained and finely diced	125 g.
2	garlic cloves, finely chopped	2
2 tbsp.	finely chopped fresh parsley	30 ml.

Prepare the stuffing by first pounding the reserved chicken liver and egg yolks to a smooth paste. Mix together the bread crumbs, salt pork, garlic and parsley with the liver paste. For greater elegance and flavor, instead of simply placing the stuffing in the bird's cavity, you can introduce it carefully under the skin of the breast and the inside of the thighs, and slip a slice of bread liberally rubbed with garlic into the cavity. Sew up the skin with thick cotton thread, and allow this amiable creature to rest in a cool place overnight.

The next day, choose a suitably sized cooking pot, which should be of earthenware. Fill it with enough water to cover the bird, and add the vegetables and seasoning. Put in your bird with due delicacy. Bring to a boil over high heat, then reduce the heat to low and cover the pot. From this point, 1½ hours of cooking at a gentle simmer will be amply sufficient.

Along with the chicken, skillfully carved, a sophisticated host may serve curried rice. It is considered bad form to eat bread with this dish: the stuffing should suffice.

In summer, the broth, skimmed of fat and chilled, constitutes one of the tastiest of cold consommés. Served hot, with croutons fried in chicken or goose fat, it also has its partisans and should not be underestimated.

GASTON DERYS
L'ART D'ÊTRE GOURMAND

Chicken with Fennel Seeds

To serve 4

3 lb.	chicken, cut into 8 serving pieces	1½ kg.
1 tsp.	fennel seeds	5 ml.
2	medium-sized onions, finely chopped	2
¼ lb.	salt pork, blanched in boiling water for 10 minutes, drained and diced	125 g.
½ cup	blanched almonds, finely chopped	125 ml.
	salt and pepper	

Place the chicken in a deep pot and add water just to cover. Boil slowly for 20 minutes, skimming frequently. Remove the chicken pieces and drain them on paper towels. Add the fennel seeds and onions to the pot, and simmer until the broth has been reduced to one third its original quantity. Strain the broth. Meanwhile, in a skillet, sauté the salt pork over moderate heat until slightly rendered. Add the almonds and chicken pieces, and sauté until golden. Pour in the broth. Season to taste. Cook for 5 minutes and serve it forth.

NAOMI BARRY AND BEPPE BELLINI
FOOD ALLA FLORENTINE

Chicken with Tarragon

Poulet à l'Estragon

To serve 4

3 to 4 lb.	chicken	1½ to 2 kg.
2 to 3 tbsp.	fresh lemon juice	30 to 45 ml.
4 tbsp.	butter	60 ml.
	salt and pepper	
2 tbsp.	chopped fresh tarragon, plus a few whole leaves	30 ml.
2	egg yolks	2
1 cup	cream	¼ liter

Rub the outside of the chicken with lemon juice. Mash the butter with salt and pepper and 1 tablespoon [15 ml.] of chopped tarragon, then put the mixture inside the bird.

Poach the chicken, with water barely to cover, until it is cooked. Leave it to cool in the stock. Take out the chicken and place it whole in a deep serving dish; strain the stock. Now beat up the egg yolks with the cream and the other tablespoon [15 ml.] of chopped tarragon. Heat about 1 cup [¼ liter] of the stock in a small pan, pour a spoonful or two into the egg-and-cream mixture, then pour all back into the pan. Stir continuously until the sauce thickens, but do not make it too thick as it will solidify slightly as it cools. Pour the sauce over the chicken and leave to get cold. Before serving, arrange tarragon leaves along the breast of the chicken.

ELIZABETH DAVID
FRENCH COUNTRY COOKING

Stewing Chicken with Rice

Poule au Riz

To serve 5 or 6

4 to 4½ lb.	stewing chicken, trussed	2 kg.
1 or 2	carrots	1 or 2
1 or 2	leeks, trimmed and washed well (optional)	1 or 2
1	large onion, studded with 1 or 2 whole cloves	1
1	bouquet garni	1
1 tbsp.	salt	15 ml.
	Rice	
3 tbsp.	butter	45 ml.
1	small onion, chopped	1
1 cup	raw unprocessed rice	¼ liter
2 cups	reserved chicken poaching stock	½ liter
	Sauce	
2 tbsp.	butter	30 ml.
1½ tbsp.	flour	22 ml.
1½ cups	reserved chicken poaching stock	375 ml.
	salt and pepper	
	grated nutmeg (optional)	
1	egg yolk	1
3 to 4 tbsp.	light cream	45 to 60 ml.
	fresh lemon juice	

Put the bird, together with the other ingredients, in a deep pan and add water to cover. Bring to a boil, skim, lower the heat and cook slowly uncovered for about 2 hours, or until the chicken is tender.

About half an hour before the chicken is cooked, prepare the rice as follows. Melt 2 tablespoons [30 ml.] of the butter in a saucepan, add the chopped onion and cook until it is golden brown. Add the rice and shake the pan over the heat for a minute or two until the grains are coated with the butter. Add hot chicken stock, cover the pan closely and cook in a medium-hot oven, preheated to 375° F. [190° C.], or on top of the stove over low heat for 20 to 25 minutes—or until the liquid is cooked away. When done, add the remaining butter to the rice, tossing all together carefully with a fork to avoid mashing the grains.

While the rice is cooking, prepare the sauce. Melt the butter, add the flour and cook until they are mixed together. Add the stock, mix all together well and cook, stirring, until the sauce is smooth and thickened. Correct the seasoning, adding a little nutmeg if desired, and continue cooking very slowly for about 10 minutes. Mix the egg yolk with the cream and combine with the sauce by adding a little hot sauce to the egg-and-cream mixture and then stirring it all carefully into the sauce. Add a few drops of lemon juice and cook just long enough to combine the ingredients, but do not allow the sauce to boil.

Make a bed of the rice in a serving dish, carve the chicken and place the pieces on top of the rice. Pour half of the sauce over the chicken and serve the remaining sauce separately.

LOUIS DIAT
FRENCH COOKING FOR AMERICANS

Chicken and Lovage

To serve 4

3 to 3½ lb.	chicken	1½ to 1¾ kg.
1	onion	1
1	carrot	1
	black peppercorns	
1	bunch lovage	1
	salt	
	Sauce	
2 tbsp.	butter	30 ml.
2 tbsp.	chopped lovage	30 ml.
1 tbsp.	flour	15 ml.
1 cup	stock reserved from poaching	¼ liter
	grated peel and juice of 2 small oranges	
¼ cup	heavy cream	50 ml.
	salt and pepper	
2 cups	chopped watercress	½ liter
½ cup	chopped mustard leaves	125 ml.
½ cup	chopped garden cress	125 ml.

Put the chicken on its back in a large saucepan with the onion, carrot, peppercorns and the bunch of lovage. Cover with water to the depth of the chicken thighs, add salt and bring the water to a boil over moderate heat. Cover the pan and poach the chicken gently, turning it once or twice, for 1 hour. Remove the chicken and keep it warm. Strain the stock.

In a small saucepan, melt the butter over moderate heat. Add the chopped lovage and cook it until it is tender. Blend in the flour and 1 cup [¼ liter] of the stock and bring to a boil, stirring. Then stir in the orange or tangerine peel, the juice and the cream. Season with salt and pepper. Keep the sauce warm, but do not let it boil again.

Disjoint the chicken and lay the pieces on a bed of chopped watercress mixed with mustard and garden cress. Pour the sauce over the top and serve immediately.

GAIL DUFF
FRESH ALL THE YEAR

Boned Chicken, Italian-Style

Pollastra Farcita Lessata all'Italiana

To bone the chicken, follow the instructions on pages 62-63.

To serve 6

4 lb.	roasting chicken	2 kg.
	salt	
3 quarts	chicken stock	3 liters
2	carrots, sliced	2
2	leeks, white parts only, sliced	2
3	ribs celery, sliced	3
3	beet leaves (optional)	3
1	onion, stuck with 1 whole clove	1

Stuffing

¼ lb.	chicken livers, chopped and sautéed in 2 tbsp. [30 ml.] butter for 3 minutes	125 g.
½ cup	lean salt pork, blanched in boiling water for 10 minutes, drained and diced	125 ml.
½ cup	chopped prosciutto or other smoked ham	125 ml.
1 tbsp.	chopped fresh parsley	15 ml.
1	garlic clove, crushed	1
1	onion, chopped	1
2 cups	fresh bread cubes, soaked in milk and squeezed almost dry	½ liter
1 tsp.	salt	5 ml.
¼ tsp.	freshly ground pepper	1 ml.
	grated nutmeg	
2	egg yolks	2

Sauce

2	hard-boiled eggs	2
¼ cup	prepared mustard, preferably Dijon-style	50 ml.
3 tbsp.	wine vinegar	45 ml.
¾ cup	oil	175 ml.
2 tbsp.	finely chopped onion	30 ml.
1 tsp.	salt	5 ml.
¼ tsp.	freshly ground white pepper	1 ml.

Bone the chicken whole, without breaking the skin. If desired, the drumstick and wing bones may be left intact to give the chicken its original appearance after it is stuffed.

Mix all of the stuffing ingredients in a bowl, season the cavity of the chicken with salt, and then stuff it loosely. Sew the openings with string and wrap the chicken in cheesecloth, tying it securely so that it will hold its shape during the cooking. Place it in a large, heavy pot with the stock and aromatic vegetables, bring to a boil, reduce the heat and simmer uncovered for 1½ hours.

Prepare the sauce while the chicken is cooking. Mash the hard-boiled egg yolks and mix them with the mustard and vinegar in a bowl. Pour in the oil in a slow stream, beating constantly, so that the mixture develops the smoothness and consistency of mayonnaise. Chop the egg whites and add them to the sauce along with the finely chopped onion, salt and white pepper.

Unwrap the chicken on a warmed serving platter. Carve it crosswise into slices and spoon a little of the strained cooking liquid over each serving. Serve the sauce separately.

LUIGI CARNACINA
GREAT ITALIAN COOKING

Chicken Casserole

Pepitoria de Gallina

To serve 4

3 lb.	roasting chicken	1½ kg.
	bouquet garni of parsley sprigs, thyme sprigs and a bay leaf, tied together in a bunch	
	salt and pepper	
1	carrot	1
1	small onion	1
2 tbsp.	lard	30 ml.
3½ oz.	ham, cut into cubes	100 g.
2 tbsp.	chopped fresh parsley	30 ml.
4 or 5	garlic cloves	4 or 5
10	hazelnuts, toasted	10
1	whole clove	1
2	hard-boiled egg yolks	2
	reserved chicken poaching stock	
2	raw egg yolks, lightly beaten	2

First poach the chicken in water containing the bunch of herbs, salt, pepper, carrot and onion until it is almost cooked (about 50 minutes). Remove the chicken, and strain and reserve the stock.

Heat the lard in a big saucepan or casserole, then fry the ham and a little of the chopped parsley. Put in the chicken and carefully brown it on all sides.

In a large mortar make a paste with the garlic and hazelnuts, the clove, hard-boiled egg yolks and the rest of the chopped parsley. Dilute the paste with two or more ladles of the chicken stock and pour this sauce over the chicken in the casserole. Cover; cook gently for 20 minutes. Remove from the heat and stir in the raw egg yolks. Serve immediately.

ANNA MACMIADHACHÁIN
SPANISH REGIONAL COOKERY

❖

Stuffed Chicken

Little is known about Apicius, the First Century Roman gourmet and writer whose cookbook furnishes this recipe for stuffed chicken; however, his discourses on cooking have come down to us through a succession of translators. The edition used here is a recent translation by Barbara Flower and Elisabeth Rosenbaum of a Fourth or Fifth Century compilation of his work.

Apicius is not specific but, prepared in this way, chicken can be either pot roasted or poached. Not all of the ingredients cited are familiar today. Spelt—"bearded wheat" or "german wheat"—is a small, hard wheat grain similar in flavor to barley; barley or rice can be substituted. Liquamen is the name of the salty fermented fish sauce the ancient Romans used as a seasoning. An alternative is pounded anchovies.

To serve 4

4 lb.	roasting chicken	2 kg.
	Stuffing	
3 or 4	sprigs lovage	3 or 4
	pepper	
1	small piece fresh ginger root, chopped	1
¼ lb.	lean veal or pork, finely chopped	125 g.
3 cups	boiled spelt grits	¾ liter
1	lamb's brain or ½ calf's brain, cooked in chicken stock and roughly cut up	1
2	eggs	2
2 tsp.	*liquamen*	10 ml.
2 tbsp.	oil	30 ml.
	whole peppercorns	
½ cup	pine nuts	125 ml.

Using a large mortar and pestle, pound the lovage, pepper, ginger, chopped meat and boiled spelt grits to a paste; then pound in the brain, break the eggs into the mortar and work

all this into a smooth mixture. Blend it with the *liquamen* and add the oil, peppercorns and pine nuts. Stuff the chicken with this mixture, leaving a little room. Cook it.

BARBARA FLOWER AND ELISABETH ROSENBAUM
THE ROMAN COOKERY BOOK

❖

Ribbed Macaroni with Chicken, Gypsy-Style

Rigatoni con Pollo alla Zingara

The rigatoni called for in this recipe is a kind of thick, ribbed macaroni about 2 inches [5 cm.] long. It is obtainable wherever Italian foods are sold, but any large macaroni product can be substituted for rigatoni.

To serve 4

3 lb.	chicken, cut into serving pieces	1½ kg.
2 tbsp.	butter	30 ml.
2 tbsp.	olive oil	30 ml.
½ cup	dry white wine	125 ml.
2	garlic cloves, chopped	2
	ground sage and dried rosemary	
1 tsp.	salt	5 ml.
	freshly ground black pepper	
2 cups	chicken stock	½ liter
3	anchovy fillets, soaked in cold water for 10 minutes and patted dry	3
½ tbsp.	wine vinegar	7 ml.
6	plum tomatoes, peeled and diced	6
½ lb.	rigatoni	¼ kg.
	Asiago or Parmesan cheese, grated	

In a deep saucepan heat the butter and oil; sauté the chicken pieces in it, browning them evenly. Pour in the wine and continue cooking, uncovered, until the wine evaporates. Add the garlic, a pinch each of the sage and rosemary, the salt, a liberal amount of pepper and the chicken stock. Cover the pan and simmer for 1 hour, or until the chicken is fork-tender. Transfer the chicken to a warm platter in a low oven.

Chop the anchovies, then mash them into a paste in the vinegar. Stir this into the sauce; add the tomatoes. Simmer over low heat, uncovered, stirring often, for 20 minutes, or until the sauce is smooth and thick. Meanwhile, cook the rigatoni al dente, drain it and place it in a large hot bowl. Pour in two thirds of the sauce; toss well. Serve immediately in hot soup bowls. Pass the cheese, to be sprinkled on the pasta, at the table. The chicken, topped with the remaining sauce, comes as the second course.

JACK DENTON SCOTT
THE COMPLETE BOOK OF PASTA

Cooked Chicken Breasts in Cream Sauce

Filet de Poularde à la Béchamel

To serve 4

2	poached chicken breasts, skinned, boned and cut into bite-sized pieces	2
2 tbsp.	butter	30 ml.
1 tbsp.	flour	15 ml.
2 tbsp.	finely chopped fresh parsley	30 ml.
3 or 4	scallions, finely chopped	3 or 4
1 tbsp.	finely chopped shallots	15 ml.
1	garlic clove, finely chopped	1
	salt and pepper	
	grated nutmeg	
1	egg yolk, beaten	1
½ cup	heavy cream	125 ml.
2 tbsp.	fresh lemon juice	30 ml.

Melt the butter in a heavy saucepan. Stir in the flour, parsley, scallions, shallots, garlic, salt, pepper and a pinch of nutmeg. Cook gently over very low heat for a few minutes. Mix the egg yolk with the cream and gradually stir into the mixture in the pan. Continue stirring until the sauce has a consistency that will coat the spoon. Add the chicken breasts and lemon juice, stir until heated through, then serve.

BERTRAND GUÉGAN
LA FLEUR DE LA CUISINE FRANÇAISE

Chicken with Eggs, Lemons and Olives

Djej Masquid Bil Beid

Preserved lemons are one of the indispensable ingredients of Moroccan cooking. Their unique pickled taste and special silken texture cannot be duplicated with fresh lemons or limes. They may be used as a flavoring element in stews, marinades, pilafs and salad dressings.

The important thing in preserving lemons yourself is to be certain they are completely covered with salted lemon juice. With my recipe you can use the lemon pickling juice over and over again. (As a matter of fact, I keep a jar of juice in the kitchen and, whenever I have a half lemon left over, I toss it into the jar and let it marinate with the rest.)

Sometimes you will see a sort of lacy, white substance clinging to preserved lemons in the jar; it is perfectly harmless, but should be rinsed off for esthetic reasons just before the lemons are used. Preserved lemons are rinsed, in any case, to rid them of their salty taste. Cook them with both pulps and rinds, if desired.

Preserved lemons

5	lemons	5
¼ cup	salt (more if desired)	50 ml.

Safi spice mixture (optional)

1	cinnamon stick	1
3	whole cloves	3
5 or 6	coriander seeds	5 or 6
3 or 4	black peppercorns	3 or 4
1	bay leaf	1
	fresh lemon juice, if necessary	

If you wish to soften the peel, soak the lemons in water for three days, changing the water daily.

Quarter each lemon from the top to within ½ inch [1 cm.] of the bottom, sprinkle salt on the exposed flesh, then close up the fruit again. Place 1 tablespoon [15 ml.] of salt on the bottom of a sterilized 1-pint [½-liter] mason jar. Pack in the lemons and push them down, adding more salt and the optional spices between layers. Pressing the lemons down releases their juices and makes room for the remaining lemons. (If the juice from the fruit does not cover them, add fresh lemon juice.) Leave some air space before sealing the jar.

Let the lemons ripen for 30 days in a warm place, turning the jar upside down each day to distribute the salt and juice.

To use, rinse the lemons, as needed, under running water—removing and discarding the pulp, if desired. There is no need to refrigerate after opening. Preserved lemons will keep up to a year, and the pickling juice can be used two or three times over the course of a year.

To serve 6

two 3 lb.	chickens, cut into serving pieces	two 1½ kg.
1	large bunch parsley, chopped	1
3	garlic cloves, chopped	3
1	Spanish onion, grated	1
	salt	
¾ tsp.	ground ginger	4 ml.
¾ tsp.	freshly ground black pepper	4 ml.
⅛ tsp.	ground saffron	½ ml.
3	large cinnamon sticks or 6 small ones	3
4 tbsp.	butter, melted	60 ml.
2 cups	water	½ liter
10	eggs	10
2	preserved lemons	2
8	red-brown olives, such as Kalamatas, pitted and chopped	8
½ cup	fresh lemon juice	125 ml.

Place the chicken pieces in a fireproof casserole. Add two thirds of the parsley, and the garlic, onion, salt, ground spices, cinnamon sticks and half of the butter. Add the water and bring to a boil. Simmer, covered, for about 1 hour or until the chicken is very tender and the flesh almost falling off the bone. (During the cooking you may need to add more water.)

Preheat the oven to 350° F. [180° C.]. Transfer the chicken (but not the sauce) to a heatproof serving dish. Remove any loose bones and the cinnamon sticks from the casserole and boil the liquid rapidly, uncovered, to reduce it to 2 cups [½ liter] of thick, rich sauce. Pour the sauce over the chicken.

Beat the eggs to a froth with the remaining parsley. Rinse and dice the preserved lemons, using the pulp if desired. Stir the lemons and chopped olives into the eggs, and pour the mixture over the chickens. Cover with aluminum foil and bake on the middle shelf of the oven for 20 minutes.

Raise the oven heat to its highest setting, remove the aluminum cover and sprinkle the egg mixture with the remaining melted butter. Transfer the dish to the upper shelf of the oven and bake for 10 minutes more, or until the eggs are completely set and the chickens have browned slightly. Sprinkle with lemon juice and serve at once.

PAULA WOLFERT
COUSCOUS AND OTHER GOOD FOOD FROM MOROCCO

Spanish Chicken Sauté with Rice

Poulet au Riz à l'Espagnole

For instructions on preparing artichokes, see page 11.

To serve 4

3 lb.	chicken, cut into serving pieces	1½ kg.
¼ cup	olive oil	50 ml.
2	onions, chopped	2
2	garlic cloves, finely chopped	2
4	tomatoes, peeled, seeded and roughly chopped	4
4	fresh artichoke hearts	4
4	sweet red peppers, quartered, seeded and deribbed	4
½ cup	freshly shelled peas	125 ml.
	ground saffron	
	salt and pepper	
1 cup	raw unprocessed rice	¼ liter
2 cups	water	½ liter

In a fireproof casserole, sauté the chicken pieces in the olive oil. As soon as they are brown, add the onions, garlic, tomatoes, artichoke hearts, peppers, peas and a good pinch of saffron. Season with salt and pepper, add the rice and lightly brown all ingredients.

Add the water and bring the contents of the casserole to a

fast boil, then complete the cooking by covering the casserole and placing it in a moderate oven, which has been preheated to 350° F. [180° C.], for around 20 to 30 minutes.

Note: this recipe is a good one for making sure that the grains of rice remain separate, providing the casserole is taken out of the oven about 2 minutes before the rice is completely cooked. Serve immediately.

LÉON ISNARD
LA CUISINE FRANÇAISE ET AFRICAINE

Chicken with Mutton

This is a very old manor-house recipe from the North of England and originally did not include tomatoes, which were not known, but it is much improved by their flavor and color. Early versions have turnips and carrots or any vegetables available. This dish can be heated up perfectly.

To serve 8, or to serve 4 twice

3 to 4 lb.	stewing chicken	1½ to 2 kg.
1½ lb.	lean mutton shoulder (or substitute lamb shoulder), boned and cut into 4 pieces	¾ kg.
3	medium-sized tomatoes, peeled	3
4	medium-sized onions, sliced	4
½ lb.	fresh mushrooms	¼ kg.
1	large zucchini, peeled, halved lengthwise, seeded and cubed	1
½	garlic clove, crushed	½
	salt and pepper	
1½ cups	dry white wine or dry hard cider	375 ml.
½ cup	dried navy beans or dried split peas	125 ml.

Put the chicken in a deep and large casserole, and fit the mutton or lamb pieces around it. Add the tomatoes, onion, mushrooms, zucchini, crushed garlic and plenty of salt and pepper. Pour in the white wine or cider, and leave overnight. Leave the dried peas or beans soaking separately in water.

In the morning, drain the beans, parboil them for 10 minutes, add them to the casserole and fill with enough water to cover. Peas should be drained, but do not need parboiling. Bake at 200° F. [100° C.]. Leave all day in the oven.

To serve, in the evening, lift out the chicken and divide it into joints, removing the rather glutinous skin. The chicken will almost fall apart without being carved. Arrange the pieces with the mutton, carved into thick slices, on a large shallow dish, with the vegetables around them in a border. Stir and season the stock, and pour over all, serving the surplus separately. The stock can be thickened if preferred.

The dish needs only boiled potatoes as accompaniment.

ELISABETH AYRTON
THE COOKERY OF ENGLAND

Williamsburg Chicken Pudding

This recipe has been adapted from the original version in Mrs. Mary Randolph's "Virginia Housewife," 1831.

To serve 4 to 6

4 to 5 lb.	chicken, cut into serving pieces	2 to 2½ kg.
1	onion	1
	celery tops	
	parsley sprigs	
1 tsp.	dried thyme	5 ml.
	salt and pepper	
	Batter	
2 cups	milk	½ liter
3	eggs, well beaten	3
¼ cup	flour	50 ml.
4 tbsp.	butter, melted	60 ml.
1 tsp.	salt	5 ml.

Put the chicken pieces in a pot with water to cover, along with the onion, a few celery tops and parsley sprigs, the thyme, salt and pepper. Simmer gently, uncovered, until the meat is just tender.

Take the chicken pieces from the broth, remove the skin and place the pieces in a shallow baking dish. Pour in 1 cup [¼ liter] of the strained poaching broth. Make a batter with milk, eggs, flour, melted butter and salt. Pour this over the chicken and bake in a moderate oven, preheated to 350° F. [180° C.], for about 35 minutes or until the batter topping is set and a knife inserted into the center comes out clean.

Serve immediately with a gravy made by thickening the remaining broth with a butter-and-flour roux.

MRS. HELEN CLAIRE BULLOCK
THE WILLIAMSBURG ART OF COOKERY

Chicken Curry
Murgi Survedar

The coconut milk called for in this recipe may be obtained from stores that specialize in Caribbean or Oriental foods. Or you can make it at home from a fresh coconut; 1 cup [¼ liter] of grated coconut mixed with 1 cup [¼ liter] of water will yield about 1 cup [¼ liter] of coconut milk. Grate the coconut meat without removing the brown skin. Measure the volume of the coconut meat and mix it with an equal volume of hot, but not boiling, tap water. (Do not use the liquid from the coconut.) Press the mixture through a fine sieve lined with a double layer of dampened cheesecloth.

To serve 4

1½ lb.	chicken pieces	¾ kg.
2 tsp.	finely chopped garlic	10 ml.
1 tbsp.	chopped fresh ginger root (or substitute 1 tsp. [5 ml.] ground ginger)	15 ml.
1 tbsp.	vegetable oil	15 ml.
2 tsp.	salt	10 ml.
½ tsp.	ground turmeric	2 ml.
8	unsalted cashew nuts	8
8	blanched almonds	8
3 cups	water	¾ liter
6 tbsp.	clarified butter	90 ml.
5 tbsp.	coarsely chopped onion	75 ml.
¼ cup	unflavored yogurt, beaten smooth with a fork	50 ml.
1 cup	coconut milk	¼ liter
2 tbsp.	chopped coriander leaves (optional)	30 ml.
	Spicy paste	
1 tbsp.	poppy seeds	15 ml.
4	whole cloves	4
1	cinnamon stick 1¼ inches [3 cm.] long (or substitute ¼ tsp. [1 ml.] ground cinnamon)	1
4	cardamom pods, husked and the seeds reserved (or substitute ¼ tsp. [1 ml.] ground cardamom)	4
½ tsp.	peppercorns	2 ml.
2 tsp.	finely chopped fresh ginger root (or substitute ½ tsp. [2 ml.] ground ginger)	10 ml.
8	garlic cloves	8
3 tbsp.	finely chopped onion	45 ml.
¼ cup	water	50 ml.

Drop the garlic, ginger and oil into a blender and purée them. Pour the purée into a heavy, medium-sized pot and sauté over medium heat for 5 minutes. Add the chicken pieces, salt, turmeric, cashews and almonds. Stir to mix well. Raise the heat and continue frying until the chicken is golden and all the natural liquid has evaporated. Add the water. Cover and simmer until just tender. Remove the chicken and nuts, drain and reserve them. Strain the broth, reduce it to 1 cup [¼ liter] and reserve separately.

To make the spicy paste, drop into the blender, one by one as listed, the poppy seeds, cloves, cinnamon, cardamom, peppercorns, ginger, garlic and finely chopped onion. Pulverize each ingredient before adding the next. Add the water and blend to a smooth, thick paste. Set aside.

In a heavy, medium-sized saucepan, heat the clarified butter and fry the coarsely chopped onion until it is just turning color. Off the heat, stir in the spicy paste. Return the pan to the heat and continue frying, scraping and turning the mixture with a spatula. Add a tablespoon of water whenever necessary to prevent sticking. Continue thus until butter bubbles up to the top of the spicy paste and it moves as a single mass when stirred.

Off the heat, add the drained chicken and nuts. Stir the mixture and add the yogurt. Return the pan to a medium heat. When the yogurt is absorbed, add the broth, spoon by spoon, and finally the coconut milk. Stir constantly until the chicken is tender and enveloped in a rich, golden sauce. Serve hot over rice. Garnish with the coriander leaves just before serving.

SHIVAJI RAO AND SHALINI DEVI HOLKAR
COOKING OF THE MAHARAJAS

Creamed Chicken

The sauce must be satin smooth, thoughtfully seasoned and not too thick. Stir frequently as you make it and add more liquid if necessary.

To serve 4

1½ cups	cooked chicken, cubed	375 ml.
2 tbsp.	butter or chicken fat	30 ml.
3 tbsp.	flour	45 ml.
1 cup	milk or chicken stock (or ½ cup [125 ml.] milk combined with ½ cup stock)	¼ liter
⅓ cup	cream	75 ml.
	salt and pepper	

In a large saucepan or top of a double boiler, melt the butter or chicken fat. Add the flour and stir until evenly blended. Stirring constantly, gradually add the milk or chicken stock, or a mixture of both, and cook over low heat until the sauce thickens. Bring to the boiling point and cook for two minutes. Add the cream, the cubed chicken, and salt and pepper to taste. Simmer at least ½ hour over low heat on a fireproof mat or in the double boiler, so that the chicken will absorb some of the sauce and be moist.

Serve on toast, waffles, hot biscuits or rice. Add a curl of crisp bacon or a sprig of parsley or watercress. Or decorate with paprika or a strip of pimento.

To vary, add diced cooked ham, chopped hard-cooked eggs, sliced cooked celery, cooked peas or sautéed mushrooms. To make blanquette of chicken, stir in 1 egg yolk, lightly beaten with 1 tablespoon [15 ml.] milk or cream, just before serving. Sprinkle with chopped parsley. For scalloped chicken, spoon the creamed chicken into a buttered baking dish. Sprinkle with buttered crumbs. Bake in an oven, preheated to 375° F. [180° C.], until the crumbs are brown.

WILMA LORD PERKINS
THE FANNIE FARMER COOKBOOK

Chicken Gratin with Cheese

Poulet au Fromage

To serve 4 to 6

two 3 lb.	chickens, split down the back and flattened	two 1½ kg.
6 tbsp.	butter	90 ml.
⅓ cup	dry white wine	75 ml.
⅓ cup	veal or chicken stock	75 ml.
1	bouquet garni	1
1	onion, chopped	1
1	small garlic clove, finely chopped	1
2	whole cloves	2
1	bay leaf	1
	fresh thyme	
	fresh basil	
	salt and coarsely ground pepper	
1 tbsp.	flour	15 ml.
¾ cup	grated Gruyère cheese	175 ml.

Brown the chickens in a casserole in 4 tablespoons [60 ml.] of the butter. Moisten the chickens with the wine and stock; add the bouquet garni, onion, garlic, cloves, bay leaf and a pinch each of thyme and basil. Season with salt and pepper. Bring to a boil over high heat. Cover the casserole and cook for 1 hour in a slow oven, preheated to 300° F. [150° C.].

Remove the chickens from the casserole and add a *beurre manié*—the remaining butter mixed with the flour—to the cooking liquid. Bring the sauce mixture to a boil over moderate heat, stirring constantly. Pour some of the sauce into the bottom of a heatproof serving dish and over it sprinkle half the cheese. Place the chickens on top and pour the rest of the sauce over them; then sprinkle on the remaining cheese. Put the dish in a moderate oven preheated to 350° F. [180° C.] to heat through and finish under the broiler until the cheese is golden brown. Serve very hot.

OFFRAY AINÉ
LE CUISINIER MÉRIDIONAL

Chicken Croquettes

To make 9 croquettes

2 cups	finely diced leftover cooked chicken	½ liter
¼ cup	butter	50 ml.
⅓ cup	flour	75 ml.
1 tsp.	salt	5 ml.
1 cup	milk	¼ liter
1 tbsp.	grated onion	15 ml.
1 tbsp.	fresh lemon juice	15 ml.
1 tbsp.	chopped fresh parsley or tarragon	15 ml.
1	egg, lightly beaten	1
⅓ cup	fresh bread crumbs	75 ml.
⅓ cup	vegetable oil	75 ml.

Melt the butter in a small pan set over moderate heat and blend in the flour and salt. Stir in the milk gradually and cook, stirring, until the mixture thickens. Cook over low heat for 3 minutes, then remove and cool it.

Stir in the chicken, onion, lemon juice and parsley. Spread the mixture evenly in an 8-inch [20-cm.] pan. Chill.

Shape the mixture into nine cutlets. Dip each one first in beaten egg and then in bread crumbs. Fry the breaded cutlets in hot oil until brown.

JEAN HEWITT
THE NEW YORK TIMES LARGE TYPE COOKBOOK

Chicken, Ham and Veal Pie

Pâté-chaud de Poulets dans un Plat

To serve 4 to 6

two 2 lb.	chickens, cut into serving pieces	two 1 kg.
	salt and pepper	
4	slices prosciutto	4
2	thin veal scallops, finely diced	2
1	shallot, finely chopped	1
3 or 4	hard-boiled eggs, quartered	3 or 4
½ cup	chicken or veal stock	125 ml.
	short-crust or rough puff pastry dough (recipe, page 167)	
1	egg, mixed with a little water	1

Cut the wing tips from the chickens; break the leg joints and remove the thigh bones. Salt and pepper the chicken pieces.

Line the bottom of a heatproof casserole with the slices of prosciutto and cover these with veal. Sprinkle in the shallot and season with salt and pepper. Add the dark-meat chicken pieces, then the breast pieces and wings. Tuck the eggs into the spaces around the chicken; then pour in the stock. Roll out the pastry dough.

Moisten the edge of the casserole with water and cover the edge with a strip of pastry. Dampen the top of this strip with water and cover the casserole with a lid of pastry. Seal well, trim and pinch the edges of the pastry. Decorate the pie with leaves made of the pastry and glaze the surface with the egg mixed with water.

Cook in a moderate oven preheated to 350° F. [180° C.] for 1 hour, remembering to cover the pastry with a sheet of parchment paper as soon as it becomes golden brown so that the crust does not burn.

URBAIN DUBOIS
ÉCOLE DES CUISINIÈRES

Shaker Chicken Pudding

The Shakers—or Shaking Quakers—settled in America from Europe during the 18th and 19th Centuries. Their distinctive fare, like the functional and attractive furniture for which they are also famous, expressed their belief in the rich rewards of simple living.

To serve 4 to 6

2 to 3 cups	cooked chicken meat, diced	½ to ¾ liter
1	apple, diced (about ½ cup [125 ml.])	1
1	onion, chopped (about ½ cup [125 ml.])	1
1	rib celery, chopped (about ½ cup [125 ml.])	1
8 tbsp.	butter	120 ml.
½ cup	apple cider	125 ml.
½ tsp.	salt	2 ml.
¼ tsp.	pepper	1 ml.
	grated nutmeg	
1 cup	bread crumbs	¼ liter
Sauce		
2 tbsp.	flour	30 ml.
2 tbsp.	butter	30 ml.
1 cup	heavy cream	¼ liter

Prepare the chicken meat, preferably from a freshly poached chicken. Gently sauté the apple, onion and celery in 4 tablespoons [60 ml.] of butter until they are soft. Add the cider, salt, pepper and a pinch of nutmeg. Simmer, covered, for 30 minutes or until the vegetables are very soft. Uncover the pot and continue to cook this mixture until it is thickened.

To make the sauce, cook the flour and 2 tablespoons [30 ml.] of butter in a saucepan for a few minutes, stirring until the mixture just begins to change color. Add the cream and cook, stirring, until the sauce thickens. Mix into this sauce the cooked vegetable hash and the chicken.

Pour the mixture into a buttered baking dish, and sprinkle with bread crumbs and the remaining 2 tablespoons [30 ml.] of butter, melted. Bake in an oven, preheated to 350° F. [180° C.], for 20 minutes or until browned.

CARL LYREN
365 WAYS TO COOK CHICKEN

Charter Pie

This Cornish recipe is from a Victorian recipe book compiled by Lady Sarah Lindsey.

To serve 8 to 10		
two 3 lb.	chickens, cut into serving pieces	two 1½ kg.
1	large onion, finely chopped	1
6 tbsp.	butter	90 ml.
	flour	
	salt and pepper	
2	bunches parsley, finely chopped	2
1 cup	milk	¼ liter
2 cups	heavy cream	½ liter
½ cup	light cream (or substitute 1 lightly beaten egg)	125 ml.
	short-crust pastry (recipe, page 167)	

Make the pastry and leave it to rest.

In a skillet over moderate heat, sweat the onion in half of the butter until the onion is transparent. Put it into a deep pie dish. Add the rest of the butter to the skillet and fry the chicken, which should first be rolled in flour seasoned with salt and pepper. When the pieces are lightly browned, lay them on top of the onion in the dish. Simmer the parsley for 3 minutes in the milk. Pour the parsley, milk and half the heavy cream over the chicken. Season well.

Put a pastry rim around the pie dish, moisten it and put on the pastry lid (see that the chicken bones do not pierce it). Decorate and make a central hole, which should be kept open with a small roll of white cardboard. Brush the pastry lid with light cream or beaten egg, and put the pie into a pre-heated hot oven at 425° F. [220° C.] for 15 minutes. Cover the top of the pie with paper or foil to protect it and lower the heat to about 350° F. [180° C.]. Leave for an hour.

Just before serving, heat the rest of the heavy cream and pour it into the pie by way of the central hole, after removing the roll of cardboard.

Charter pie is very good cold; the sauce sets to become an excellent jelly.

JANE GRIGSON
GOOD THINGS

Romertopf's Beggar Chicken

Five-spice powder is a Chinese seasoning made up of ground star anise, Szechwan pepper, fennel seeds, cinnamon and cloves, and is obtainable at Oriental food stores. You can substitute anise seed, pulverized with a mortar and pestle.

To serve 3 or 4		
4 lb.	chicken, cut into serving pieces	2 kg.
	arrowroot mixed with a little water	
	blanched almonds and sesame seeds (optional)	

Marinade		
1 tsp.	sesame-seed oil	5 ml.
1 tbsp.	dry sherry	15 ml.
¼ tsp.	five-spice powder	1 ml.
¼ tsp.	white pepper	1 ml.
1	garlic clove, crushed	1
¼ cup	soy sauce	50 ml.
1 tsp.	grated fresh ginger root	5 ml.

In a nonmetal bowl, combine the ingredients for the marinade. Mix well and marinate the chicken pieces for at least half a day, turning frequently. (Do not add any salt—there is enough in any good soy sauce.)

When you are ready to cook the chicken, presoak a clay pot, top and bottom, in water for 15 minutes. Add the chicken and the marinade to the pot. Place the covered pot in a cold oven. Set the oven temperature to 450° F. [230° C.]. Cook for 45 minutes after the oven reaches 450° F.

Remove the pot from the oven, uncover and pour off the liquid into a saucepan. Return the pot to the oven, uncovered, for a further 10 minutes of cooking to brown the chicken. Meanwhile, bring the liquid in the saucepan to a simmer and thicken with arrowroot.

Serve the chicken with rice, liberally drenched with the sauce. For a Chinese touch, sprinkle the chicken with almonds and sesame seeds.

GEORGIA MACLEOD SALES AND GROVER SALES
THE CLAY-POT COOKBOOK

Chicken Loaf with Watercress Sauce

To serve 6 to 8

2 lb.	chicken breasts, skinned, halved and boned	1 kg.
1 cup	finely chopped onions	¼ liter
2	egg yolks	2
2 cups	fine fresh bread crumbs	½ liter
⅔ cup	heavy cream	150 ml.
1	bunch watercress, finely chopped	1
¼ tsp.	grated nutmeg	1 ml.
	salt and freshly ground pepper	

Watercress sauce

6 tbsp.	butter	90 ml.
6 tbsp.	flour	90 ml.
3 cups	chicken stock	¾ liter
1	bunch watercress	1
1 cup	heavy cream	¼ liter
	salt and freshly ground pepper	
¼ tsp.	grated nutmeg	1 ml.

Preheat the oven to 400° F. [200° C.]. Cut the halved chicken breasts into cubes. Place them in an electric blender or food processor and grind to a smooth paste. This may have to be done in two or more steps.

Scrape the mixture into a mixing bowl, then add the remaining ingredients and blend together well. Pour the mixture into a 6-cup [1½-liter] loaf pan and cover with wax paper. Add a close-fitting lid. Stand the mold in a roasting pan and pour boiling water around it to a level of about one third the depth of the mold. Bake for 1½ hours, or until the loaf is set and cooked through.

To make the watercress sauce, melt 4 tablespoons [60 ml.] of the butter in a saucepan and add the flour, stirring with a wire whisk. When the flour and butter are blended, add the stock, stirring rapidly with the whisk. Simmer the sauce for about 20 minutes, stirring often.

Meanwhile, cut off and discard the tough bottom stems of the watercress. Drop the cress into a small saucepan of boiling water and simmer for about 30 seconds. Drain, squeeze to extract most of the liquid, and chop the cress. Set it aside.

Add the cream to the sauce. Add salt and pepper to taste, and the nutmeg. Simmer for about 15 minutes. Strain the sauce through a very fine sieve. Return it to the saucepan and stir in the watercress. Swirl in the remaining butter.

Serve the loaf sliced and hot, with the watercress sauce.

CRAIG CLAIBORNE
CRAIG CLAIBORNE'S FAVORITES FROM THE NEW YORK TIMES

Fried-and-Roasted Breaded Chicken

To serve 8

two 1½ to 2 lb.	chickens, quartered	two ¾ to 1 kg.
16 tbsp.	butter	240 ml.
	flour	
2	eggs	2
	fine dry bread crumbs	
1 cup	sour cream	¼ liter

Melt the butter in a skillet. Flour each chicken piece thoroughly. Beat the eggs in a shallow dish, coat the floured chicken thoroughly with egg and then cover thickly with dry bread crumbs. It is important that the chicken be thoroughly covered with flour, then with egg, then with bread crumbs. Put the pieces in the melted butter and brown them lightly on both sides. Remove them to a heatproof earthenware dish, with the wings and legs lying at the outer edges of the dish. Put the dish in an oven preheated to 300° F. [150° C.] and roast for 1½ to 2 hours, basting frequently with sour cream.

ALICE B. TOKLAS
THE ALICE B. TOKLAS COOK BOOK

Chicken Calypso

To serve 6

3 to 4 lb.	chicken, cut into serving pieces	1½ to 2 kg.
⅓ cup	olive oil	75 ml.
2 cups	raw unprocessed rice	½ liter
1	medium-sized onion, finely chopped	1
1	garlic clove, finely chopped	1
1	green pepper, halved, seeded, deribbed and finely chopped	1
1	small fresh green chili, stemmed, seeded and finely chopped	1
½ lb.	fresh mushrooms, sliced (about 2½ cups [625 ml.])	¼ kg.
½ tsp.	ground saffron	2 ml.
1	strip of lime peel, about 2 inches [5 cm.] long	1
1 tbsp.	strained fresh lime juice	15 ml.
¼ tsp.	Angostura bitters	1 ml.
1 quart	chicken stock	1 liter
	salt and freshly ground pepper	
3 tbsp.	light rum	45 ml.

Heat 3 tablespoons [45 ml.] of the olive oil in a skillet and sauté the chicken pieces until brown all over. Remove them to a heavy, fireproof casserole. Add the rice, onion, garlic, green pepper and hot green chili to the oil remaining in the skillet; sauté, stirring, until the oil is absorbed, being careful not to let the rice scorch. Add to the chicken in the casserole.

Add the remaining 2 tablespoons [30 ml.] of oil to the skillet and sauté the mushrooms over fairly high heat for 5 minutes. Add them to the casserole with the saffron, lime peel, lime juice, bitters and chicken stock. Salt and pepper to taste. Bring to a boil. Then cover and simmer gently until the rice and chicken are tender, and the liquid is absorbed—about 30 minutes. Add the rum and cook, uncovered, for 5 minutes longer.

ELISABETH LAMBERT ORTIZ
THE COMPLETE BOOK OF CARIBBEAN COOKING

Steamed Chicken Stuffed with Parsley

Poulet Farci au Persil et Cuit à la Vapeur

To make the preserved lemon called for in this dish, follow the directions in the recipe on page 136 for chicken with eggs, lemons and olives.

To serve 6 to 8

two 3 lb.	roasting chickens	two 1½ kg.
6	medium-sized tomatoes, peeled, seeded and chopped	6
⅔ cup	finely chopped fresh parsley	150 ml.
2	ribs celery, finely chopped	2
	peel of 1 preserved lemon, finely chopped	
	salt	
1 tsp.	freshly ground black pepper	5 ml.
½ tsp.	cayenne pepper	2 ml.
2 tbsp.	butter, divided into 2 chunks (or knobs)	30 ml.
	ground cumin seed	

Mix the tomatoes with the parsley, celery and lemon peel. Season with salt, black pepper and cayenne pepper. Stuff each chicken with this mixture, along with a knob of butter.

Place the chickens in the top of a *couscoussier* or other type of steamer containing 3 to 4 quarts [3 to 4 liters] of boiling water. Seal together the top and bottom sections of the steamer by means of a strip of cloth soaked in a flour-and-water paste. Cover the chickens with a clean damp cloth and put the lid on.

Cook over a moderate heat. Check the chickens after 1½ hours. If the flesh can be easily detached from the bones, the chickens are done. Remove the steamer from the stove. Put the chickens on a warmed platter and serve at once, with a bowl containing a mixture of salt and cumin for seasoning.

LATIFA BENNANI SMIRES
LA CUISINE MAROCAINE

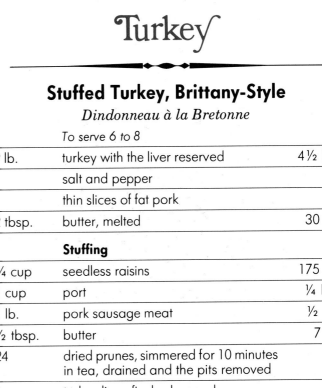

Turkey

Stuffed Turkey, Brittany-Style

Dindonneau à la Bretonne

To serve 6 to 8

9 lb.	turkey with the liver reserved	4½ kg.
	salt and pepper	
	thin slices of fat pork	
2 tbsp.	butter, melted	30 ml.
	Stuffing	
¾ cup	seedless raisins	175 ml.
1 cup	port	¼ liter
1 lb.	pork sausage meat	½ kg.
½ tbsp.	butter	7 ml.
24	dried prunes, simmered for 10 minutes in tea, drained and the pits removed	24
1	turkey liver, finely chopped	1
1 tsp.	dried thyme	5 ml.
	salt and pepper	

To make the stuffing, cover the raisins with port and let them macerate for 5 to 6 hours. Lightly cook the sausage meat in butter. Add the raisins and port, the prunes, liver, thyme, salt and pepper to the sausage and mix well. Stuff the turkey with this mixture and season the bird with salt and pepper. Truss the bird, set it in a large roasting pan and cover the breast with slices of fat pork. Pour melted butter over the turkey, place it in a moderate oven preheated to 350° F. [180° C.] and cook for about 3 hours. Baste frequently with the pan juices; from time to time moisten with a spoonful of water. Serve when the turkey is done and a golden color, steaming all over. Serve the juices separately, but—above all—do not add stock or any other liquid to them.

ÉDOUARD NIGNON
ÉLOGES DE LA CUISINE FRANÇAISE

James Beard's Favorite Roast Turkey

Much of this fashion of roasting a turkey came from my family. I have changed and embellished it a bit, and the final recipe is the one I use for Thanksgiving or other traditional holiday dinners.

To serve 8 to 10

18 to 20 lb.	turkey with the liver, gizzard and heart reserved	8 to 9 kg.
1	onion, stuck with 2 whole cloves	1
1	sprig parsley	1
	salt	
½ tsp.	dried thyme	2 ml.
1 quart	water	1 liter
½	lemon	½
8 to 12 tbsp.	butter, softened	120 to 180 ml.
	freshly ground pepper	
	strips of fresh or salt pork (or substitute bacon rinds)	
¼ cup	flour	50 ml.
¼ cup	Cognac or Madeira (optional)	50 ml.

Stuffing

1 to 1½ cups	butter	275 to 375 ml.
1 cup	finely chopped shallots (or substitute finely chopped scallions)	250 ml.
1½ tbsp.	dried tarragon, or 3 tbsp. [45 ml.] fresh tarragon, finely chopped	22 ml.
	salt	
1½ tsp.	freshly ground pepper	7 ml.
½ cup	pine nuts	125 ml.
10 to 12 cups	fresh bread crumbs	2½ to 3 liters
1 or 2	garlic cloves, finely chopped (optional)	1 or 2

Make the stuffing first. Melt ½ cup [125 ml.] of the butter in a heavy skillet—a 12-inch [30-cm.] one if possible. Add the shallots or scallions and the tarragon, and allow to cook until the shallots are just wilted. Add 1 tablespoon [15 ml.] of salt, the pepper and pine nuts, and then additional melted butter as needed: I should say another ½ cup to 1 cup [125 to 250 ml.], depending on the amount the shallots have absorbed. Finally, add the crumbs and toss well. Taste the mixture and, if required, add more of any of the ingredients. A clove or two of garlic may also be added to the mixture.

Remove the neck from the bird, if that has not already

been done, and put the neck in a 2-quart [2-liter] saucepan with the liver, gizzard, heart, and the onion, parsley, 2 teaspoons [10 ml.] of salt and the thyme. Add the water, bring to a boil and boil for 5 minutes, skimming. Then reduce the heat and simmer, covered, for 1 hour. Drain and reserve the stock for the sauce. If you like, chop the gizzard, heart and liver to add to the sauce.

Rub the inside of the turkey with the lemon. Fill the body cavity and neck cavity with stuffing, but not too tightly—the crumbs should remain somewhat loose. Truss the turkey. Close the vent of the bird; either secure with skewers and twine or sew it up. Tie the legs together firmly, and then tie them to the tail of the bird. Massage the turkey well with about 4 tablespoons [60 ml.] softened butter, and then salt and pepper it. Line a rack with strips of fresh or salt pork or with bacon rind, which you can sometimes buy from your butcher when he cuts down a whole slab.

Set the rack in a fairly shallow roasting pan and place the turkey, breast side down, on the rack. Roast for 1 hour in an oven preheated to 350° F. [180° C.]. Remove the pan from the oven, turn the turkey on one side and rub with half of the remaining softened butter. Return the turkey to the oven and roast for another hour. Remove the pan from the oven, turn the turkey on its back and rub the breast with the remaining butter. Return to the oven and continue roasting till the turkey is done.

Remove from the oven and place on a hot platter. Allow the turkey to rest for 15 minutes if being served hot. If being served tepid, let it cool gently at room temperature. Remove all the twine and skewers.

For the sauce, pour off all the fat, save 4 tablespoons [60 ml.], from the roasting pan. Discard the excess fat. Over medium heat, add the flour to the pan and blend thoroughly, scraping to loosen bits of caramelized dripping. If there are any juices on the platter beneath the turkey, add those (skimmed of fat) as well. Gradually stir in 2 cups [½ liter] or more of the turkey stock and cook, stirring constantly, till the mixture thickens. Correct the seasoning. Add the giblets, if you like, and Cognac or Madeira, and simmer about 4 or 5 minutes. Serve with the turkey and stuffing.

JAMES BEARD
JAMES BEARD'S AMERICAN COOKERY

Fillets of Turkey, Bologna-Style

Filetti Di Tacchino Alla Bolognese

To serve 4 to 6

3 to 4 lb.	turkey breast, sliced into fillets ⅓ inch [1 cm.] thick	1½ to 2 kg.
	bread crumbs	
1	large egg, beaten with ¼ tsp. [1 ml.] salt and a pinch of pepper	1
¾ cup	olive oil	175 ml.
½ lb.	mozzarella, thinly sliced	¼ kg.
⅓ lb.	prosciutto or Canadian bacon, thinly sliced	150 g.

Dip the turkey fillets into the egg, then into the bread crumbs, and fry a few at a time in hot oil until golden on both sides. Arrange the fillets in a single layer in a large, well-buttered baking dish. Cut the prosciutto or Canadian bacon slices to the same size as the fillets and place a slice on top of each fillet, then cover with a slice of mozzarella cheese. Place in a preheated 350° F. [180° C.] oven for 20 minutes. If you wish, serve the fillets with a drop of warm tomato sauce on top of each one.

MARIA LUISA TAGLIENTI
THE ITALIAN COOKBOOK

Turkey Goulash

Porkölt von Puter

This recipe, originally from Hungary, also works well with other poultry and game. The paprikaspeck called for is a smoked fat bacon that has been rubbed with paprika prior to cooking; it is popular in Central European cooking.

To serve 8

8 lb.	turkey, cut into serving pieces	4 kg.
1 lb.	*paprikaspeck* (or substitute other bacon and rub it with Hungarian paprika), cut into strips	½ kg.
2 cups	chicken or turkey stock	½ liter
¼ cup	sour cream	50 ml.
¼ cup	Tokay or Muscat	50 ml.

Wrap each of the turkey pieces with *paprikaspeck*. Brown the pieces well on all sides in a pan. Remove the pieces to a casserole. Add 1½ cups [375 ml.] of stock, cover and braise the pieces slowly in an oven preheated to 300° F. [150° C.] for 1½ to 2 hours or until tender. Halfway through the braising add the sour cream.

When the braising is completed, remove the turkey, add the remaining stock and the wine to deglaze the deposits in the casserole, and bring to a boil. This liquid can be served as a gravy with no thickening.

IDA SCHULZE
DAS NEUE KOCHBUCH FÜR DIE DEUTSCHE KÜCHE

Turkey Turnovers

To serve 4

1½ cups	leftover cooked turkey meat (white and/or dark), chopped	375 ml.
1 tbsp.	finely chopped fresh parsley	15 ml.
1 tbsp.	finely cut fresh chives	15 ml.
1 tbsp.	finely chopped white boiling onion	15 ml.
1 tbsp.	chopped green pepper	15 ml.
½ cup	leftover turkey gravy	125 ml.
2 tbsp.	dry sherry	30 ml.
	salt and pepper	
1	egg yolk	1
2 tbsp.	heavy cream	30 ml.

Pastry

1 cup	flour	¼ liter
¼ tsp.	salt	1 ml.
6 tbsp.	unsalted butter	90 ml.
⅓ to ½ cup	ice water	75 to 125 ml.

Mix the turkey, parsley, chives, onion and green pepper with the turkey gravy. Add the sherry and season well to taste. Preheat the oven to 375° F. [190° C.].

For the pastry, sift the flour and salt into a bowl. Cut the butter into the flour and rub the mixture with your finger tips until it resembles coarse cornmeal. Add just enough ice water (the least possible amount) to work the ingredients quickly into a firm dough.

On a lightly floured board, roll out the dough very thin, about ⅛ inch [3 mm.] thick, and cut it into 4-inch [10-cm.] squares. Put 1 tablespoon [15 ml.] of the turkey filling on each square. Fold the dough over the filling into a triangle. Brush the edges with a little water and seal them securely.

Beat the egg yolk with the cream and use it to brush the tops of the turnovers. Bake them on an ungreased baking sheet for about 15 minutes or until they are golden brown.

To serve, pile the freshly baked turnovers on a hot folded napkin on a warmed serving plate and serve immediately.

DIONE LUCAS AND MARION GORMAN
THE DIONE LUCAS BOOK OF FRENCH COOKING

Gratin of Vine Leaves Stuffed with Turkey

Boulettes de Dinde au Yaourt

A recipe by E. Nizan of the Comédie Française.

	To serve 4	
1 lb.	raw turkey breast meat, finely chopped	½ kg.
1	large onion, finely chopped	1
2	slices French or Italian bread, crusts removed, soaked in milk and squeezed almost dry	2
2	eggs	2
	salt and pepper	
12	tender young fresh grapevine leaves, parboiled for 5 minutes, drained and patted dry	12
2 tbsp.	butter	30 ml.
2 tbsp.	fresh lemon juice	30 ml.
½ cup	hot water	125 ml.
	unflavored yogurt	

Prepare the stuffing for the vine leaves by mixing the turkey, onion, soaked bread and eggs. Season the mixture and work it together well. Place some stuffing on each vine leaf and roll up the leaf into a parcel.

Melt the butter in a casserole, preferably earthenware, and put in the stuffed vine leaves carefully, so that the parcels do not come apart. Add the lemon juice. Cover and cook over very low heat for 2 hours, adding a little hot water from time to time. The sauce should reduce while cooking. Brown the surface of the parcels lightly by placing the casserole under the broiler for 10 minutes before serving. Serve the stuffed vine leaves very hot, accompanied by yogurt.

GASTON DERYS
L'ART D'ETRE GOURMAND

Turkey Breast in a Piquant Sauce

Piccata di Petto di Tacchino

	To serve 6	
4 to 5 lb.	raw turkey breast	2 to 2½ kg.
	flour	
8 tbsp.	unsalted butter	125 ml.
1 tbsp.	olive oil	15 ml.
½ cup	dry white wine	125 ml.
¼ cup	fresh lemon juice	50 ml.
	salt	

Slice the breast into 12 thin slices no more than ⅛ inch [3 mm.] thick. Pound the slices gently with the side of the blade of a big butcher knife or with the smooth side of a meat mallet. Dust them with flour, patting on the flour to make sure it sticks.

Melt the butter in a big skillet over medium heat, adding the olive oil to help prevent the butter from browning. Sauté the slices in the butter and oil, turning them when the edges get white (this takes about 3 minutes). Cook the slices another 3 minutes on the other side. Since hardly anyone but a restaurant chef has huge skillets, you will probably have to cook the slices in two or three batches. Remove each batch to a warmed platter.

When the last slices are cooked, do not remove them from the pan. Just add the wine, and stir and cook for a moment. Then add the lemon juice and stir again. Taste the sauce on a bit of bread and, if desired, add salt. Put all the cooked slices back in the pan and see that each one is coated with the sauce. Simmer about 2 minutes. Serve hot with the sauce.

MARGARET AND G. FRANCO ROMAGNOLI
THE ROMAGNOLIS' TABLE

Turkey Chili

	To serve 8 to 10	
5 to 6 lb.	turkey, quartered	2½ to 3 kg.
1	onion, stuck with 2 or 3 whole cloves	1
2	ribs celery	2
2 or 3	sprigs parsley	2 or 3
2	small dried hot chilies	2
	salt	
2 tbsp.	chili powder	30 ml.
½ cup	canned, drained green chilies, finely chopped	125 ml.
1 cup	almonds, ground	¼ liter
½ cup	peanuts, ground	125 ml.
1	large onion, finely chopped	1
3	garlic cloves, finely chopped	3
2	green peppers, halved, seeded, deribbed and finely chopped	2
¼ cup	olive oil	50 ml.
1 cup	small pitted green olives	¼ liter
½ cup	blanched almonds	125 ml.

Cover the turkey pieces with water and add the onion stuck with cloves, the celery, parsley and hot peppers. Bring to a boil. Reduce the heat, skim off any scum that may rise to the top and cover the pot. Simmer until the turkey is tender but not falling from the bones. Remove the turkey pieces and cool until they can be handled. Remove the meat from the bones in good-sized pieces.

Reduce the broth by half over high heat. You should have about 1 quart [1 liter] of broth. Strain and adjust the salt. Add the chili powder, the green chilies and the ground nuts. Simmer until the mixture is thick, smooth and well blended in flavor. Taste for seasoning; you may find you wish to add more chili powder. Sauté the onion, garlic and green peppers in the olive oil. Add to the sauce and cook for 5 minutes. Add the turkey meat and heat thoroughly. Add the olives and blanched almonds, and reheat for 3 minutes.

JOSÉ WILSON (EDITOR)
HOUSE AND GARDEN'S NEW COOK BOOK

Turkey Daube

Dindonneau en Daube

Goose can be substituted for turkey, but cooking time should be reduced. The daube may be served cold or hot, if reheated in the oven at 325° F. [160° C.], or over a very low heat.

To serve 8 to 10

8 lb.	turkey, cut into serving pieces	4 kg.
	salt and pepper	
	mixed spices	
3½ oz.	bacon rind in one piece, blanched in boiling water for 5 minutes, drained and cut into 1-inch [1-cm.] squares	100 g.
3½ oz.	lean salt pork, blanched in boiling water for 10 minutes, drained, cut into cubes and lightly sautéed in butter	100 g.
2 cups	veal stock	½ liter

Marinade

2 to 3 tbsp.	brandy	30 to 45 ml.
2 to 3 tbsp.	olive oil	30 to 45 ml.
2	medium-sized onions, chopped	2
2	shallots, chopped	2
2	carrots, chopped	2
2½ cups	dry white wine	¾ liter
	bouquet garni, made of 2 sprigs parsley, 2 sprigs thyme and 1 bay leaf	
1	garlic clove, crushed	1
	orange peel	

Put the turkey pieces into a bowl with a little salt, pepper and mixed spices. Add the brandy, oil, chopped vegetables,

wine, bouquet garni, garlic and a few strips of orange peel. Leave to marinate for 2 to 3 hours.

Put alternate layers of turkey, bacon rind and salt pork into a large casserole, tucking the bouquet garni into the center. Add the marinade and the stock. Cover very tightly and cook in a moderate oven, preheated to 325° F. [160° C.], for 2 to 2½ hours. Remove the bouquet garni and leave the turkey to cool in the liquid.

AUGUSTE ESCOFFIER
MA CUISINE

Turkey Tetrazzini-Style

To serve 4

1 cup	thin strips of leftover cooked turkey	¼ liter
½ cup	chopped, cooked spaghetti	125 ml.
½ cup	sliced, sautéed fresh mushrooms	125 ml.
2 tbsp.	bread crumbs, mixed with softened butter	30 ml.
4 to 5 tbsp.	grated Parmesan cheese	60 to 75 ml.

Cream sauce

1 cup	heavy cream	¼ liter
2 or 3	thin onion slices	2 or 3
3	sprigs parsley	3
½	bay leaf	½
1	whole clove	1
2 tbsp.	butter	30 ml.
3 tbsp.	flour	45 ml.
	salt and pepper	
	grated nutmeg	

Make a cream sauce by first scalding the cream containing the onion, parsley, bay leaf and clove and then straining it. Melt the butter in a small pan, stir in the flour and let this roux cook briefly before stirring in the flavored cream. Simmer for 2 or 3 minutes, then season the sauce to taste with salt, pepper and a dash of nutmeg. Stir in the turkey, spaghetti and mushrooms. Mix well and turn the mixture into a buttered baking dish or six individual baking dishes. Sprinkle with the buttered bread crumbs mixed with the Parmesan cheese and bake in a preheated moderate oven at 375° F. [190° C.] for 10 to 15 minutes or until the crumbs are brown. Serve at once, while still bubbling.

LOUIS P. DE GOUY
THE GOLD COOKBOOK

Stuffed Turkey
Yemistes Yallopoules

To serve 15

12 to 14 lb.	turkey with the giblets reserved	5½ to 6½ kg.
1	lemon, halved	1
	salt and pepper	
	butter, melted	
Meat stuffing		
4 to 6 tbsp.	butter	60 to 90 ml.
2	onions, finely chopped	2
6 oz.	lean ground lamb	175 g.
	reserved turkey heart and liver, finely chopped	
1 lb.	fresh chestnuts, shells slit, boiled for 5 minutes, peeled and broken into pieces	½ kg.
1 tbsp.	pine nuts	15 ml.
2 cups	strained turkey broth, made by simmering the reserved turkey neck and gizzard in 3 cups [¾ liter] water for 45 minutes	½ liter
½ cup	raw unprocessed rice	125 ml.
1	lamb liver, minced	1
1 cup	fresh bread crumbs	¼ liter
2	cooking apples, peeled, cored and finely chopped	2

Wash the turkey in cold water, pat it dry inside and out, and leave it for 30 minutes while you cook your stuffing.

For the stuffing, heat the butter in a skillet and fry the onions until they begin to change color, then add the ground lamb and simmer gently for 15 minutes. Add the turkey heart and liver, the chestnuts and pine nuts and simmer for another 5 minutes. Add the broth and bring this to a boil. Add the rice and cook quickly for 10 minutes, then add the lamb liver, bread crumbs and apples. Stir well.

To stuff the turkey, slit the skin at the back of the neck and cut off the neck down to the turkey's shoulders if the neck has not already been removed. Lightly fill the cavity, remembering that the stuffing always swells and too much swelling might cause the neck skin to burst. Sew (or pin with a skewer) the neck flap to the back of the turkey. Just as lightly, fill the body cavity and sew or skewer this together.

Tie the legs to the tail and fix the wings snugly to the body. Do not bring the cord across the breast lest it mark the skin. Rub the turkey with cut lemon, salt, pepper and melted butter and place it in a large, shallow pan in a moderate oven. Roast it according to its weight when stuffed, allowing 25 to 30 minutes per pound.

Greeks prefer to have plenty of stuffing so that it can be cooked separately and served with the turkey. If you find you have made too much stuffing for your turkey, it can be roasted in a pan for 45 minutes or so and served with the turkey. Or it can be made into rissoles by shaping it into small balls, dipping them into beaten egg and bread crumbs, and then frying them in butter, to be served as a garnish.

ROBIN HOWE
GREEK COOKING

Rock Cornish Game Hen

Roast Rock Cornish Game Hens with Pine-Nut Stuffing

To serve 4

4	Rock Cornish game hens, about 1 lb. [½ kg.] each	4
2 tsp.	salt	10 ml.
4 tbsp.	melted butter	60 ml.
	watercress	
Stuffing		
5 tbsp.	butter	75 ml.
1 cup	raw unprocessed long-grain rice	¼ liter
2 cups	chicken stock	½ liter
1 tsp.	salt	5 ml.
1 cup	finely chopped onion	¼ liter
½ cup	pine nuts	125 ml.
6 tbsp.	finely chopped fresh parsley	90 ml.

For the stuffing, melt 3 tablespoons [45 ml.] of the butter in a 2-quart [2-liter] heavy casserole or saucepan over moderate heat. Add the rice and stir constantly for 2 to 3 minutes, or until most of the rice has turned milky and opaque. Do not let it brown. Then pour in the chicken stock, add the salt and bring to a boil, stirring occasionally. Cover the pan tightly, reduce the heat to its lowest point and simmer for 18 to 20 minutes or until the rice has absorbed all the liquid.

Meanwhile, in a small skillet melt the remaining 2 tablespoons [30 ml.] of butter and when the foam subsides add the onion. Cook over moderate heat for 8 to 10 minutes, then add the pine nuts. Cook 2 or 3 minutes longer, stirring, until the nuts are lightly browned.

Combine the cooked rice, the onion, pine nuts and the parsley. Mix gently but thoroughly. Taste for seasoning.

Preheat the oven to 400° F. [200° C.]. Sprinkle the inside

of each bird with ½ teaspoon [2 ml.] of salt, then pack the cavities loosely with the stuffing; they should be no more than three quarters full. Skewer or sew the openings with cotton thread, truss the birds securely and brush them with the melted butter. Place them on their sides on a rack set in a shallow roasting pan just large enough to hold them.

Roast the birds in the middle of the oven for 15 minutes, then turn them on the other side and brush them with butter again. Roast for another 15 minutes. Turn them breast up, brush with the remaining butter and salt each bird lightly. Roast, basting occasionally with the drippings in the bottom of the pan, for 15 to 20 minutes longer, or until the birds are golden brown all over and tender. Test for doneness by piercing the fleshy part of a thigh with the point of a sharp knife. The juice that spurts out should be yellow. If it is pink, roast a few minutes longer.

Transfer the birds to a warm serving platter, pour the pan juices over them and serve, garnished with watercress.

FOODS OF THE WORLD/AMERICAN COOKING

Barbecued Game Hens

The technique for impaling six Rock Cornish game hens on a spit is shown on page 51.

	To serve 6	
6	Rock Cornish game hens	6
6	small onions	6
	celery leaves	
1½ cups	butter	375 ml.
2 tsp.	dried tarragon	10 ml.
1 tsp.	dried thyme	5 ml.
¼ cup	fresh lemon juice	50 ml.
1 tsp.	paprika	5 ml.
1 tsp.	salt	5 ml.
	freshly ground black pepper	

An hour or so before dinner, stuff the cavity of each game hen with an onion and a few celery leaves and tie the wings and feet. Impale the hens on the spit. Put the butter into a small skillet or saucepan and sprinkle the herbs over it, rubbing the leaves between your fingers to release their flavor. Melt the butter over low heat, stirring it to blend the herb flavors through. Remove from the stove and stir in the lemon juice, paprika, salt and pepper.

When the coals for the barbecue are gray, brush the hens liberally with butter and start them roasting. Using a pastry brush, baste frequently with the butter. Roast for 45 minutes to an hour or until the skin is well browned and the drumsticks can be moved easily.

ELEANOR GRAVES
GREAT DINNERS FROM LIFE

Poached Rock Cornish Hens

The technique for stuffing poultry under the breast skin is demonstrated on page 37.

	To serve 6	
3	Rock Cornish game hens	3
9 tbsp.	butter	135 ml.
3 tbsp.	dried tarragon	45 ml.
3 tbsp.	finely chopped fresh parsley	45 ml.
	salt and pepper	
6 tbsp.	fine fresh bread crumbs	90 ml.
1	lemon, halved	1
5 qts.	lukewarm chicken stock	5 liters
¼ cup	vinegar	50 ml.
2	shallots, finely chopped	2
Velouté sauce		
3 tbsp.	butter	45 ml.
3 tbsp.	flour	45 ml.
1½ cups	reserved chicken poaching stock	375 ml.

Start this preparation several hours before you plan to cook the birds. Cream 6 tablespoons [90 ml.] of the butter and add 1½ teaspoons [7 ml.] of tarragon, 1 tablespoon [15 ml.] of the chopped parsley, 1 teaspoon [5 ml.] salt and ¼ teaspoon [1 ml.] of pepper. Blend in the bread crumbs. Divide the mixture into six portions and stuff them under the breast skin of the hens, one portion on each side. Pat each breast flat. Let the birds rest at room temperature or in the refrigerator for several hours to absorb the flavor from the stuffing.

Salt and pepper the cavity of each bird. Rub the hens with the cut sides of the halved lemon. Truss, and wrap the hens in parchment paper. Tie the paper securely. Immerse the birds in the lukewarm stock, bring to a boil, reduce the heat and barely simmer for 30 to 35 minutes.

Meanwhile, combine the vinegar, chopped shallots and the remaining 1½ teaspoons [7 ml.] of tarragon in a small enameled or stainless-steel saucepan. Cook until all but 1 tablespoon [15 ml.] of the liquid has evaporated.

To prepare a velouté sauce, make a roux with the butter and flour, and cook for 10 to 12 minutes. Add the hot stock and bring to a boil over medium heat. Let simmer for 30 minutes. Skim off the skin that forms on the surface as frequently as possible. Add the reduced mixture to the velouté and simmer together for 5 minutes. Strain the sauce into a sauceboat; blend in the remaining chopped parsley and the remaining butter. Serve half a bird to each person.

MADELEINE KAMMAN
THE MAKING OF A COOK

Squab

Squabs with Rice

This unusual dish from Shakespeare's day is taken from a cookbook published in 1609.

	To serve 4	
4	squabs	4
4	bunches thyme, parsley and marjoram	4
2 tbsp.	butter	30 ml.
1 tbsp.	vegetable oil	15 ml.
	Mutton stock	
	meaty mutton or lamb bones	
1 quart	water	1 liter
1	bouquet garni	1
1	medium-sized carrot, sliced	1
1	medium-sized onion, sliced	1
	Rice pudding	
¼ cup	raw unprocessed long-grain rice	50 ml.
2 cups	light cream (or cream and milk)	½ liter
½ tsp.	ground mace	2 ml.
1	large lemon, peeled thinly	1

Simmer the stock ingredients for 3 to 4 hours (this can be done in advance). Strain and reduce the stock to 3 cups [¾ liter]. Season with salt and black pepper.

To prepare the rice pudding: put the rice, cream, lemon peel and mace into a casserole. Cook in the oven at 250° F. [120° C.]. Stir the crust occasionally and, if the rice becomes too dry, add some creamy milk. Leave for 2 to 3 hours—the slower a rice pudding is cooked, the better it tastes.

Insert the bunches of sweet herbs into the squabs' cavities. Then brown the squabs all over in the butter and oil. Next tuck them closely together in a casserole, breasts down, and pour in the boiling mutton stock, which should barely cover them. Simmer with the rice until cooked, either on top of the stove or in an oven preheated to 375° F. [190° C.]; in the latter case, it is important that the casserole should be at a boil when you put it in.

When the flesh begins to show signs of parting from the breastbone, separate them completely, so that each squab is divided into two large pieces. Lay them on a serving dish and keep them warm.

Reduce the stock until it has a good strong flavor. It can be thickened a little if you like, but I think that a strongly flavored thin gravy is preferable since the rice will provide the desirable thickness.

Season the rice pudding with sugar and more mace to taste. Smother the squabs with the pudding and squeeze the peeled lemon over it.

No green vegetables should be served with this dish. They could come beforehand, or afterwards, as an entirely separate course.

JANE GRIGSON
GOOD THINGS

Braised Stuffed Squabs, Catalan-Style

Pigeonneau à la Catalane

This dish may be served directly from the casserole. Alternatively, strain, degrease and reduce the braising liquid, pour the sauce over the squabs and garnish with the garlic cloves.

	To serve 4	
4	squabs with the livers reserved	4
2 tbsp.	butter or rendered goose fat	30 ml.
2 to 3 tbsp.	diced smoked ham	30 to 45 ml.
1 tbsp.	flour	15 ml.
⅓ cup	dry white wine	75 ml.
¼ cup	chicken or veal stock	50 ml.
24	garlic cloves, peeled, blanched for 5 minutes in boiling salted water and drained	24
1	bouquet garni	1
	Stuffing	
	reserved squab livers, finely chopped	
1 tbsp.	finely chopped, cooked smoked ham	15 ml.
1 cup	fresh bread crumbs	¼ liter
1	egg	1
1 tbsp.	finely chopped fresh parsley	15 ml.
½ tsp.	finely chopped garlic	2 ml.
	salt and pepper	
	dried thyme and finely crumbled bay leaf	
1 tsp.	Cognac	5 ml.

Mix together all the stuffing ingredients, adding a pinch each of the thyme and bay leaf. Stuff the squabs and truss them. In a fireproof earthenware casserole, lightly fry the squabs in the butter (or goose fat, as is done in Catalan country) with the fresh ham. When the squabs are golden brown on all sides, remove them to a warm platter. Add the flour to the fat in the casserole and cook, stirring over low heat until golden. Add the wine and stock, and mix well.

Return the squabs to the casserole and add the garlic cloves. Do not be afraid of using this quantity of garlic; when blanched, garlic has neither the bitterness nor the pungency that it has when fried raw. Add the bouquet garni and cook, covered, in the oven at 325° F. [170° C.] for 45 minutes.

PROSPER MONTAGNÉ
MON MENU

Squab Pie

Adapted from an old recipe from Lynchburg, Virginia.

	To serve 4	
2	squabs	2
	salt and pepper	
1	onion, studded with 2 or 3 whole cloves	1
2 tbsp.	butter	30 ml.
2 tbsp.	finely chopped fresh parsley	30 ml.
2 tbsp.	finely chopped fresh thyme	30 ml.
2	hard-boiled eggs	2
½ cup	milk or cream	125 ml.
2 tbsp.	cracker crumbs or crushed water biscuits	30 ml.
	short-crust pastry (recipe, page 167)	

Put the squabs in a saucepan with a tight-fitting lid. Cover with boiling water and boil slowly till tender, with a little salt, an onion and a few cloves. Then take them out, drain and dry, and put in each squab a teaspoon [5 ml.] of butter, pepper, salt, chopped parsley and thyme. Then put into the cavity of each squab a hard-boiled egg, and truss the birds.

Lay the squabs in a large, round earthenware baking dish, 3 to 4 inches [8 to 10 cm.] deep. Strain over them the liquid in which they were simmered. Add the remaining butter and the milk or cream. Add the cracker crumbs (or crushed water biscuits), the remaining parsley and thyme, and a little salt. Put in a few pieces of short-crust pastry.

Cover with short-crust pastry and bake in an oven preheated to 350° F. [180° C.] for 30 to 40 minutes.

MRS. HELEN CLAIRE BULLOCK
THE WILLIAMSBURG ART OF COOKERY

Braised Squab

Pigeon Bressane

	To serve 6	
6	squabs with the livers and hearts reserved	6
1 tbsp.	butter	15 ml.
1 tsp.	salt	5 ml.
1 tsp.	freshly ground white pepper	5 ml.
1	carrot, diced	1
1	onion, diced	1
½ cup	dry white wine	125 ml.
½ cup	water	125 ml.
	Stuffing	
3 tbsp.	unsalted butter	45 ml.
1½ cups	finely diced fresh mushrooms	375 ml.
¼ tsp.	salt	1 ml.
	freshly ground black pepper	
	reserved squab livers and hearts, coarsely chopped	
¾ cup	chopped onions	175 ml.
¾ cup	raw unprocessed rice	175 ml.
1½ cups	chicken stock	375 ml.

To prepare the stuffing, melt 1 tablespoon [15 ml.] of the butter in a saucepan, add the mushrooms and sauté for 5 to 6 minutes until all of the liquid from the mushrooms has evaporated. Add the salt and a pinch of black pepper, the chopped livers and hearts of the squabs, and sauté for 2 minutes over medium heat. Set aside.

Melt 2 tablespoons [30 ml.] of butter in another saucepan, add the onions and cook for 1 minute. Add the rice and mix well so that all the grains are coated with butter. Add the stock and bring to a boil. Cover and simmer slowly on top of the stove for 20 minutes. Combine with the mushroom mixture and check the seasoning. Loosely fill each squab with this stuffing and truss them in the normal way.

Season the squabs with salt and pepper. Melt 1 tablespoon [15 ml.] butter in a large fireproof casserole and sauté the squabs over medium heat for about 10 minutes or until they are browned on all sides. Add the carrot and onion, cover, reduce the heat and simmer for 15 minutes. Add the wine and water, cover and simmer for another 30 minutes.

Arrange the squabs on a warmed serving platter, remove the trussing strings, strain the juices and pour over the squabs. Serve immediately.

JACQUES PÉPIN
A FRENCH CHEF COOKS AT HOME

Guinea Hen

Roast Guinea Hen with Bacon

Pintade Rôtie au Lard Fumé

To serve 3 or 4

3 lb.	guinea hen with the wishbone removed (or substitute two 1½ to 2 lb. [¾ to 1 kg.] guinea hens)	1½ kg.
	salt and freshly ground pepper	
	dried oregano	
2 tbsp.	butter	30 ml.
1 tsp.	oil	5 ml.
	thin slices bacon	
⅓ cup	dry white wine	75 ml.

Sprinkle salt, pepper and a pinch of oregano into the bird's cavity and add the knob of butter. Truss the bird. Rub it with a few drops of oil; sprinkle it on all sides with salt, pepper and a little oregano. Press bacon slices, lengthwise, over the entire breast, tying around a couple of lengths of cotton string to hold them in place.

Roast the bird in an oven preheated to 375° F. [190° C.]; to contain the bird, use a heavy, shallow pan (gratin dish, small skillet, etc.) approximating as near as possible the size of the bird itself. Roast from 45 to 50 minutes (30 minutes for small hens). Remove the bacon slices for the last 8 to 10 minutes of cooking time to permit the breast to brown lightly.

Clip the trussing strings and pull them out. Transfer the bird to a heated platter. Skim a few tablespoons of excess fat from the roasting pan, add the white wine, and scrape and stir over high heat until all adherent material is dissolved and the wine is reduced by about half. Send this juice to the table in a heated sauceboat and serve the guinea hen with a chestnut purée.

RICHARD OLNEY
THE FRENCH MENU COOKBOOK

Stuffed Guinea Hen with Raspberry Sauce

Poulet d'Inde à la Framboise Farci

This recipe dates from the mid-17th Century, when poulet d'Inde meant either guinea hen or turkey. A guinea hen is used here. The bird is boned, using the method shown on pages 62-63. The raspberry vinegar called for is made by steeping fresh raspberries in red wine vinegar for a month at room temperature. Strain the vinegar before using it.

To serve 2

3 lb.	guinea hen, boned	1½ kg.
3 oz.	fresh pork fat, chopped	100 g.
4 oz.	lean ground veal	125 g.
	salt and pepper	
1 or 2	whole cloves, pounded to a powder	1 or 2
1 tbsp.	capers, rinsed and drained well	15 ml.
3	egg yolks	3
1 cup	veal or chicken stock	¼ liter
¼ lb.	fresh mushrooms, sliced (about 1¼ cups [¼ liter])	125 g.
1	bouquet garni	1
1 oz.	lean salt pork without the rind, blanched in boiling water for 5 minutes, drained and chopped	50 g.
1 tbsp.	flour	15 ml.
2 tbsp.	red wine vinegar, preferably raspberry vinegar	30 ml.
1 tbsp.	fresh lemon juice	15 ml.
	fresh raspberries	

Remove the breast flesh from the bird without damaging the skin, then chop the flesh and mix it with the chopped pork fat and ground veal. Add salt and pepper, cloves and capers, and mix in the egg yolks. Stuff the guinea hen with this mixture, truss the bird and place it in a pan in a fairly hot oven, preheated to 400° F. [200° C.], for about 30 minutes, basting after the first 20 minutes.

Transfer the bird to a heavy fireproof casserole. Pour half the stock over it and add the mushrooms and bouquet garni. Gently braise on top of the stove, covered, for 15 minutes, basting regularly.

To make the sauce, heat the salt pork in a skillet. When the fat has been rendered, remove the pork and stir the flour into the fat. As soon as this is lightly browned, dilute it with the remaining stock and the vinegar. Simmer gently, then pour it into the casserole with the lemon juice.

Sprinkle a handful of fresh raspberries on top of the guinea hen and serve at once.

LA VARENNE
LE CUISINIER FRANÇOIS

Duck

Peppery Duck

Pepereend

This dish is greatly improved if the strained cooking liquid is degreased, cleansed and reduced before adding the red pepper, green peppercorns and stuffed olives.

To serve 4

4½ lb.	duck, trussed	2 kg.
1	onion, sliced	1
1 tbsp.	butter	15 ml.
4	thin slices lean salt pork, blanched in boiling water for 10 minutes and drained	4
1	carrot, sliced	1
1	bouquet garni of parsley, thyme and bay leaf	1
	salt and pepper	
½ cup	dry white wine	125 ml.
1 cup	beef stock	¼ liter
1	small sweet red pepper, halved, seeded, deribbed and diced	1
1 tbsp.	green peppercorns, rinsed and drained	15 ml.
12	stuffed green olives, rinsed and drained	12

Fry the onion slices in the butter until they are transparent. Line the bottom of a heatproof casserole with the salt pork. Spread the carrot and onion slices, with the butter, on top of the salt pork and add the bouquet garni. Rub the duck all over with salt and pepper and place in the casserole. Cover and bake in an oven preheated to 425° F. [220° C.] for 15 minutes to color the duck.

Remove the lid, add the wine to the casserole and boil for a few minutes over high heat to reduce the liquid slightly. Add the stock and bring to a boil. Cover the casserole and place it in a hot oven, 375° F. [190° C.], for 45 minutes.

Remove the duck and cover with foil to keep it warm. Carefully strain and skim the cooking liquid and return it to the casserole. Mix in the diced red pepper, green peppercorns and olives. Return the duck to the casserole, cover and place it in the oven for a further 15 minutes at 350° F. [180° C.].

Carve the duck, arrange the pieces in a warmed oval dish and cover the pieces with the sauce. Serve with boiled rice and diced cucumber that has been simmered in butter with a pinch of ground fennel seeds, salt, pepper and sugar.

HUGH JANS
VRIJ NEDERLAND

Basic Roast Duckling and Sauce

To serve 4

4 to 5 lb.	duckling with the gizzard, heart and liver reserved and chopped	2 to 2½ kg.
1 tsp.	salt	5 ml.
¼ tsp.	pepper	1 ml.
½ tsp.	dried rosemary	2 ml.

Basic duck sauce

1	rib celery, coarsely chopped	1
1	carrot, coarsely chopped	1
1	onion, coarsely chopped	1
1	tomato, coarsely chopped	1
1 cup	beef stock	¼ liter

Elderberry and ginger sauce

	basic duck sauce	
3 tbsp.	sugar	45 ml.
1 tbsp.	butter	15 ml.
⅓ cup	cider vinegar	75 ml.
1 cup	elderberry preserves	250 ml.
3 tbsp.	brandy	45 ml.
1 tsp.	finely chopped fresh ginger root (or substitute ½ tsp. [2 ml.] ground ginger)	5 ml.

Preheat the oven to 450° F. [230° C.].

Trim the duck of excess fat at the base of the tail and inside. Rub it inside and out with salt, pepper and rosemary. Prick the skin on the thighs and breast to allow the fat to drain. Place the duck and giblets in a pan and roast for 1½ hours. Remove the duck from the pan and keep it warm.

Pour off all but about 2 tablespoons [30 ml.] of fat from the roasting pan. Add the chopped vegetables and sauté for 10 minutes, stirring constantly. Add the beef stock. Stir, scraping up the brown bits in the pan, then strain the contents into a saucepan.

This basic duck sauce may be served as is, or turned into elderberry and ginger sauce as follows: melt the sugar and butter in a saucepan and cook, stirring, until the mixture is brown. Add the vinegar and continue to cook over high heat until the mixture is reduced by half. Stir in the elderberry preserves, the basic duck sauce, the brandy and ginger. Lower the heat and simmer for 10 minutes. Taste the sauce and add salt if necessary.

Cut the duck into quarters using poultry shears, pour the sauce over it and serve.

ALBERT STOCKLI
SPLENDID FARE, THE ALBERT STOCKLI COOKBOOK

Duck with Green Peas

Canetons Nantais

To serve 2 or 3

6 to 7 lb.	duck	3 kg.
4 lb.	fresh peas, shelled	2 kg.
12	small boiling onions	12
2 tbsp.	butter	30 ml.
5	slices lean bacon, cut into small pieces, blanched in boiling water for 5 minutes and drained	5
1	bouquet of winter savory	1
¼ cup	veal or chicken stock	50 ml.

In a large casserole roast the duck in an oven preheated to 425° F. [220° C.]. When the duck is two thirds cooked, after about 45 minutes, take the casserole from the oven and degrease the juices in it.

Reduce the oven temperature to 350° F. [180° C.]. Now cook the green peas in boiling water for a few minutes and drain them. Also, lightly cook the onions in the butter. Mix together the bacon pieces, the onions and the peas, and put them around the duck in the casserole. Finally, do not forget to add the bouquet of savory, which is indispensable for green peas cooked in this way. Season the duck and vegetables, moisten them with the stock, then return the casserole to the oven and cook very slowly, uncovered, until the duck is perfectly done—about 20 to 30 minutes.

AUSTIN DE CROZE
LES PLATS RÉGIONAUX DE FRANCE

Broiled Long Island Duckling

To serve 4

5 to 6 lb.	duckling, cut into quarters	2½ to 3 kg.
	salt, preferably coarse salt	
	Marinade	
¾ cup	vegetable oil	175 ml.
½ cup	red wine vinegar	125 ml.
1 tsp.	salt	5 ml.
	freshly ground black pepper	
1	large onion, thinly sliced	1
3	large garlic cloves, thinly sliced	3
2	large bay leaves, coarsely crumbled	2

In a shallow bowl, large enough to hold the duck quarters in one layer, make the marinade by mixing together the oil, vinegar, salt and a few grindings of pepper. Stir in the onion, garlic and bay leaves. Lay the duck pieces in this marinade,

baste thoroughly and marinate at room temperature for at least 3 hours, turning the pieces every half hour.

When you are ready to broil the duck, remove the pieces from the marinade. Strain the marinade through a fine sieve and discard the vegetables. Preheat the broiler to its highest setting. Arrange the duck pieces, skin side down, on the broiler rack, sprinkle lightly with salt and broil 4 inches [9 cm.] from the heat source for about 35 minutes, regulating the heat or lowering the rack so that the duck browns slowly without burning. Baste every 10 minutes or so with the marinade. Turn the pieces over, sprinkle with salt again and broil for a further 10 to 15 minutes, basting two or three times with the marinade. When the duck is tender and a deep golden brown, arrange the pieces on a heated serving platter. Moisten with a tablespoon [15 ml.] or so of the pan drippings if you wish and serve at once.

FOODS OF THE WORLD/AMERICAN COOKING

Spitted Curried Duck

Curry powder may be made of as many as 20 different spices, the most common of which are ginger, turmeric, fenugreek, cloves, cumin, cinnamon, and red and black pepper. The best curries to use for spicy effect are those made in, or in the style of, Madras, India.

To serve 2

4 to 5 lb.	duck	2 to 2½ kg.
1 tbsp.	curry powder	15 ml.
2	garlic cloves, finely chopped	2
1 tsp.	turmeric	5 ml.
½ tsp.	Tabasco sauce	2 ml.
	Basting sauce	
½ cup	honey	125 ml.
¼ cup	fresh strained orange juice	50 ml.
¼ cup	fresh strained lemon juice	50 ml.
1½ tbsp.	curry powder	22 ml.
	chutney	

Prepare the duck by rubbing it inside and out with 1 tablespoon [15 ml.] of curry powder to which you have added the garlic cloves, turmeric and Tabasco. Truss and spit the duck. Roast over medium coals for about 1½ hours. Prick the skin from time to time. During the last half hour of roasting, baste the duck with a mixture of honey, orange juice, lemon juice and the remaining 1½ tablespoons [22 ml.] of curry powder. Serve with chutney and Chinese fried rice.

JAMES BEARD
JAMES BEARD'S TREASURY OF OUTDOOR COOKING

Roast Honey Duck

To serve 6 to 8

4 to 5 lb.	duck	2 to 2½ kg.
	salt	
2	garlic cloves, crushed	2
2 or 3	scallions, finely chopped	2 or 3
3 tbsp.	soy sauce	45 ml.
3 tbsp.	dry sherry	45 ml.
2 tbsp.	honey	30 ml.
1 cup	boiling water	¼ liter

Wipe the duck with a damp cloth. Rub it lightly, inside and out, with salt. Preheat the oven to 350° F. [180° C.].

Combine the garlic and scallions with the soy sauce and sherry. Divide this soy mixture in half.

Mix the honey with one half of the soy mixture. Rub some of this sauce into the duck skin and let the bird stand a few minutes until dry. Then repeat. For basting the bird, add the boiling water to the remainder of the combined sauce.

Pour the remaining half of the soy mixture into the duck cavity. Place the bird on a rack over a drip pan containing several inches [5 to 8 cm.] of water.

Roast until done (about 1¾ to 2 hours), basting with the reserved combined sauce at 15-minute intervals. Add more water to the drip pan as it evaporates.

GLORIA BLEY MILLER
THE THOUSAND RECIPE CHINESE COOKBOOK

Four Countries Duck

Vierländer Ente

When making the sauce to accompany this duck, thoroughly degrease the roasting juices before deglazing the pan with the stock and sour cream.

To serve 3 or 4

4 lb.	duck	2 kg.
6 tbsp.	butter	90 ml.
2 cups	chicken or veal stock	½ liter
⅓ cup	sour cream	75 ml.
	Stuffing	
½ lb.	lean boneless ham, diced	¼ kg.
4 tbsp.	butter	60 ml.
3	medium-sized apples, peeled, cored and cut into rings	3
¼ cup	bread crumbs	50 ml.

Rub the duck all over with the 6 tablespoons [90 ml.] of butter. To make the stuffing, fry the ham in the 4 tablespoons

[60 ml.] of butter, then mix it with the apples and bread crumbs. Stuff the duck with this mixture and sew up. Roast the duck for about 1 hour in an oven preheated to 425° F. [220° C.]. When the duck is fully cooked, transfer it to a warmed platter. Make a sauce with the roasting juices, stock and sour cream. Serve the sauce separately.

MARIA ELISABETH STRAUB
GRÖNEN AAL UND RODE GRÜTT

Holstein Duck

Ente auf Holsteiner Art

A simple method for making a sauce from pan juices appears on page 21, Steps 4-6.

To serve 2 or 3

3 to 4 lb.	duck with the liver and gizzard reserved	1½ to 2 kg.
	salt and pepper	
	dried marjoram	
¼ cup	salt water, made with 2 tsp. [10 ml.] salt	50 ml.
1 cup	sour cream	¼ liter
	Stuffing	
	reserved duck liver and gizzard, chopped	
6	cooking apples, peeled, cored and cut into small pieces	6
1	medium-sized onion, chopped	1
½ lb.	smoked ham, finely diced	¼ kg.
2	eggs	2
2 tbsp.	fresh bread crumbs	30 ml.

Season the duck inside and out with a mixture of salt, pepper and marjoram. Mix together the liver and gizzard, apples, onion, diced ham, eggs and bread crumbs. Stuff the duck with this mixture and sew it up. Place it breast down in a roasting pan that has been rinsed with water, pour a few spoonfuls of water over the duck and place in a moderate oven preheated to 350° F. [180° C.]. Turn the duck breast side up after 15 minutes and prick below the wings and legs. Baste frequently with the cooking juices. Add a little water as soon as the cooking juices begin to brown.

After roasting for 60 to 70 minutes or until the juices run clear when the thigh is pricked, pour the salt water over the duck so that the skin becomes crisp. Roast for another 10 minutes, remove the duck from the oven and set it on a warmed platter. Degrease the pan juices, deglaze with a little water and reduce the sauce until it is syrupy. Add the sour cream and season the sauce with salt and marjoram.

JUTTA KÜRTZ
DAS KOCHBUCH AUS SCHLESWIG-HOLSTEIN

Ducks à la Mode

This recipe was recorded by Mrs. Glasse, a celebrated English cookery writer, in 1747. I give it first in her own words, then conclude with a few clarifying notes:

"Take two fine ducks, cut them into squares, fry them in butter a little brown, then pour out all the fat, and throw a little flour over them; add half a pint of good gravy, a quarter of a pint of red wine, two shallots, an anchovy and a bundle of sweet herbs; cover them close and let them stew for a quarter of an hour; take out the herbs, skim off the fat and let your sauce be as thick as cream. Send it to table and garnish with lemon."

	To serve 6 to 8	
two 7 lb.	ducks	two 3 kg.
6 tbsp.	butter	90 ml.
	flour	
1 cup	veal or chicken stock	¼ liter
½ cup	dry red wine	125 ml.
2	shallots, finely chopped (or substitute 1 chopped onion)	2
4 or 5	anchovy fillets, soaked in cold water for 10 minutes and drained	4 or 5
1	bouquet garni of thyme, parsley, marjoram and sage	1
	salt and pepper	
1	lemon, quartered	1

Cut the ducks down the backs and then across with poultry shears or disjoint them in the ordinary way. They are better if lightly floured before browning and again after, as Mrs. Glasse suggests. An onion may replace the shallot.

For the bundle of sweet herbs use a prepared bouquet garni or a bundle of thyme, parsley, marjoram and sage.

I don't think a quarter of an hour is long enough to stew the ducks; I stew them for 30 minutes. Many of Mrs. Glasse's recipes give very short cooking times.

Thicken the sauce, in the usual way, to the consistency of cream and season well. She doesn't mention pepper and salt, but assumes it. Better seasoned at the end, as the anchovies make it fairly salty. The dish is very good indeed.

ELISABETH AYRTON
THE COOKERY OF ENGLAND

Roasted Stuffed Boneless Duck

Instructions for boning a duck appear on pages 62-63. Dried Chinese mushrooms, glutinous rice and Chinese sausages are readily obtainable from Oriental food stores.

The technique of boning and stuffing is the same throughout China, but the stuffings used differ from region to region. This recipe is Cantonese in origin.

	To serve 4 to 6	
5 lb.	duck	2½ kg.
½ cup	dried Chinese mushrooms	125 ml.
1 cup	warm water	¼ liter
2 cups	raw glutinous rice (or substitute raw short-grain rice)	½ liter
4 cups	cold water	1 liter
4	Chinese sausages (or substitute sweet Italian sausages)	4
2 tbsp.	vegetable oil	30 ml.
4 tsp.	salt	20 ml.
1	slice fresh ginger root, about ½ inch [1 cm.] thick	1

Soak the dried mushrooms in the warm water for 20 minutes. Drain the mushrooms and cut off the stems. Cut each mushroom into dice.

Using a 2-quart [2-liter] saucepan, put the rice in 3 cups [¾ liter] of the cold water. Bring to a boil, then cover and simmer for 10 minutes. Turn off the heat, without uncovering or disturbing the rice, and let the rice rest for 20 minutes.

In a small skillet, boil the Chinese sausages in the remaining 1 cup [¼ liter] of water for 6 minutes. Discard the water. Cool and then cut into little dice.

In a wok or skillet, stir fry the mushrooms in oil for 1 minute. Add the sausages and mix. Then add the cooked rice and mix well. Add 2 teaspoons [10 ml.] of salt and mix again.

Remove the bones of the duck, leaving the meat and skin intact. Turn the duck inside out and rub with ginger. Then sprinkle the remaining 2 teaspoons [10 ml.] of the salt all over the inside. Turn the duck skin side out. Stuff, using up all the stuffing, then truss. Cover a cake rack with foil, then cut slits in the foil for air circulation.

Preheat the oven to 375° F. [190° C.]. Pour cold water to a depth of about ½ inch [1 cm.] in the bottom of a roasting pan. Place the duck on the rack above the water and roast for 1½ hours, adding boiling water to the pan if it becomes dry.

To serve, cut the stuffed duck with a knife or metal spoon into six equal pieces.

GRACE ZIA CHU
MADAME CHU'S CHINESE COOKING SCHOOL

Peking Duck

The malt sugar called for in this recipe resembles honey; the plum sauce, bean paste and hoisin sauce are sweet condiments. All are obtainable in Oriental food stores.

Peking duck is a world-famous dish that is, in fact, simple to cook. It should be noted that Peking duck has achieved its justifiable fame not only because of the way it is prepared but also because of the way it is eaten: wrapped in a pancake. The pancakes are smaller and—because no egg is used—drier than those used in egg rolls.

To serve 4

3 to 4 lb.	duck	1½ to 2 kg.
1 tsp.	malt sugar	5 ml.
2 tbsp.	soy sauce	30 ml.
½ cup	plum sauce	125 ml.
½ cup	sweet red-bean paste or *hoisin* sauce	125 ml.
10	scallions, trimmed and quartered lengthwise	10
1	small cucumber, peeled and cut lengthwise into thin strips about 2 inches [5 cm.] long	1

Pancakes

2 cups	flour	½ liter
1 cup	boiling water	¼ liter
	vegetable oil or sesame oil	

Clean the duck and place it in a basin. Boil a large kettle of water and pour it over the duck, dousing it thoroughly. Remove the bird immediately and dry it inside and out with a paper towel. Hang it by the neck overnight in an airy place.

Dissolve the malt sugar in the soy sauce and rub the duck with this mixture. When this coating has dried, place the duck on a wire rack in a roasting pan and put it in an oven, preheated to 375° F. [190° C.], to roast for 1 hour. Do not baste the duck or open the oven door.

While the duck is roasting, make the pancakes. Put the flour in a bowl and gradually add the boiling water. Mix well with a wooden spoon, but do not knead the dough. Cover with a cloth and leave to stand for 20 minutes.

Form the dough into a long roll about 2 inches [5 cm.] in diameter. Cut off ½-inch [1-cm.] rounds from the roll. Roll the rounds into balls and flatten them into round cakes ¼ inch [6 mm.] thick.

When you have used up the dough, dust each cake with flour and roll it out into a paper-thin pancake. Lightly brush a heavy skillet with oil, and cook the pancakes over low heat for 1¼ minutes on each side. They are ready when parts of the pancakes start to curl and bubble slightly. Stack the cooked pancakes and cover with a damp cloth until required.

To serve the duck, first slice off the crisp skin in 1- to 2-inch [3- to 5-cm.] squares, and then slice off the meat. Place the skin and the meat on two separate warmed dishes and bring to the table.

The plum sauce, the bean paste (or *hoisin* sauce), the scallions and cucumber strips should all be laid out in separate small dishes. Spread a spoonful of sauce on each pancake, lay strips of cucumber and scallions down the center, add duck skin and meat, and roll up the pancake.

After the duck carcass has been stripped of its meat, it is usually boiled with a large amount of cabbage and, traditionally, served as a soup to end the meal.

KENNETH LO
CHINESE FOOD

Orange Barbecue Duck

To serve 4

6 lb.	duck	2½ kg.
	salt and pepper	
½ cup	fresh orange juice	125 ml.
½ cup	chicken stock	125 ml.

Barbecue sauce

½	orange	½
1 cup	fresh orange juice	¼ liter
¼ cup	port	50 ml.
¼ cup	currant jelly	50 ml.
3 tbsp.	fresh lemon juice	45 ml.
¼ tsp.	ground ginger	1 ml.
	cayenne pepper	
	black pepper	
	salt	

Rub the duck lightly inside and out with salt and pepper. Prick the skin thoroughly to allow the excess fat to run off. For an outdoor barbecue, roast the duck on an electric spit over a drip pan; or roast it in an oven preheated to 325° F. [160° C.]. Allow 25 minutes per pound. Baste the duck several times during the roasting with a mixture made of ½ cup [125 ml.] of orange juice and the chicken stock.

To prepare the barbecue sauce, peel the orange zest from the skin of the orange half. Cut the zest into slivers, simmer it for 3 minutes in a little water and drain. Skim the fat from the juices left in the roasting pan. Add to them the orange zest, 1 cup [¼ liter] of orange juice, the port, currant jelly, lemon juice and ginger. Add cayenne pepper, black pepper and salt to taste. Simmer the sauce while the duck is being carved and serve immediately.

NARCISSE CHAMBERLAIN AND NARCISSA G. CHAMBERLAIN
THE CHAMBERLAIN SAMPLER OF AMERICAN COOKING

Duck in Almond Sauce

Pato en Salsa de Almendras

To serve 4

5 to 6 lb.	duck, cut into serving pieces, with the liver reserved and coarsely chopped	2½ to 3 kg.
	flour seasoned with salt and pepper	
6 tbsp.	lard	90 ml.
1	onion, sliced and separated into rings	1
2	garlic cloves, chopped	2
4	tomatoes, peeled and chopped (or substitute 1⅓ cups [325 ml.] chopped, drained, canned tomatoes)	4
14 or 15	blanched almonds, toasted in a moderate oven for 10 minutes	14 or 15
¼ cup	dry sherry	50 ml.
1 tbsp.	chopped fresh parsley	15 ml.
	chicken or veal stock, or water (optional)	

Remove any surplus fat from the duck pieces. Wash and dry the pieces, and dip them into well-seasoned flour. Heat the lard in a large, shallow and fireproof earthenware dish or—failing this—a heavy-based saucepan, and gently fry the liver. Remove the liver with a perforated spoon and set aside.

Put the onion and garlic into the fireproof dish, and fry them gently until the onion begins to soften. Take them out—draining off as much fat as possible—and put them aside with the liver. Put the pieces of duck into the fat remaining in the dish, adding a little more lard if necessary, and brown the pieces carefully on all sides. Add the tomatoes. Lower the heat and leave to cook gently with a lid covering the dish.

Meanwhile, pound together the liver, onion, garlic and almonds in a large mortar (or use an electric blender) to make a smooth paste. Moisten this mixture with the sherry and add it to the duck. Stir in the chopped parsley and adjust the seasoning. Cover the dish and simmer gently for about an hour or until the duck is tender. It may be necessary to add a little stock or water during the cooking. If you have used an earthenware dish, you may take it straight to the table. Otherwise transfer the duck and sauce to a warmed serving bowl. Creamed potatoes go well with this.

ANNA MACMIADHACHÁIN
SPANISH REGIONAL COOKERY

Braised Duck with Orange

Canard à l'Orange ou à la Bigarade

It is customary to use Seville oranges, which are slightly bitter, for this recipe; but ordinary oranges may be substituted.

Instead of browning the duck on the stove top, you can roast it to draw off excess fat, then braise it (pages 64-65).

To serve 4

5 to 6 lb.	duck, trussed	2½ kg.
3 tbsp.	butter or lard	45 ml.
1	carrot, sliced	1
1	large onion, sliced	1
	salt and pepper	
¾ cup	dry white wine	200 ml.
1¼ cups	stock, preferably veal or duck	300 ml.
1 tsp.	cornstarch, mixed with a little water	5 ml.
2 tbsp.	fresh Seville orange juice	30 ml.
1 tbsp.	Seville orange zest, cut into thin strips and blanched in boiling water for 2 minutes	15 ml.

Place the duck in a heavy enameled casserole with the butter or lard and the carrot and onion slices. Cook over high heat, turning the bird until it is well browned all over. Drain off the excess fat. Season the duck with salt and pepper. Add the white wine and reduce it to three quarters of its original volume while continuing to turn the duck. Then add the stock and let the duck cook very gently, covered.

When the duck is done—after about 1½ hours—transfer it to a warmed platter and cover it loosely with foil to keep it hot. Add a little water to the braising liquid to increase its volume to about 1 cup [¼ liter]. Strain the liquid into a small pan and degrease. Thicken the liquid with cornstarch, simmer for 2 minutes, and finally add the orange juice and zest. Serve the duck on the platter, with the sauce separate.

J. B. REBOUL
LA CUISINIÈRE PROVENÇALE

Aromatic Roast Duck, Cantonese-Style

To serve 6

4 lb.	duck	2 kg.
½ cup	soy sauce	125 ml.
2 tbsp.	dry white wine	30 ml.
1	small garlic clove	1
½ tbsp.	soybean paste	7 ml.
1 tsp.	sugar	5 ml.
1 tsp.	grated orange peel	5 ml.
1	scallion, trimmed	1
1	piece fresh ginger root, peeled	1
⅓ cup	oil	75 ml.

Place the soy sauce, wine, garlic, bean paste, sugar, orange peel, scallion and ginger root in the duck's cavity. Close the opening and sew it up.

Brush the duck's skin with oil. Roast the bird in an oven preheated to 325° F. [160° C.] for 1 hour, brushing the skin with oil every 10 minutes. Let the bird cool; then chill it and cut into small pieces. Serve cold.

YU WEN MEI AND CHARLOTTE ADAMS
100 MOST HONORABLE CHINESE RECIPES

Duck in Sour-Sweet Sauce

Anitra in Agrodolce

To serve 3 or 4

4 to 5 lb.	duck	2 to 2½ kg.
2	large onions, thinly sliced	2
4 tbsp.	butter	60 ml.
	salt and pepper	
	flour	
	ground cloves	
1½ cups	veal or chicken broth (or substitute water)	375 ml.
2 tbsp.	finely chopped fresh mint	30 ml.
2 tbsp.	sugar	30 ml.
2 tbsp.	wine vinegar	30 ml.

In a large casserole or saucepan, melt the onions in the heated butter. Season the duck with salt and pepper, roll it in flour and put it to brown with the onions. Add a pinch of ground cloves. When the duck is well browned, pour in the heated broth or water, cover the pan and cook gently for 2 to 3 hours. Turn the duck over from time to time so that it cooks evenly. When it is tender, remove it from the pan and keep it warm in the oven. Pour off as much fat as possible from the sauce and stir in the chopped mint. Have the sugar ready, caramelized—that is, heated in a pan with a little water until it turns taffy colored. Stir this into the sauce and add the vinegar. See that the seasoning is right and serve the sauce separately as soon as it has acquired a thick, syrup-like consistency.

This dish is also excellent cold. Instead of pouring off the fat before adding the mint, sugar and vinegar, make the sauce as directed and remove the fat—it makes the most delicious frying fat—when the sauce is cold.

ELIZABETH DAVID
ITALIAN FOOD

Braised Duck with Walnut and Pomegranate Sauce, Iranian-Style

Fesenjan

Pomegranate syrup is made from the fruit's juice. It is obtainable at stores that sell Middle Eastern foods.

To serve 4

4½ to 5 lb.	duck, cut into quarters and trimmed of all exposed fat	2 to 2½ kg.
¼ cup	olive oil	50 ml.
2	medium-sized onions, cut into slices ¼ inch [6 mm.] thick	2
½ tsp.	ground turmeric	2 ml.
1 lb.	shelled walnuts, pulverized in a blender or with a mortar and pestle	½ kg.
1 quart	water	1 liter
2 tsp.	salt	10 ml.
	freshly ground black pepper	
¼ cup	bottled pomegranate syrup	50 ml.
⅓ cup	fresh lemon juice	75 ml.
¼ cup	sugar	50 ml.
1 tbsp.	coarsely chopped walnuts (optional)	15 ml.

In a heavy 12- to 14-inch [30- to 35-cm.] skillet, heat the olive oil over moderate heat. Add the onions and turmeric. Stirring frequently, cook for 8 to 10 minutes, or until the onions are richly browned. With a slotted spoon, transfer them to a heavy, heatproof 5- to 6-quart [5- to 6-liter] casserole and set the skillet aside. Add the pulverized walnuts, the water, salt and a few grindings of pepper to the casserole and stir until thoroughly blended. Bring to a boil over high heat, reduce the heat to low and simmer, partially covered, for 20 minutes.

Meanwhile, return the skillet to the stove, heat the oil remaining in the pan until a light haze forms above it and add the duck. Brown the duck lightly, turning it with tongs or a spoon and adding more oil if necessary. Regulate the heat so that the duck colors evenly without burning.

Transfer the duck to the simmering walnut mixture, turning the pieces about with a spoon to coat them evenly. Bring to a boil, reduce the heat to low, cover tightly and simmer for 1½ hours or until the duck is almost tender.

With a large spoon, skim as much fat as possible from the surface of the walnut sauce. Combine the pomegranate syrup, lemon juice and sugar. Add them to the sauce. Simmer for 30 minutes longer and taste for seasoning.

To serve, arrange the pieces of duck on a warmed deep platter and moisten with 1 cup [¼ liter] or so of the sauce. Sprinkle the duck, if you like, with coarsely chopped walnuts. Pour the rest of the sauce into a bowl or sauceboat and serve it separately.

FOODS OF THE WORLD/MIDDLE EASTERN COOKING

Duck with Figs

Le Canard à la Mantouane

To serve 4

5 to 6 lb.	duck	2½ to 3 kg.
24	dried figs	24
2 cups	port	½ liter
4 tbsp.	butter	60 ml.
2 cups	velouté sauce *(recipe, page 168)*	½ liter

Soak the figs in the port for 36 hours, in a covered bowl.

In a heavy fireproof casserole brown the duck in butter. Cook over moderate heat; after 15 minutes, sprinkle some of the port from the figs over the duck. Continue adding port at frequent intervals for 20 to 30 minutes until all the wine has been used. Place the figs around the bird, add the velouté sauce and cover the casserole. Braise in an oven, preheated to 350° F. [180° C.], for 45 minutes, basting frequently.

Place the duck on a platter, put the figs around it and pour the degreased cooking liquid over them.

ÉDOUARD NIGNON
L'HEPTAMERON DES GOURMETS
OU LES DÉLICES DE LA CUISINE FRANÇAISE

Roast Goose with Potato Stuffing

Gänsebraten mit Kartoffelfüllung

To serve 7 or 8

10 lb.	goose	5 kg.
	Stuffing	
3	medium-sized potatoes, diced small	3
⅓ cup	finely chopped onion	75 ml.
3 tbsp.	finely chopped fresh parsley	45 ml.
2 tbsp.	butter	30 ml.
	salt and pepper	
	dried marjoram	

Boil the potatoes in salted water for 8 minutes and drain them. In a large skillet, fry the onion and parsley gently in butter. Add the potatoes, shake the skillet to coat the potatoes evenly, season them and add a small pinch of marjoram. Season the goose with salt. Place the potato stuffing in the goose and sew it up. Truss and roast the goose as usual.

HANS KARL ADAM
DAS KOCHBUCH AUS SCHWABEN

Michaelmas Goose

There is an old saying in Ireland that if you eat goose on Michaelmas Day (September 29) you will never want for money all year round. At that time of the year Irish geese weigh about 10 pounds [5 kg.] each and are very tender. The traditional stuffing for this dish is potato, which cuts the grease and absorbs the rich flavor of the bird.

To serve 6

10 lb.	goose with the liver reserved, and the goose neck, gizzard and heart cooked in salted water for 20 minutes, strained and the stock reserved	5 kg.
4 to 5 tbsp.	oil	60 to 75 ml.
	Stuffing	
3 to 4	medium-sized potatoes, boiled, peeled and cut into chunks	3 to 4
1	medium-sized onion, finely chopped	1
4 oz.	lean salt pork, blanched in boiling water for 5 minutes, drained and finely diced	125 g.
	salt and pepper	
	reserved goose liver, chopped	
1 tbsp.	finely chopped fresh parsley	15 ml.
1 tsp.	finely chopped sage	5 ml.
	Onion sauce	
4	onions, sliced	4
½ cup	milk	125 ml.
½ cup	water	125 ml.
1	turnip, sliced	1
2 tbsp.	butter	30 ml.
	grated nutmeg	
	salt and pepper	
	cream (optional)	
	Applesauce	
2	cooking apples, peeled and cored	2
½ cup	water	125 ml.
2 tbsp.	butter	30 ml.
2 tbsp.	sugar	30 ml.
	grated nutmeg	
	salt	

Mix all the stuffing ingredients together and season very highly, then put the stuffing into the breast cavity of the bird and secure the vent. Place the bird in a roasting pan with a scant cup [¼ liter] of the goose-giblet stock. Cover the bird with foil and roast in a hot oven preheated to 400° F. [200° C.] for 30 minutes, then lower the heat to 350° F. [180° C.] and cook for 20 minutes to the pound. Baste at least twice during the cooking and add another scant cup of stock if the pan is running dry. Remove the foil for the last 15 minutes to allow the skin to crisp up.

In the 18th and 19th Centuries, onion sauce was always served with goose. The onions were cooked in half milk and half water with a slice of turnip. When soft the onions were mashed, mixed with a knob of butter, a pinch of nutmeg, salt and pepper, and beaten until smooth—sometimes finished with a little cream.

Nowadays applesauce is a more usual accompaniment to the goose. To prepare the applesauce, cook the peeled and cored apples in water until tender. Sieve or mash them and add the butter, sugar and a pinch each of nutmeg and salt. Reheat the sauce and serve hot.

THEODORA FITZGIBBON
A TASTE OF IRELAND

Goose or Turkey a la Daube

This recipe has been adapted from E. Smith's "Compleat Housewife," Williamsburg, 1742.

To serve 6 to 8

10 lb.	goose or turkey, trussed	5 kg.
5 or 6	slices bacon	5 or 6
1 quart	dry white wine	1 liter
2 to 3 quarts	goose, turkey or veal stock	2 to 3 liters
2 cups	vinegar	½ liter
¼ tsp.	ground allspice	1 ml.
2	bay leaves	2
¼ tsp.	finely chopped fresh marjoram	1 ml.
¼ tsp.	finely chopped fresh winter savory	1 ml.
1 bunch	scallions, trimmed	1 bunch
½ lb.	sliced fresh mushrooms (about 2½ cups [625 ml.]), sautéed	¼ kg.
1	lemon, peeled and diced	1
2 or 3	anchovies, rinsed with water, drained and pounded to a paste	2 or 3
2 tbsp.	butter, cooked over low heat until brown	30 ml.
1	lemon, thinly sliced	1

Lard the goose or turkey with the bacon, and half-roast it at 375° F. [190° C.] for about 1 hour; then take it off the spit or

out of the oven, and put it in as small a pot as will hold it. Add the white wine and enough strong broth to cover the bird. Add the vinegar, allspice, bay leaves, marjoram, winter savory and scallions. Simmer over low heat for another hour.

When the bird is ready, lay it in the serving dish and make a sauce by adding the mushrooms, diced lemon and the pounded anchovies to some of the cooking liquor (about 3 cups [¾ liter]). Thicken the sauce by swirling in the brown butter off the heat and serve with the bird. Garnish the bird with slices of lemon.

MRS. HELEN CLAIRE BULLOCK
THE WILLIAMSBURG ART OF COOKERY

Roast Goose

Oie Rôtie

Despite its name, this Jewish recipe from Poland first braises the goose pieces for at least an hour and only roasts them for a few minutes before serving. The broth may be saved for soup.

To serve 6 to 8

7 to 9 lb.	goose, cut into 8 pieces, with the giblets reserved	3 to 4 kg.
	salt	
1 cup	pearl barley, washed and drained	¼ liter
2 or 3	onions, cut into pieces	2 or 3
2 or 3	carrots, cut into pieces	2 or 3
2 or 3	leeks, cut into pieces	2 or 3
1	bouquet garni	1
4 quarts	salted water	4 liters

Put the barley, vegetables, bouquet garni and the giblets in the salted water, and simmer for at least 4 hours. In the meantime, salt the goose pieces and let them stand at room temperature for 30 minutes; then wash them in cold running water. Place the goose pieces in the barley broth and cook at a simmer until the flesh is tender. The time required will vary with the type of goose and its age: young geese are tender after an hour; older birds may need 2 hours or more.

When you judge that the goose is ready to eat, remove it from the pot. Drain the pieces and place them on a heatproof dish. Baste them with goose fat skimmed from the broth and place them in a very hot oven, preheated to 450° F. [230° C.], until they are brown. Serve without any garnish.

The same treatment is suitable for stewing chicken, turkey or duck; and the dish is as good cold as hot.

ÉDOUARD DE POMIANE
CUISINE JUIVE GHETTOS MODERNES

Roast Goose with Giblet Sauce

You can substitute 1 teaspoon [5 ml.] of cornstarch for 2 teaspoons [10 ml.] of potato starch.

To serve 6 to 8

10 to 12 lb.	goose with the giblets reserved	4½ to 6 kg.
8	apples, peeled, cored and quartered	8
1 tbsp.	salt	15 ml.
1 tbsp.	butter	15 ml.
1 cup	boiling water	¼ liter
1	bunch watercress	1

Giblet sauce

	reserved goose giblets	
2 cups	chicken stock	½ liter
1	onion	1
	salt	
	dried thyme	
½	carrot	½
½	rib celery	½
2 tbsp.	butter	30 ml.
¼ cup	goose fat, reserved from roasting	50 ml.
2 tsp.	potato starch	10 ml.

Stuff the apples into the cavity of the goose and truss the legs with string. Secure the neck skin to the back with a skewer and twist the wings behind the back. Rub the bird with salt and prick it all over with a fork. Spread the butter over the breast and place the bird on a rack in a roasting pan. Add boiling water to the pan and put the goose in an oven preheated to 375° F. [190° C.]. Count 20 minutes per pound cooking time. Turn the goose so that it browns lightly on all sides and baste frequently with the simmering giblet stock.

To make the giblet stock, simmer the neck, heart and gizzard in chicken stock to cover, adding the onion, salt to taste, a pinch of thyme, the carrot and the celery. After 2 hours, strain the stock and set it aside. Chop the heart and gizzard and set them aside. Sauté the liver in the butter, chop it and add to the heart and gizzard.

When the goose is done, remove the trussing strings and skewer, place the bird on a warmed serving platter and let it rest while you complete the giblet sauce.

Pour off all but about ¼ cup [50 ml.] of fat from the roasting pan and stir into it the potato starch. Cook, stirring, over high heat for about 5 minutes. Gradually add about 1 cup [¼ liter] of strained giblet stock to the pan and cook, stirring, for another 5 minutes. Add the chopped giblets and serve the sauce separately. Decorate the platter with watercress and place paper frills on the goose drumsticks.

JULIE DANNENBAUM
MENUS FOR ALL OCCASIONS

Old-fashioned Braised Goose

La Compôte d'Oie Comme Autrefois

The marc called for in the following recipe is a pungent brandy distilled from the grapeskins and seeds after wine is made.

To serve 6

7 to 9 lb.	goose	3 to 4 kg.
4 tbsp.	butter	60 ml.
8	medium-sized onions, finely chopped	8
20	shallots, finely chopped	20
10	garlic cloves, finely chopped	10
1 quart	dry white wine	1 liter
6	large, ripe tomatoes, peeled, seeded and chopped	6
1	bouquet garni	1
	salt and pepper	
½ cup	marc	125 ml.

Brown the goose lightly in butter in a large fireproof casserole. Add the onions, shallots and garlic, and fry for a few minutes more until they are soft but not browned.

Pour in the wine and add the tomatoes and bouquet garni. Salt and pepper lightly, cover the casserole, and braise in a low oven at 250° F. [120° C.] for about 5 hours or until the goose flesh separates from the bones. Remove and bone the goose, discarding the bones. Keep the meat warm in a covered dish.

Reduce the liquid in the casserole to a syrupy consistency, and add the marc. Remove the bouquet garni, taste the sauce and adjust the seasoning. Pour the sauce over the goose. Serve very hot.

MAURICE BÉGUIN
LA CUISINE EN POITOU

Goose with Pears

To serve 6

7 to 9 lb.	goose	3 to 4 kg.
	salt	
1	large onion	1
1	carrot	1
6	pears	6
1	lemon, halved	1
2 tbsp.	Cognac	30 ml.
1 cup	chicken stock	¼ liter

Preheat the oven to 350° F. [180° C.].

Wipe the goose with a damp cloth. Remove the visible fat from inside the bird and set the fat aside to be rendered for another use. Salt the cavity of the bird, and place the onion and carrot inside. Puncture the skin of the goose in several places, especially below the legs and breast, to allow fat to run off during roasting. (Fat that has dripped from the goose should be removed frequently and carefully saved.)

Place the goose on a rack in a shallow roasting pan and roast it, allowing 20 minutes to the pound. A meat thermometer should register 180° F. [85° C.] when the goose is done.

About 30 minutes before the goose is done, cut the pears in halves or quarters, scoop out the cores with a spoon, and rub the cut fruit with the lemon. Put a cup of the goose fat you have been taking from the roasting pan into a baking dish and add the pears, coating them with the fat. Bake them for 20 to 30 minutes, or until the pears are tender, in the same oven as the goose.

In a saucepan over medium heat, reduce the Cognac by half and sprinkle it over the pears when they are done.

When the goose is done, transfer it to a warm platter. After pouring off the last of the fat in the pan, scrape loose the juices that have solidified on the bottom of the pan and combine them over low heat with the chicken stock.

Carve the goose. Remove the baked pears from the fat. Mix the goose slices with the pears. Pour the hot juices over all and serve.

LEE FOSTER (EDITOR)
THE CORRESPONDENTS' CHOICE

Poached Goose with Garlic Cream Sauce

L'Oie à l'Instar de Visé

This is a traditional Belgian dish. The recipe given here is from Maurice des Ombiaux, a noted gastronome of the 1920s and 1930s. The method for binding the sauce with egg yolks and cream is shown on page 58.

To serve 6 to 8

10 lb.	goose	5 kg.
1	bouquet garni	1
2	large onions	2
4	carrots	4
1	whole bulb of garlic, unpeeled and in 1 piece	1
	peppercorns	
1 tbsp.	butter	15 ml.
	Sauce	
15	garlic cloves, peeled	15
1 quart	milk	1 liter
5	egg yolks	5
¾ cup	heavy cream	175 ml.

Place the goose in a cooking pot containing salted water. Bring to a boil, skimming off any scum that rises to the surface. Add the bouquet garni, onions, carrots, the whole garlic bulb and a few peppercorns. Reduce the heat to low and simmer, covered, for 2 hours or until the goose is tender. Remove the goose, cut it into serving pieces, pat the pieces dry and brown them lightly in a skillet with the butter.

Meanwhile, prepare the sauce by first simmering the garlic cloves in the milk for about 15 minutes. Add the egg yolks mixed with the cream to bind the sauce.

Arrange the goose pieces on a platter. Pour on the butter from the skillet, then add the sauce, garlic and all.

GASTON DERYS
L'ART D'ÊTRE GOURMAND

Sweet and Sour Goose Legs

Goosküül Söötsuur

Turkey legs may be substituted for goose legs.

To serve 4

4	whole goose legs	4
4 tbsp.	butter	60 ml.
1 tbsp.	sugar	15 ml.
½ tbsp.	cornstarch, mixed with a little water	7 ml.
	Stock	
1 cup	white vinegar	¼ liter
¼ cup	sugar	50 ml.
2	large onions, peeled	2
2	bay leaves	2
1 tbsp.	mustard seeds	15 ml.
¼ tsp.	ground cinnamon	1 ml.
1 tsp.	salt	5 ml.

Put all the stock ingredients into a pan. Add the goose legs to the pan, cover with water and bring to a boil, skimming frequently. Reduce the heat and simmer gently, uncovered, for 2 hours. Remove the goose legs, cool, cover them with foil and refrigerate. Strain the stock, discarding the seasonings, and refrigerate it for a few hours or until the fat rises to the top and solidifies. Then brown the legs in butter in a deep heavy skillet, sprinkling them with a little of the sugar. Skim the solidified fat from the cold stock and put it in the skillet with the goose legs. Add the remaining sugar, letting it caramelize over moderate heat. Transfer the goose legs to a warmed platter, pour 1½ cups [⅓ liter] of the vinegary stock into the skillet and stir in the cornstarch mixture to thicken the sauce. Simmer a few minutes and pour the sauce over the goose pieces. Serve with fried potatoes.

JUTTA KÜRTZ
DAS KOCHBUCH AUS SCHLESWIG-HOLSTEIN

Ragout of Goose with Apples

Ragoût d'Oie aux Pommes

To serve 6 to 8

10 to 12 lb.	goose, cut into serving pieces	5 to 6 kg.
	salt	
¼ cup	rendered goose fat	50 ml.
2	large onions, thinly sliced	2
10 to 12 lb.	cooking apples, peeled, cored and cut into eighths	5 to 6 kg.
2 tsp.	Hungarian paprika	10 ml.
½ cup	water	125 ml.

Salt the pieces of goose, leave them for 30 minutes, then rinse them in cold water and dry them. In a large heatproof casserole or deep pot, brown the goose pieces in the goose fat. Add the onions and sauté until they are a golden color. Salt lightly. Add the apples, sprinkle with the paprika and pour in the water. Cover and cook slowly for at least 2 hours, or until the goose is tender. Add more salt to correct the seasoning if this is necessary.

You may have to add a little extra water from time to time during the cooking, but when the goose is ready to serve there should be no water left in the casserole; the apples should be bathed only in the goose fat.

ÉDOUARD DE POMIANE
CUISINE JUIVE GHETTOS MODERNES

Stuffed Goose Neck

You may not often eat goose; but when you do, make sure you are given the whole of the neck with the bird. The skin of the neck can make a wonderful meal. Stuff it with chopped goose liver, minced pork or veal, onion and herbs, and serve it hot with red cabbage or cold with salad. Thin slices of stuffed goose neck are delicious to serve as an hors d'oeuvre.

To serve 4

1	goose neck	1
1	goose liver, finely chopped	1
1	medium-sized onion, finely chopped	1
1 tbsp.	chopped fresh parsley	15 ml.
	rubbed sage	
	salt and pepper	
3 tbsp.	fresh white bread crumbs	45 ml.
2	eggs, beaten	2
½ cup	rendered goose fat	125 ml.

Peel off the skin from the goose neck (use the bones for stock). Combine the liver, onion, parsley, a pinch of sage,

salt, pepper and bread crumbs. Bind with the beaten eggs and pack the stuffing into the neck skin.

Sew up each end of the neck and roast it in the goose fat, basting frequently, for 40 minutes in a moderate oven preheated to 375° F. [190° C.].

Remove the stitches and slice the neck before serving.

MARIKA HANBURY TENISON
LEFT OVER FOR TOMORROW

Preserved Goose

Confit d'Oie

To serve 8 to 10

12 to 15 lb.	goose	6 to 7 kg.
½ cup	water	125 ml.
	coarse salt	
3	garlic cloves	3
12	peppercorns	12
2	whole cloves	2
1	bay leaf	1
	dried thyme	

Clean the goose. Remove the fat from inside and from around the gizzard and melt it over gentle heat, after adding the water. There should be at least 1 quart [1 liter] of goose fat; if not, add melted fresh pork fat. Set the pan aside to cool.

In the meantime, cut the goose into four pieces, making two breast pieces and two whole leg pieces. Rub the pieces generously with coarse salt. Place them in a bowl with the garlic, peppercorns, cloves, bay leaf and a little thyme. Leave the goose pieces in the bowl in a cold place or refrigerator for 24 hours, moving the pieces occasionally so that each is kept covered with salt.

After 24 hours wipe off the salt and dry the pieces with a towel; cook them in the fat for 1 hour or until done, simmering slowly and never allowing the fat to get hot enough to fry the meat. To test when done, pierce with a metal skewer. If the juice that flows out when the skewer is withdrawn is clear and shows no pink color, the goose is cooked enough. Remove the goose pieces from the fat, drain them and separate the meat from the bones.

Strain the fat and separate it from the gravy. It is very important that no gravy at all be left in the fat. Pour about 1 inch [2½ cm.] of the clear, melted fat into a large jar and let it harden. Place the pieces of meat on this, then pour in the remaining fat, making sure that none of the meat is uncovered and that none touches the sides of the jar. Let the jar stand in a cold place for about 2 days, then pour in more fat to fill any interstices that were formed by the cooling of the fat. Cover closely with wax paper and keep in the refrigerator or other cold place until ready to use.

LOUIS DIAT
FRENCH COOKING FOR AMERICANS

Sauces and Stuffings

Bread Sauce

Bread sauce is a traditional English accompaniment to roast birds—served as cranberry sauce is in the United States.

To serve 4

3 to 4 tbsp.	fresh white bread crumbs	45 to 60 ml.
3	whole cloves	3
1	medium-sized onion	1
1	bay leaf	1
2 cups	milk	½ liter
	salt and pepper	
	cayenne pepper or grated nutmeg	
1 tbsp.	butter	15 ml.
1 tbsp.	cream	15 ml.

Stick the cloves into the onion and put it with the bay leaf and milk into a saucepan. Cover and simmer over very low heat for 15 to 20 minutes or until the milk is well flavored.

Remove the onion and bay leaf and stir the crumbs into the milk. Simmer over low heat for about 5 minutes or until the sauce is thickened and creamy, stirring constantly.

Remove the pan from the heat and season the sauce with salt and pepper, and nutmeg or cayenne pepper. Blend in the butter and cream. Reheat the sauce gently and serve at once. Note: if a thicker sauce is wanted, add 1 or 2 more tablespoons [15 ml. or 30 ml.] of bread crumbs. If a thinner sauce is called for, decrease the bread crumbs. The main thing is to have a sauce that is well flavored with onion and seasonings.

NIKA STANDEN HAZELTON
THE CONTINENTAL FLAVOUR

Oyster Stuffing for Turkey

To make about 5 cups [1 ½ liters] stuffing

1 pint	shucked oysters, drained (about 18 oysters)	½ liter
2 cups	unsalted soda-cracker crumbs or crumbled water biscuits	½ liter
1 cup	light cream	¼ liter
4 tbsp.	butter, melted	60 ml.
	salt and pepper	

Place the oysters and the cracker crumbs in a large bowl. Pour in the cream and butter, season with salt and pepper,

and mix all the ingredients gently together. Set the mixture aside for about 1 hour before use to allow flavors to mingle.

MRS. HELEN CLAIRE BULLOCK
THE WILLIAMSBURG ART OF COOKERY

Barbecue Glazing Sauce

To make about 2 ½ cups [½ liter] sauce

3	garlic cloves, finely chopped	3
¼ cup	olive oil	50 ml.
1 tsp.	salt	5 ml.
1 tsp.	freshly ground pepper	5 ml.
¼ tsp.	dried oregano	1 ml.
1 tbsp.	chopped fresh basil	15 ml.
1½ cups	puréed tomatoes	375 ml.
¼ cup	strained honey	50 ml.
	juice of 2 limes	
½ cup	dry red wine	125 ml.
¼ cup	finely chopped fresh parsley	50 ml.

Sauté the garlic in olive oil. Add the salt, black pepper, oregano, basil, puréed tomatoes and honey. Simmer for 15 minutes and add the lime juice and red wine. Blend well and simmer for another 10 minutes. Taste for seasoning. Just before removing from the heat, add the parsley.

JULIETTE ELKON
THE HONEY COOKBOOK

Soyer's Recipe for Goose Stuffing

To make about 6 to 7 cups
[1 ½ liters] stuffing

4	apples, peeled and cored	4
4	onions	4
4	sage leaves	4
4	lemon thyme leaves	4
4 or 5	medium-sized potatoes, boiled, peeled and mashed	4 or 5
	salt and pepper	

Boil the apples, onions, sage and thyme in a stewpan with sufficient water to cover them. When done, pulp them through a sieve, after first removing the sage and thyme. Then add sufficient pulp of potatoes to cause the stuffing to be sufficiently dry without sticking to the hand. Add pepper and salt, and stuff the bird.

MRS. ISABELLA BEETON
THE BOOK OF HOUSEHOLD MANAGEMENT

Louisiana Yam and Apple Stuffing

*Enough for 2 ducklings, 2 capons, or
a 12-pound [5-kg.] turkey*

4 cups	diced, peeled apples	1 liter
1 cup	chopped celery	¼ liter
1 cup	water	¼ liter
6	large yams (about 3 lb. [1½ kg.])	6
2 tbsp.	fresh lemon juice	15 ml.
1 tsp.	ground cinnamon	5 ml.
8 tbsp.	butter	120 ml.
1 cup	brown sugar	¼ liter
	salt	
1 cup	chopped pecans	¼ liter
	grated peel of 1 lemon	

Simmer the apples and celery in the water until just tender. Drain, reserving the liquid. Meanwhile, boil the yams in water to cover for approximately 25 minutes or until they are tender when pierced with a fork. Peel the yams into a bowl and mash them together with the lemon juice, cinnamon, butter, brown sugar and salt. Moisten with the apple and celery liquid. Stir in the apples, celery, pecans and lemon peel. Taste and correct the seasoning.

THE JUNIOR LEAGUE OF NEW ORLEANS INC.
THE PLANTATION COOKBOOK

Sage and Onion Stuffing

*To make about 6 cups [1 ½ liters] —
enough for 1 goose or 2 ducks*

4	large onions	4
10	fresh sage leaves	10
2 cups	fresh bread crumbs	½ liter
	salt and pepper to taste	
3 tbsp.	butter	45 ml.
1	egg yolk	1

Peel the onions and put them into boiling water. Let them simmer for 5 minutes or rather longer. Just before they are taken out, put in the sage leaves for a minute or two to take off their rawness. Drain, then chop the onions and sage very fine, add the bread crumbs, seasoning and butter, and work the whole together with the yolk of an egg. The stuffing will now be ready for use. It should be rather highly seasoned, and the sage leaves should be very finely chopped.

Many cooks do not parboil the onions in the manner just stated, but merely use them raw. The stuffing then, however, is not nearly so mild and, to many tastes, its strong flavor would be very objectionable. When made for goose, a portion of the liver of the bird, simmered for a few minutes and very finely minced, is frequently added to this stuffing; and where economy is studied, the egg yolk may be dispensed with.

MRS. ISABELLA BEETON
THE BOOK OF HOUSEHOLD MANAGEMENT

Corn-Bread Stuffing

*Enough for a 12- to 14-pound
[6-kg.] turkey*

	turkey neck, gizzard and liver	
1 cup	finely chopped scallions	¼ liter
1 cup	finely chopped celery	¼ liter
½ cup	finely chopped green pepper	125 ml.
4 tbsp.	butter	60 ml.
24	shucked oysters, drained (with the liquor reserved) and chopped	24
	salt and pepper	
	milk (optional)	
	Corn bread	
½ cup	flour	125 ml.
1 cup	white cornmeal	¼ liter
1 tsp.	baking powder	5 ml.
½ tsp.	baking soda	2 ml.
1 tsp.	salt	5 ml.
1 cup	buttermilk	¼ liter
1	egg	1
2 tbsp.	shortening, melted	30 ml.

The corn-bread batter can be prepared several hours ahead. Put the flour, cornmeal, baking powder, soda and salt into a sifter and sift together into a bowl. Add the buttermilk and stir well. Add the egg and shortening and beat well.

Pour the mixture into a hot, greased 9-inch [23-cm.] iron skillet. Bake in an oven, preheated to 400° F. [200° C.], for approximately 20 minutes or until brown. Remove the corn bread from the skillet, cool and crumble it.

Boil the turkey neck and gizzard for about 20 to 30 minutes in enough water to obtain about ½ cup [125 ml.] of stock. Strain the stock. Chop the liver and, when it has cooled, the gizzard. In a large skillet, sauté the scallions, celery and green pepper in the butter until they are soft and transparent. Add the liver, gizzard and oysters, stirring for 1 or 2 minutes. Remove from the heat and mix in the crumbled corn bread. Add salt and pepper to taste. Moisten to the desired consistency with stock, oyster liquor or milk.

THE JUNIOR LEAGUE OF NEW ORLEANS INC.
THE PLANTATION COOKBOOK

Cranberry Sauce

To make about 1 ½ cups [375 ml.] sauce

2 cups	firm unblemished fresh cranberries	½ liter
1 cup	sugar	¼ liter
½ cup	water	125 ml.
1 tsp.	finely grated fresh orange peel	5 ml.

Wash the cranberries in a colander under cold running water. Combine the berries with the sugar and water in a small, heavy, enameled or stainless-steel saucepan. Stirring frequently, bring them to a boil over high heat. Then reduce the heat to low and, still stirring from time to time, simmer uncovered for 4 or 5 minutes or until the skins of the cranberries begin to pop and the berries are tender. Do not overcook them to the point where they become mushy.

Remove the pan from the heat and stir in the orange peel. With a rubber spatula, scrape the entire contents of the pan into a small bowl. Refrigerate for 2 or 3 hours or until the sauce is thoroughly chilled.

FOODS OF THE WORLD/AMERICAN COOKING: NEW ENGLAND

Stuffing for Poached Chicken

Farce pour Poule au Pot

This recipe is from a book published anonymously in 1922, but thought to have been written by gastronome Leo Larguier.

To make 3 to 4 cups [¾ to 1 liter] stuffing

about 50	black olives, pitted and chopped	about 50
1	garlic clove, finely chopped	1
1	medium-sized onion, chopped	1
3	slices stale French or Italian bread, crusts removed, soaked in warm water, then squeezed almost dry	3
1 tbsp.	chopped fresh parsley	15 ml.
	salt and pepper	
1	egg, lightly beaten	1
	grated nutmeg	

Mix together the olives, garlic, onion, bread, parsley, salt and pepper. Add the egg to bind the mixture and add a suspicion of freshly grated nutmeg.

CLARISSE OU LA VIEILLE CUISINIÈRE

Standard Preparations

Short-Crust and Rough Puff Pastry

One simple formula produces dough both for plain short-crust pastry and for rough puff pastry. The difference is in how you roll it out.

To make enough pastry to cover an 8-inch [20-cm.] pie

1 cup	flour	¼ liter
¼ tsp.	salt	1 ml.
8 tbsp.	cold unsalted butter, cut into small pieces	120 ml.
3 to 4 tbsp.	cold water	45 to 60 ml.

Mix the flour and salt in a mixing bowl. Add the butter and cut it into the flour rapidly, using two table knives, until the butter is in tiny pieces. Do not work for more than a few minutes. Add half the water and, with a fork, quickly blend it into the flour-and-butter mixture. Add just enough of the rest of the water to enable you to gather the dough together with your hands into a firm ball. Wrap the dough in plastic film or wax paper and refrigerate it for 2 to 3 hours, or put it in the freezer for 20 minutes until the outside surface is slightly frozen.

To roll out short-crust pastry: Remove the ball of pastry dough from the refrigerator or freezer and put it on a cool, floured surface (a marble slab is ideal). Press the dough out partially with your hand, then give it a few gentle smacks with the rolling pin to flatten it and render it more supple. Roll out the dough from the center, until the pastry forms a circle about ½ inch [1 cm.] thick. Turn the pastry over so that both sides are floured and then continue rolling until the circle is about ⅛ inch [3 mm.] thick. Roll the pastry onto the rolling pin, lift, and unroll it over the piepan. Trim the pastry to within ½ inch [1 cm.] of the rim, roll the edges under, press firmly with thumb and forefinger to crimp the edges.

To roll out rough puff pastry: Place the dough on a cool, floured surface and smack it flat with the rolling pin. Turn the dough over to make sure that both sides are well floured. Roll out the pastry rapidly into a rectangle about 1 foot [30 cm.] long and 5 to 6 inches [13 to 15 cm.] wide. Fold the two short ends to meet each other in the center, then fold again to align the folded edges with each other. Following the direction of the fold lines, roll the pastry into a rectangle again, fold again in the same way and refrigerate for at least 30 minutes. Repeat this process two or three times before using the pastry. Always let the pastry dough rest in the refrigerator between rollings.

Velouté Sauce

To make 1 ½ to 2 quarts [1 ½ to 2 liters] sauce

4 tbsp.	butter	60 ml.
¼ cup	flour	50 ml.
2 quarts	veal or chicken stock	2 liters

Melt the butter in a heavy saucepan over low heat and stir in the flour until this roux mixture is smooth. Cook, stirring constantly, for 2 to 3 minutes. When the roux stops foaming and is a light golden color, pour in the stock and whisk continuously until the mixture reaches a boil. Move the saucepan half off the heat, so that the liquid on one side of the pan maintains a steady, but very light boil. Skim off fat and impurities that form on the surface of the other, calm side of the liquid. From time to time spoon off the skin. Cook for 30 minutes or until the sauce is the desired consistency.

Veal Stock

To make 2 to 3 quarts [2 to 3 liters] stock

1	veal knuckle bone, sawed into 2-inch [5-cm.] pieces	1
4 lb.	meaty veal trimmings (neck, shank or rib tips)	2 kg.
3 to 5 quarts	water	3 to 5 liters
4	carrots, scraped and topped	4
2	large onions, 1 stuck with whole cloves	2
1	whole garlic bulb, unpeeled	1
1	rib celery	1
1	leek, split lengthwise into halves and washed	1
1	large bouquet garni of parsley, thyme sprigs and a bay leaf	1
	salt	

Put the bones into a heavy stockpot and place the meat on top of them. Add cold water to cover by 2 inches [5 cm.]. Bring to a boil over low heat, starting to skim before the liquid begins to boil. Keep skimming, occasionally adding a glass of cold water to the pot, until no more scum rises. Do not stir the bones and meat, lest you cloud the stock.

Add the vegetables, bouquet garni and a dash of salt to the pot, pushing them down into the liquid so that every-

thing is submerged. Continue skimming until a boil is reached. Reduce the heat to very low, and cook partially covered at a bare simmer for 4 hours, skimming off the surface fat three or four times.

Strain the stock by pouring the contents of the pot through a colander into a large bowl or clean pot. Discard the bones, veal pieces, vegetables and bouquet garni. Cool the strained stock and skim the last traces of fat from the surface. If there is any residue at the bottom of the container after the stock cools, decant the clear liquid carefully into another bowl or pot and discard the sediment.

Refrigerate the stock if you do not plan to use it immediately; it will keep safely for 3 to 4 days. To preserve the stock longer, refrigerate it for only 12 hours or until the last bits of fat solidify on the top—then you can scrape off the fat and warm the stock enough so that it may be poured into four or five pint-sized freezer containers. Be sure to cover the containers tightly. The frozen stock will keep for 6 months, while you use it—container by container—as necessary.

To reduce veal stock: Pour the stock into a wide saucepan and bring it to a boil, removing any scum or skin that forms on the surface. Continue boiling until the liquid reaches the desired consistency or quantity.

To prepare veal stock for use as an aspic glaze: Reduce the veal stock until it reaches a light, syrupy consistency. Remove the pan from the heat and test the glaze by placing a spoonful of the reduced stock on a plate, then refrigerating it for 10 minutes. If the glaze sets to a trembling jelly, it is ready for use. Otherwise, boil the liquid stock for another 5 minutes or so and test it again.

Basic White Sauce

To make about 1 ½ cups [375 ml.] sauce

2 tbsp.	butter	30 ml.
2 tbsp.	flour	30 ml.
2 cups	milk	½ liter
	salt	
	white pepper	
	grated nutmeg (optional)	
	heavy cream (optional)	

Melt the butter in a heavy saucepan. Stir in the flour and cook, stirring, over low heat for 2 to 5 minutes. Pour in all of the milk at once, whisking constantly to blend the mixture smoothly. Raise the heat and continue whisking while the sauce comes to a boil. Season with a little salt. Reduce the heat to low, and simmer for about 40 minutes, stirring every so often to prevent the sauce from sticking to the bottom of the pan. When the sauce thickens to the desired consistency, add white pepper, and a pinch of nutmeg if you like; taste for seasoning. Whisk again until the sauce is perfectly smooth, and add cream if you prefer a richer and whiter sauce.

Batter for Deep Frying

The consistency of this batter may be varied by increasing or decreasing the proportion of liquid to flour. A thin batter will cook crisper and lighter, but some of it will be lost in the oil during frying; a thicker batter clings to food better, but tends to be heavier.

	To coat about 10 chicken pieces	
1 cup	flour	¼ liter
¼ tsp.	salt	1 ml.
2	eggs, with the yolks separated from the whites	2
3 tbsp.	olive oil or melted butter	45 ml.
½ cup	beer or water	125 ml.

Mix together the flour, salt, egg yolks, and oil or butter in a bowl. Gradually add the beer or water, and whisk for only as long as it takes to produce a smooth batter. Do not overwork the mixture. Leave the batter to rest for at least 1 hour at room temperature, otherwise it will shrink away from the poultry pieces and provide an uneven coating. Beat the egg whites until they form soft peaks and fold them into the batter just before using.

Crepe Batter

	To make about ten 5- or 6-inch [13- or 15-cm.] crepes	
⅓ cup	flour	75 ml.
	salt	
3	eggs	3
1 cup	milk or water	¼ liter
1 tbsp.	brandy	15 ml.
3 tbsp.	butter, melted	45 ml.

Place the flour in a mixing bowl and make a well in the center. Add a pinch of salt, then add the eggs. Whisk from the center of the bowl gradually outward until the mixture is fairly smooth. Whisk in the milk or water gradually, then the brandy and finally the butter. The batter should have the consistency of light cream. If necessary, add more milk or water to thin the batter. Let the batter rest at room temperature for at least 30 minutes before cooking the crepes.

Chicken Stock

Chicken stock is prepared in the same way as veal stock, but it is cooked for a shorter time. Turkey, duck, goose or other poultry stocks may be made as chicken stock is. All the scum and dissolved fats must be completely removed to produce a clear and digestible liquid. Old hens and roosters will produce the richest, most flavorful version of chicken stock.

	To make about 2 quarts [2 liters] stock	
4 to 5 lb.	raw or cooked chicken carcasses, but raw trimmings, necks, gizzards and hearts	2 kg.
3 to 4 quarts	water	3 to 4 liters
4	carrots	4
2	large onions, 1 stuck with 2 cloves	2
1	large leek, split lengthwise into halves and washed	1
1	rib celery	1
1	large bouquet garni of parsley, thyme sprigs and a bay leaf	1

Put all the chicken pieces in a heavy stockpot and cover by 2 inches [5 cm.] with water. Bring to a boil over low heat, skimming to remove the scum as it rises to the surface. Occasionally add a little cold water to help precipitate the scum. Add the vegetables and bouquet garni, pushing them down into the liquid to make sure that they are all submerged. Return the liquid to a boil and simmer gently for 2 hours, skimming and degreasing as necessary. Strain the stock through a colander into a large bowl or clean pot. Discard the chicken pieces, vegetables and bouquet garni. Cool the stock and remove every trace of fat that rises to the top.

Refrigerate the stock if you do not plan to use it immediately; it will keep safely for 3 to 4 days. To preserve the stock longer, refrigerate it for only 12 hours or until the last bits of fat solidify on the top—then you can scrape off the fat and warm the stock enough so that it may be poured into four pint-sized freezer containers. Be sure to cover the containers tightly. The freezer stock will keep for 6 months, while you draw on the supply—container by container—as necessary.

Recipe Index

All recipes in the index that follows are listed by their English titles except when a dish of foreign origin, such as coq au vin, is universally recognized by its source name. Entries are organized by the types of poultry and also by the major ingredients specified in recipe titles. Sauces, marinades and stuffings are listed under separate headings. Foreign recipes are listed under the country or region of origin. Recipe credits appear on pages 174-176.

General Index/ Glossary

Included in this index to the cooking demonstrations are definitions, in italics, of special culinary terms not explained elsewhere in this volume. The Recipe Index begins on page 170.

Recipe Credits

The sources for the recipes in this volume are shown below. Page references in parentheses indicate where the recipes appear in the anthology.

Adam, Hans Karl, *Das Kochbuch aus Schwaben.* © 1976 by Verlagsteam Wolfgang Hölker. Published by Verlag Wolfgang Hölker, Münster. Translated by permission of Verlag Wolfgang Hölker (160).
Ainé, Offray, *Le Cuisinier Méridional.* Imprimeur-Libraire, 1855 (103, 139).
Ali-Bab, *Encyclopedia of Practical Gastronomy* (English translation). Translated by Elizabeth Benson. Copyright © by McGraw-Hill, Inc. Published by McGraw-Hill Book Company, N.Y. By permission of McGraw-Hill Book Co. (93).
Aresty, Esther B., *The Delectable Past.* Copyright © 1964 by Esther B. Aresty. Published by Simon & Schuster, a division of Gulf & Western Corporation. Reprinted by permission of Simon & Schuster, a division of Gulf & Western Corporation (106).
Armisen, Raymond & Martin, André, *Les Recettes de la Table Niçoise.* © Librairie Istra 1972. Published by Librairie Istra, 15 rue des Juifs, Strasbourg. Translated by permission of Librairie Istra (118).
Ayrton, Elisabeth, *The Cookery of England.* Copyright © Elisabeth Ayrton, 1974. Published by Penguin Books Ltd., London. By permission of Penguin Books Ltd. (128, 137, 156).
Barberousse, Michel, *Cuisine Normande.* Published by Éditions Barberousse, Paris. Translated by permission of Michel Barberousse (91). *Cuisine Provençale.* Privately published by Michel Barberousse, Seguret. Translated by permission of Michel Barberousse (121).
Barr, Beryl & Sachs, Barbara Turner, (Editors), *The Artists' & Writers' Cookbook.* Copyright © 1961 by William H. Ryan. Published by Angel Island Publications, Inc. By permission of Erskine Caldwell & Elizabeth Frink (99, 107).
Barry, Naomi & Bellini, Beppe, *Food alla Florentine.* Copyright © 1972 by Doubleday & Company, Inc. Published by Doubleday & Company, Inc., N.Y. Reprinted by

permission of Doubleday & Company, Inc. (132).
Beard, James, *James Beard's American Cookery.* Copyright © 1972 by James A. Beard. Published by Little, Brown and Company, Boston. By permission of Little, Brown and Company (108, 121, 144). *James Beard's Treasury of Outdoor Cooking.* Copyright © 1960 by the Golden Press, Inc. and the Ridge Press, Inc. Published by the Golden Press, Inc. and the Ridge Press, Inc. By permission of the Golden Press, Inc. and the Ridge Press, Inc. (154).
Beeton, Mrs. Isabella, *The Book of Household Management.* (1861). Reproduced in facsimile by Jonathan Cape Ltd., London (127, 165, 166).
Béguin, Maurice, *La Cuisine en Poitou.* Published by La Librairie Saint-Denis, © 1933 (162).
Bennani-Smires, Latifa, *La Cuisine Marocaine.* © Les Éditions Alpha G.E.A.M., Casablanca. Published by Les Éditions Alpha G.E.A.M., 1974. Translated by permission of Société d'Édition et de Diffusion Al Madariss, Casablanca (115, 143).
Bocuse, Paul, *Paul Bocuse's French Cooking.* English translation, copyright © 1977 by Random House, Inc. Published by Pantheon Books, Inc., N.Y. Reprinted by permission of Pantheon Books, a Division of Random House, Inc. (88).
Boni, Ada, *The Talisman Italian Cook Book.* Copyright 1950, 1978 by Crown Publishers, Inc. Published by Crown Publishers, Inc., N.Y. By permission of Crown Publishers, Inc. (101, 118).
Bullock, Mrs. Helen Claire, *The Williamsburg Art of Cookery.* Copyright 1938, © 1966 by the Colonial Williamsburg Foundation. Published by Colonial Williamsburg. Reprinted by permission of Holt, Rinehart and Winston, Publishers (138, 151, 161, 165).
Carnacina, Luigi, *Great Italian Cooking,* edited by Michael Sonino. Published in English by Abradale Press Inc., N.Y. Reproduced by permission of Aldo Garzanti Editore and Abradale Press (89, 96, 112, 134).
Carrier, Robert, *The Robert Carrier Cookery Course.* © Robert Carrier, 1974. Published by W. H. Allen & Co. Ltd., London. By permission of W. H. Allen & Co. Ltd. (98, 107).
Chamberlain, Narcisse and Narcissa G., *The Chamberlain Sampler of American Cooking.* Copyright © 1961 by Hastings House, Publishers, Inc. Published by Hastings House, Publishers, Inc. By permission of Hastings House, Publishers (157).

Chantiles, Vilma Liacouras, *The Food of Greece.* Copyright © 1975 by Vilma Liacouras Chantiles. Published by Atheneum, N.Y. By permission of Vilma Liacouras Chantiles (102, 103, 105).
Chu, Grace Zia, *Madame Chu's Chinese Cooking School.* Copyright © 1975 by Grace Zia Chu. Published by Simon & Schuster, N.Y. Reprinted by permission of Simon & Schuster, a Division of Gulf & Western Corporation (156).
Claiborne, Craig, *Craig Claiborne's Favorites from The New York Times,* Volume 1, 1975. Copyright © 1975 by The New York Times Company. Published by The New York Times Book Company, N.Y. Reprinted by permission of Times Books (142). *Craig Claiborne's Favorites from The New York Times,* Volume 2, 1976. Copyright © 1976 by The New York Times Company. Published by The New York Times Book Company, N.Y. Reprinted by permission of Times Books (124).
Clarisse ou la Vieille Cuisinière. © 1922 Éditions de l'Abeille d'Or. Published by Éditions de l'Abeille d'Or, Paris. Translated by permission of Éditions Rombaldi, Paris (167).
Courtine, Robert, *Mon Bouquet de Recettes.* © Les Nouvelles Éditions Marabout, Verviers, 1977. Published by Les Nouvelles Éditions-Marabout, Verviers. Translated by permission of Les Nouvelles Éditions, Marabout (94, 120).
Curnonsky, *A L'Infortune du Pot.* Copyright Éditions de la Couronne, 1946. Published by Éditions de la Couronne, Paris (90). *Cuisine et Vins de France.* Copyright © 1953 by Auge, Gillon, Hollier-Larousse, Moreau et Cie (Librairie Larousse) Paris. Published by Librairie Larousse, Paris. Translated by permission of Société Encyclopédique Universelle (88, 89, 124).
Cutler, Carol, *The Six-Minute Soufflé and Other Culinary Delights.* Copyright © 1976 by Carol Cutler. Published by Clarkson N. Potter, Inc., a division of Crown Publishers, Inc. By permission of Clarkson N. Potter, Inc. (110).
Dannenbaum, Julie, *Menus for All Occasions.* Copyright © 1974 by Julie Dannenbaum. Published by E. P. Dutton & Co. Inc., N.Y. Reprinted by permission of E. P. Dutton (162).
David, Elizabeth, *French Country Cooking.* Copyright © Elizabeth David, 1951. Published by Penguin Books Ltd., London. By permission of Penguin Books Ltd. (132). *Italian Food.* Copyright © Elizabeth David, 1954, 1963, 1969. Pu

d by Penguin Books Ltd., London. By permission of
ᵍuin Books Ltd. (159). Spices, Salt and Aromatics in the
sh Kitchen. Copyright © Elizabeth David, 1970. Pub-
d by Penguin Books Ltd., London. By permission of
ᵍuin Books Ltd. (114). Summer Cooking. Copyright ©
ᵇeth David, 1955. Published by Penguin Books Ltd.,
ᵗon. By permission of Penguin Books Ltd. (116).

Bonnefons, Nicholas, Les Délices de la Campagne
) (100).

Crémone, Baptiste Platine, Le Livre de Honneste
ᵗé (125).

Croze, Austin, Les Plats Régionaux de France. Pub-
d by Éditions Daniel Morcrette, B. P. 26, 95270-Lu-
ᵉs, France. Translated by permission of Éditions Dan-
orcrette (154).

Gouy, Louis P., The Gold Cook Book. Copyright
, 1969 by the author. Published by Chilton Book Com-
ᵧ. Reprinted by permission of the publisher, Chilton
ᵏ Company, Radnor, Pa. (147).

Pomiane, Édouard, Cuisine Juive Ghettos Mo-
ᵉs. Copyright © 1929 by Albin Michel. Published by
ons Albin Michel, Paris. Translated by permission of
ons Albin Michel (115, 161, 164).

s, Gaston, L'Art d'Être Gourmand. Copyright © by
ᵑ Michel 1929. Published by Éditions Albin Michel, Par-
ᵗanslated by permission of Éditions Albin Michel (128,
146, 163).

, Louis, French Cooking for Americans. Copyright
by Louis Diat. Copyright © renewed 1969 by Mrs.
s Diat. Published by J. B. Lippincott Company, N.Y. Re-
ᵉd by permission of J. B. Lippincott Company (113,
164).

ois, Urbain, L'École des Cuisinières. Published by
ᵘ, Paris, 1876 (98).

ois, Urbain and Bernard, Émile, La Cuisine
ᵗique (1881) (94).

Gail, Fresh All The Year. © Gail Duff 1976. Pub-
d by Macmillan London Ltd., 1976. By permission of
ᵐillan London Ltd. (122, 133).

n, Juliette, The Honey Cookbook. Copyright © 1955
ᵘfred A. Knopf, Inc. Published by Alfred A. Knopf, Inc.
ᵗnted by permission of Alfred A. Knopf, Inc. (165).

ffier, Auguste, A Guide to Modern Cookery. Pub-
d by William Heinemann Ltd., London. By permission
ᵗilliam Heinemann Ltd. (92, 93). Ma Cuisine. © English
ᵧ The Hamlyn Publishing Group Limited. Published by
ᵗamlyn Publishing Group Limited, London. By permis-
of The Hamlyn Publishing Group Limited (147).

ᵈ, Michael, Cooking with Michael Field. Copyright
by Frances Field; © 1972 Frances Field and Nelson
ᵇleday, Inc.; © 1978 by the estate of Frances Field.
ᵗhed by Holt, Rinehart and Winston. By permission of
ᵗ Rinehart and Winston, Publishers (111).

ᵍibbon, Theodora, A Taste of Ireland. Copyright ©
ᵇ by Theodora Fitzgibbon. Published by Houghton
ᵗin Company, Boston. Reprinted by permission of
ᵍhton Mifflin Company (161).

er, Barbara and Rosenbaum, Elisabeth, The
ᵃn Cookery Book, a critical translation of The Art of
ᵏing by Apicius. © E. Rosenbaum 1958. Published by
ᵗge G. Harrap & Co. Ltd., London. Published by
ᵗge G. Harrap & Co. Ltd. (135).

ᵈs of the World, American Cooking, Middle Eastern
ᵏing, American Cooking: New England, The Cooking of
ᵗaribbean. Copyright © 1968 Time Inc., Copyright ©
ᵗ Time Inc., Copyright © 1970 Time Inc., Copyright ©
ᵗ Time Inc. Published by Time-Life Books, Alexandria
148; 154; 110, 159; 167; 95).

ᵉr, Lee (Editor), The New York Times Correspondents'
ᵏe. Copyright © 1974 by Quadrangle/The New York
ᵉs Book Company. Published by Quadrangle/The
ᵧ York Times Book Co. Reprinted by permission of
ᵈrangle/The New York Times Book Co. (104, 109,
162).

ᵉr, Peta J. and Escudier, Jean-Noel, The Won-
ᵈ Food of Provence. Copyright © 1968 by Robert Reb-
ᵏ and Peta J. Fuller. Reprinted by permission of Houghton Mifflin
ᵖany. Reprinted by permission of Houghton Mifflin
ᵖany (91, 123).

Graves, Eleanor, Great Dinners from Life. Copyright ©
1969 Time Inc. Published by Time-Life Books, Alexandria
(97, 149).

Grigson, Jane, Good Things. Copyright © 1968, 1969,
1970, 1971 by Jane Grigson. Copyright © 1971 by Alfred
A. Knopf, Inc. Reprinted by permission of Alfred A. Knopf,
Inc. (141, 150).

Guégan, Bertrand, La Fleur de la Cuisine Française,
Volumes 1 & 2. Published by Éditions de la Sirène. Translated by permission of Éditions Henri Lefebvre (93, 136).

Guérard, Michel, Michel Guérard's Cuisine Minceur.
English translation © 1976 by William Morrow and Com-
pany, Inc. Published by William Morrow and Company,
Inc., N.Y. Originally published in French as La Grande Cui-
sine Minceur. © Éditions Robert Laffont S. A., Paris, 1976.
Reprinted by permission of William Morrow and Company,
Inc. (105).

Hazelton, Nika Standen, The Continental Flavour.
Copyright © 1961 by Nika Standen Hazelton. Published by
Penguin Books, Ltd., London. Reprinted by permission of
Penguin Books Ltd. and Curtis Brown Ltd. (126, 165). The
Swiss Cookbook. Copyright © 1967 by Nika Standen Ha-
zelton. Published by Atheneum, New York. By permission
of Atheneum (90).

Hewitt, Jean, The New York Times Large Type Cookbook. Copyright © 1968, 1971 by The New York Times
Company. Published by Golden Press, a division of Western Publishing Company, Inc. Reprinted by permission of
Quadrangle/The New York Times Book Company (140).

Hibben, Sheila, American Regional Cookery. Copyright
© 1932, 1946 by Sheila Hibben. Published by Little, Brown
and Company, Boston. By permission of McIntosh and
Otis, Inc. (99).

Holkar, Shivaji Rao and Shalini Devi, Cooking of
the Maharajas. Copyright © 1975 by Shivaji Rao Holkar
and Shalini Devi Holkar. Published by The Viking Press,
New York. Reprinted by permission of The Viking Press
(130, 138).

Howe, Robin, Greek Cooking. © Robin Howe 1960.
Published by André Deutsch Limited, London. By permission of André Deutsch Limited (148).

Isnard, Léon, La Cuisine Française et Africaine. © 1949
by Éditions Albin Michel. Published by Éditions Albin Michel, Paris. Translated by permission of Éditions Albin Michel (92, 116, 117, 137).

Jans, Hugh, Vrij Nederland (Dutch Magazine). Published by Vrij Nederland, Amsterdam. Translated by permission of Vrij Nederland and Hugh Jans (120, 153).

Jervey, Phyllis, Rice & Spice. © 1957 by Charles E. Tuttle Co., Inc. Published by Charles E. Tuttle Company Inc.,
Tokyo. By permission of Charles E. Tuttle Company Inc.
(108).

Jouveau, René, La Cuisine Provençale. Copyright ©
Bouquet & Baumgartner, Flamatt, Switzerland. Published
by Éditions du Message, 1962, Berne. Translated by permission of Bouquet & Baumgartner (119).

Junior League of New Orleans Inc., The, The Plantation Cookbook. Copyright © 1972 by The Junior League
of New Orleans, Inc. Published by Doubleday & Company, Inc., N.Y. Reprinted by permission of Doubleday &
Company, Inc. (166).

Kahn, Odette, La Petite et la Grande Cuisine. © Calmann-Lévy 1977. Published by Éditions Calmann-Lévy.
Translated by permission of Éditions Calmann-Lévy (107).

Kamman, Madeleine, The Making of a Cook. Copyright © 1971 by Madeleine M. Kamman. Reprinted by
Atheneum Publishers. Reprinted by permission of Atheneum Publishers (149).

Kramarz, Inge, The Balkan Cookbook. © 1972 by
Crown Publishers, Inc. Published by Crown Publishers, Inc.,
N.Y. By permission of Crown Publishers, Inc. (131).

Kürtz, Jutta, Das Kochbuch aus Schleswig-Holstein. ©
1976 by Verlagsteam Wolfgang Hölker. Published by Verlag Wolfgang Hölker, Münster. Translated by permission
of Wolfgang Hölker (155, 163).

Labourer, Suzanne & Boulestin, X.-M., Petits et
Grands Plats. Published by Au Sans Pareil, 1928 (126).

La Cuisine Lyonnaise. Published by Éditions Gutenberg 1947 (130).

La Varenne, Le Cuisinier François (1651) (152).

Lin, Florence, Florence Lin's Chinese One-Dish Meals.
Copyright © 1975 by Florence Lin. Published by Hawthorn
Books, Inc. By permission of Hawthorn Books, Inc. (96,
122).

Lo, Kenneth, Chinese Food. Copyright © Kenneth Lo,
1972. Published by Penguin Books Ltd., London. By permission of Penguin Books Ltd. (95, 100, 157).

L.S.R., L'Art de Bien Traiter (1674) (116).

Lucas, Dione & Gorman, Marion, The Dione Lucas
Book of French Cooking. Copyright 1947 by Dione Lucas.
Copyright © 1973 by Mark Lucas and Marion F. Gorman.
Published by Little, Brown and Company, Boston. By per-
mission of Little, Brown and Company (88, 145).

Lyren, Carl, 365 Ways to Cook Chicken. Copyright ©
1974 by Carl Lyren. Published by Doubleday & Company,
Inc., N.Y. Reprinted by permission of Doubleday & Company, Inc. (101, 140).

MacMiadhacháin, Anna, Spanish Regional Cookery.
Copyright © Anna MacMiadhacháin, 1976. Published by
Penguin Books Ltd., London. By permission of Penguin
Books Ltd. (134, 158).

Massiolot, Le Cuisinier Roial et Bourgeois (1691) (104).

Mathiot, Ginette, A Table avec Édouard de Pomiane.
Éditions Albin Michel, 1975. Published by Éditions Albin
Michel, Paris. Translated by permission of Éditions Albin
Michel (126).

McNeill, F. Marian, The Scots Kitchen. Published by
Blackie & Son Limited, London. Reproduced by permission
of Blackie & Son Limited (119).

Médecin, Jacques, La Cuisine du Comté de Nice. © Jul-
liard, 1972. Published by Penguin Books Ltd., London.
Translated by permission of Penguin Books Ltd. (92, 102).

Miller, Gloria Bley, The Thousand Recipe Chinese Cookbook. Copyright © 1966 by Gloria Bley Miller. Published by
Grosset & Dunlap, N.Y. By permission of Gloria Bley Miller
(97, 155).

Montagné, Prosper, The New Larousse Gastronomique.
English translation © 1977 by Hamlyn Publishing Group
Limited. Published by Crown Publishers, Inc. By permission
of Crown Publishers, Inc. (90, 94).

Montagné, Prosper, and Gottschalk, A., Mon
Menu—Guide d'Hygiène Alimentaire. Published by Société
d'Applications Scientifiques, Paris (150).

Nignon, Édouard, Éloges de la Cuisine Française. Published by Éditions d'Art, Paris, 1933. Translated by permission of Éditions Daniel Morcrette, B. P., 26, 95270-Lu-
zarches, France (114, 143). L'Heptameron des Gourmets ou
les Delices de la Cuisine Française. Privately printed in Paris
by Impr. G. de Malherbes, 1919 (160).

Norman, Barbara, The Spanish Cookbook. Copyright
© 1969 by Barbara Norman. Published by Bantam Books,
Inc., N.Y. By permission of Bantam Books, Inc. (117).

Oliver, Raymond, La Cuisine—sa technique, ses secrets.
Published by Éditions Bordas, Paris, 1973. Translated by
permission of Leon Amiel Publishers (114, 123).

Olney, Richard, The French Menu Cookbook. Copyright
© 1970 by Richard Olney. Published by Simon and Schuster, N.Y. By permission of John Schaffner, Literary Agent
(112, 152). Simple French Food. Copyright © 1974 by Richard Olney. Published by Atheneum, N.Y. By permission of
Atheneum (106).

Ortiz, Elisabeth Lambert, The Complete Book of Caribbean Cooking. Copyright © Elisabeth Lambert Ortiz,
1973, 1975. Published by M. Evans and Company, Inc.,
New York. By permission of John Farguharson Ltd., Literary
Agents (120, 142).

Ortiz, Elisabeth Lambert with Endo, Mitsuko, The
Complete Book of Japanese Cooking. Copyright © 1976 by
Elisabeth Lambert Ortiz. Published by M. Evans and Com-
pany, Inc., N.Y. By permission of John Farquharson Ltd.,
Literary Agents (97).

Palay, Simin, La Cuisine du Pays. © 1970 Marrimpouey
Jeune—Pau. Published by Éditions Marrimpouey Jeune et
Cie, Pau. Translated by permission of Éditions Marrim-
pouey Jeune et Cie (124).

Pellaprat, Henri Paul, The Great Book of French Cuisine. Copyright © 1966, 1971 by Rene Kramer, Publisher,
Castagnola/Lugano, Switzerland. Published by Harper &

Row, Publishers, Inc. By permission of Harper & Row, Publishers, Inc. (90).

Pépin, Jacques, A French Chef Cooks at Home. Copyright © 1975 by Jacques Pépin. Published by Simon and Schuster, N.Y. Reprinted by permission of Simon & Schuster, a Division of Gulf & Western Corporation (91, 151).

Perkins, Wilma Lord, The Fannie Farmer Cookbook. Eleventh Edition. Copyright 1896, 1900, 1901, 1902, 1903, 1904, 1905, 1906, 1912, 1914 by Fannie Farmer. Copyright 1915, 1918, 1923, 1924, 1928, 1929 by Cora D. Perkins. Copyright 1930, 1931, 1932, 1933, 1934, 1936, 1940, 1941, 1942, 1943, 1946, 1951. © 1959, 1964, 1965 by Dexter Perkins Corporation. Published by Little, Brown and Company, Boston. By permission of Little, Brown and Company (139).

Reboul, J. B., La Cuisinière Provençale. Published by Tacussel, Marseille. Translated by permission of Tacussel, Éditeur (158).

Renaudet, Les Secrets de la Bonne Table. Published by Éditions Albin Michel, Paris. Translated by permission of Éditions Albin Michel (127).

Romagnoli, Margaret and G. Franco, The Romagnolis' Table. Copyright © 1974, 1975 by Margaret and G. Franco Romagnoli. Published by Little, Brown and Company, Boston. By permission of Little, Brown and Company (109, 146).

Saint-Ange, Madame, La Cuisine de Madame Saint-Ange. © Éditions Chaix. Published by Éditions Chaix, Grenoble. Translated by permission of Éditions Chaix (111).

St. Paul's Greek Orthodox Church, The Women of, The Art of Greek Cookery. Copyright © 1961, 1963 by St. Paul's Greek Orthodox Church, Hempstead, N.Y. Published by Doubleday & Company, Inc. Reprinted by permission of Doubleday & Company, Inc. (108).

Sales, Georgia MacLeod and Grover, The Clay-Pot Cookbook. Copyright © 1974 by Georgia MacLeod Sales and Grover Sales. Published by Atheneum, N.Y. By permission of Atheneum (141).

Salta, Romeo, The Pleasures of Italian Cooking. © Romeo Salta, 1962. Published by Macmillan Publishing Co., N.Y. By permission of Macmillan Publishing Co., Inc. (100).

Sandler, Sandra Takako, The American Book of Japanese Cooking. Copyright © 1974 by Sandra Sandler. Published by Stackpole Books, Harrisburg. By permission of Stackpole Books (111).

Sarvis, Shirley, A Taste of Portugal. Copyright © 1967 Shirley Sarvis. Published by Charles Scribner's Sons, N.Y. By permission of Shirley Sarvis (122).

Schulze, Ida, Das neue Kochbuch für die deutsche Küche. Published by Verlag von Velhagen & Klasing, West Berlin. Translated by permission of Verlag von Velhagen & Klasing (145).

Scott, Jack Denton, The Complete Book of Pasta. Copyright © 1968 by Jack Denton Scott. Published by William Morrow & Company, Inc., New York. Reprinted by permission of Jack Denton Scott and William Morrow and Company, Inc. (135).

Serra, Victoria, translated by Gili, Elizabeth, Tia Victoria's Spanish Kitchen. Copyright © Elizabeth Gili 1963. Published by Kaye & Ward Ltd., London. By permission of Kaye & Ward Ltd. and Elizabeth Gili (125).

Singh, Dharamjit, Indian Cookery. Copyright © Dharamjit Singh, 1970. Published by Penguin Books Ltd., London. By permission of Penguin Books Ltd. (125).

Snow, Jane Moss, A Family Harvest. Copyright © 1976 by Jane Moss Snow. Published by The Bobbs-Merrill Company, Inc., Ind. Reprinted by permission of The Bobbs-Merrill Company, Inc. (96, 102).

Stockli, Albert, Splendid Fare, The Albert Stockli Cookbook. Copyright © 1970 by Albert Stockli, Inc. Published by Alfred A. Knopf, Inc. By permission of Alfred A. Knopf, Inc. (153).

Straub, Maria Elisabeth, Grönen Aal und Rode Grütt. © LN-Verlag Lübecker Nachrichten GmbH, Lübeck, 1971. Published by LN-Verlag Lübeck. Translated by permission of LN-Verlag Lübeck (155).

Taglienti, Maria Luisa, The Italian Cookbook. Copyright © 1955 by Maria Luisa Taglienti. Published by Random House, Inc. Reprinted by permission of Random House, Inc. (145).

Tante Marguerite, La Cuisine de la Bonne Ménagère. Published by Éditions de L'Épi, Paris (1929) (129).

Tendret, Lucien, La Table au Pays de Brillat-Savarin. Published by Librairie Dardel, Chambery, 1934. Translated by permission of Éditions Rabelais Grancher (118, 119).

Tenison, Marika Hanbury, Left Over for Tomorrow. Copyright © Marika Hanbury Tenison. Published by Penguin Books Ltd., London. By permission of Penguin Books Ltd. (164).

Toklas, Alice B., The Alice B. Toklas Cook Book. Copyright © 1954 by Alice B. Toklas. Published by Harper & Row, Publishers, Inc., N.Y. By permission of Harper & Row, Publishers, Inc. (142).

Watt, Alexander, The Art of Simple French Cookery. 1960 by Alexander Watt. Published by Doubleday & Company, Inc., N.Y. Reprinted by permission of Doubleday & Company, Inc. (129).

Wilson, José (Editor), House and Garden's New Cook Book. Copyright © 1967 by The Condé Nast Publications Inc. Published by The Condé Nast Publications Inc. By permission of The Condé Nast Publications Inc. (14). House and Garden's Party Menu Cookbook. Copyright 1973 by The Condé Nast Publications Inc. Published The Condé Nast Publications Inc., N.Y. By permission The Condé Nast Publications Inc. (109).

Wolfert, Paula, Couscous and Other Good Food from Morocco. Copyright © 1973 by Paula Wolfert. Published Harper & Row, Publishers, Inc. By permission of Harper & Row, Publishers, Inc. (130, 131, 136).

Yu Wen Mei & Adams, Charlotte, 100 Most Honorable Chinese Recipes. Copyright © 1963 by Charlotte Adams. Published by Thomas Y. Crowell Company, Inc., N.Y. Reprinted by permission of Curtis Brown, Ltd. (101, 159).